ANIMAL DEFENSES

HOW ANIMALS PROTECT THEMSELVES

WRITTEN BY ETTA KANER

ILLUSTRATED BY PAT STEPHENS

Kids Can Press

My thanks to Kimberly Baily and Bob Johnson of the Toronto Zoo for their helpful comments, to Pat Stephens for making the animals so lifelike, and to my editor, Laurie Wark, for her patience, persistence, flexibility and good humor.

For David

Text © 1999 Etta Kaner
Illustrations © 1999 Pat Stephens

Kids Can Press acknowledges the financial support of the Ontario Arts Council, the Canada Council for the Arts and the Government of Canada, through the BPIDP, for our publishing activity.

Published in Canada by
Kids Can Press Ltd.
29 Birch Avenue
Toronto, ON M4V 1E2

Published in the U.S. by
Kids Can Press Ltd.
2250 Military Road
Tonawanda, NY 14150

Kids Can Press is a Nelvana company

Edited by Laurie Wark
Designed by Marie Bartholomew
Printed and bound in Hong Kong, China by Book Art Inc., Toronto

The hardcover edition of this book is smyth sewn casebound.
The paperback edition of this book is limp sewn with a drawn-on cover.

CM   99 0 9 8 7 6 5 4 3 2
CM PA   99 0 9 8 7 6 5 4 3 2 1

Canadian Cataloguing in Publication Data

Kaner, Etta
    Animal defenses

Includes index.
ISBN 1-55074-419-4 (bound)
ISBN 1-55074-421-6 (pbk.)

1. Animal defenses – Juvenile literature. 2. Animal Weapons – Juvenile literature. I. Stephens, Pat. II. Title.

QL759.K36 1999   j591.47   C98-932032-4

Contents

Introduction

What do you do when you are afraid? Do you yell for help? Do you hide? Do you run away? Some animals do these things too when they are afraid. But many animals defend themselves in more unusual ways. Some animals change color to make it hard for a predator, or enemy, to see them in their environment. An octopus can do this in seconds. Other animals pretend to be something they're not. An inchworm holds itself stiff to look like a stick. Some animals even have partnerships with other animals. Buffalo depend on birds to warn them of danger. And some crabs use an animal called an anemone like a sword. These are just a few of the strange ways in which animals defend themselves. Read on to find out more about the amazing world of animal defense.

Blue-ringed octopus in camouflage colors

Blue-ringed octopus

Putting on a show

Imagine that you are a very small animal. A bird is about to attack and it's too late to run. What do you do? You try to look dangerous, even though you're not. You hope that your new look will frighten away your enemy. Many harmless animals bluff like this in different ways.

Toad

Citrus swallowtail caterpillar

When a toad is cornered by a snake, it may puff itself up and stretch out its hind legs. The toad becomes about three times bigger than usual. This makes it look too big for the snake to swallow. If the toad is lucky, the snake slithers away to pick on someone its own size.

The citrus swallowtail caterpillar scares away hungry birds by acting like a snake. It lifts up the front of its body and sticks out a bright red organ that looks like a snake's forked tongue. It flickers the fake tongue back and forth and gives off a terrible smell. This is enough to turn birds away.

The blue-tongued skink of Australia is a slow-moving lizard. When frightened, it opens its mouth wide, hisses and sticks out a huge, bright blue tongue. It's not trying to be rude. It just wants to scare its attacker. Most hungry birds and mammals leave it alone. Wouldn't you?

Strange but true

When a predator gets too close to the African cut-throat finch, the bird imitates a snake. It hisses and wriggles its body just like a snake.

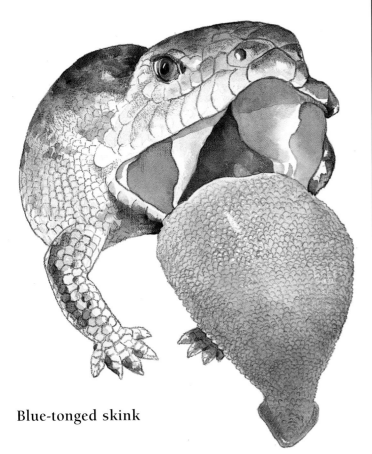

Blue-tonged skink

Some stick insects, or walkingsticks, try to look like scorpions. They curve up their abdomens and wave their tails in the air. They look as if they are about to attack. No animal wants to tangle with a deadly scorpion, so it leaves the walkingstick alone.

Walkingstick

Putting on a show

When resting on a branch, the eyed hawkmoth looks like a crumpled dead leaf. If a bird gets too close, the moth quickly uncovers its back wings. Suddenly, two huge eyespots stare out at the bird. They look as if they belong to an owl or a hawk. Now the bird wants to protect itself and it makes a fast exit.

Can you find me?

If an animal is not a fast mover, what does it do when a predator is close by? It hides. Some animals hide in their homes. Others don't go anywhere to hide. They just stay very still. Since they look a lot like their surroundings, their enemies don't see them. This is called camouflage.

Three-toed sloth

In the South American rain forest, this three-toed sloth spends most of its time hanging from a branch. It moves so little that tiny plants called algae grow on its long gray hairs. This makes the sloth look like the gray-green lichen plants that grow on branches around it. The sloth looks so much like a plant that some moths live in its fur.

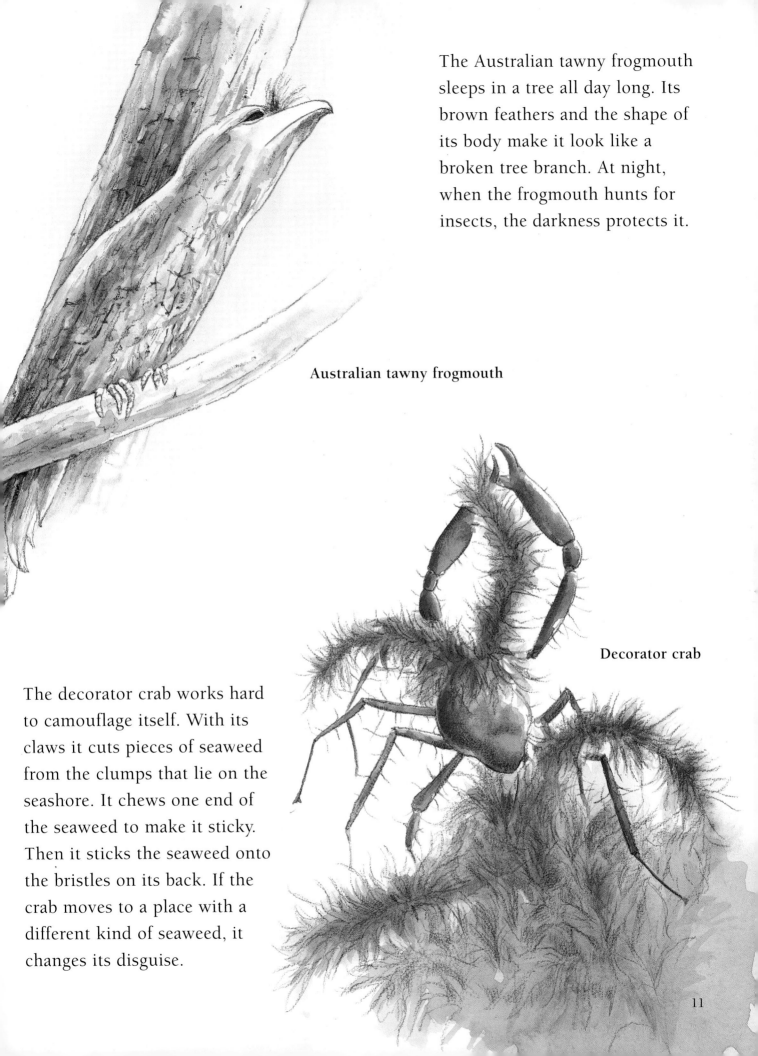

The Australian tawny frogmouth sleeps in a tree all day long. Its brown feathers and the shape of its body make it look like a broken tree branch. At night, when the frogmouth hunts for insects, the darkness protects it.

Australian tawny frogmouth

Decorator crab

The decorator crab works hard to camouflage itself. With its claws it cuts pieces of seaweed from the clumps that lie on the seashore. It chews one end of the seaweed to make it sticky. Then it sticks the seaweed onto the bristles on its back. If the crab moves to a place with a different kind of seaweed, it changes its disguise.

11

Can you find me?

As the flounder hunts for food on the ocean floor, it rests on different backgrounds. If it sees a sandy seabed, the flounder's skin changes to look like sand. On a rocky bottom, its skin looks like tiny rocks. A flounder can even look like a checkerboard if it rests on one for a while.

Flounder

Prairie dogs live in burrows, or tunnels, under the ground in North America. A prairie dog can get into or out of its burrow through two or three holes. By standing on a mound of earth at one of these holes, a prairie dog keeps a lookout for enemies. As soon as it sees a hawk or a fox, it gives a warning bark. All of the prairie dogs in the area dive into their burrows and stay there until the coast is clear.

Prairie dog

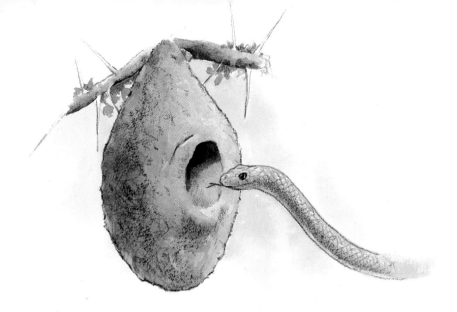

Nest of a Cape penduline tit

In South Africa, the nest of the Cape penduline tit has two entrances — a fake one and a real one. The fake one is a large hole in the side of the nest. If a snake enters it to steal the bird's eggs, surprise — it hits a wall. The real entrance is a tiny slit just above the false one. After the tit squeezes in or out, the real entrance closes up tight.

Chuckwalla

The chuckwalla doesn't have a home in which to hide. This lizard lives in a rocky American desert. When it sees a predator, the chuckwalla runs to the closest rock crevice and wedges itself in. Then it blows itself up with air. The chuckwalla's body becomes so tightly wedged between the rocks that it is impossible for the predator to pull it out.

Strange but true

Some snakes and lizards only half hide from their enemies. They wriggle their bodies into sand so that only the tops of their heads and their eyes are above the sand. By lying still, they can look out for danger and strike out at any passing meal.

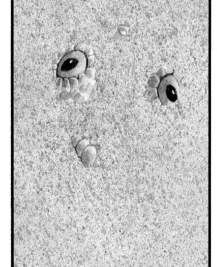

13

Can you find me?

A beaver's home, or lodge, is built from tree branches and mud. The dome-shaped lodge is built in a pond. Even though the lodge is in water, there is a dry, cozy room inside. The only way to get into this room is by diving deep and swimming up a tunnel that leads to it. A beaver has no trouble doing this. But there's no way a bear or a mountain lion can follow it.

Copycats

Is being a copycat always a bad thing? Not if you're an animal. In fact, that's how many animals survive. They look and act like animals that make their predators sick. So predators stay away from both them and their poisonous look-alikes.

Viceroy butterfly

Monarch butterfly

The viceroy butterfly looks like the monarch butterfly, doesn't it? Birds find it hard to tell them apart too. While the viceroy is harmless, the monarch is poisonous. Birds have learned to avoid eating both butterflies. They don't want to take a chance on getting ill by eating the wrong one.

Ant

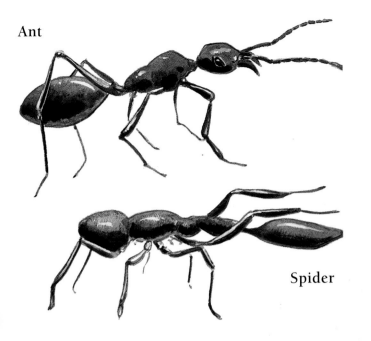

Spider

Many spiders copy ants. But it's not easy. Ants have six legs. Spiders have eight. Ants have antennae. Spiders don't. A spider must hold two legs in front of its head to look like antennae. It moves them from side to side and scurries around like an ant. Why do spiders imitate ants if they have to work so hard at it? Birds and lizards eat spiders, but they don't touch ants. They know that ants bite, sting and sometimes spray acid.

Hoverfly

Honeybee

The hoverfly looks and acts like a honeybee. It drinks nectar from flowers and buzzes a warning when threatened. But the hoverfly is harmless. It has no sting. Luckily, birds don't seem to know this. They are fooled into thinking that the hoverfly is a harmful honeybee, and leave it alone.

Copycats

At first glance, these two snakes look like twins. But they're not. The king snake is harmless, while the coral snake has a venomous bite. Animals can't tell the difference between them, so they stay clear of both. How can you tell the difference? This old saying might help, "If red touches yellow, avoid the fellow."

Coral snake

King snake

You can't hurt me

Just as you wear a helmet to protect your head, some animals have protective gear too. But animals' gear is made from shells, bone or spines, and can cover most of their body.

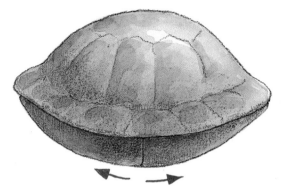

Box turtle

The three-toed box turtle has a top shell, or carapace, like all turtles. But its bottom shell, or plastron, is different. It has a hinge in the middle. This lets the turtle fold up the front and back of its plastron. The top and bottom shells are sealed together and the turtle's body is safe from any predator.

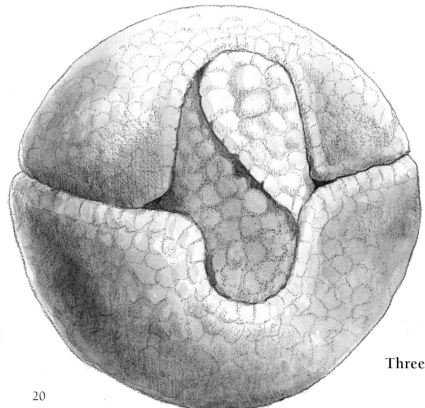

When the three-banded armadillo from South America is attacked, it rolls itself into a ball. Three bands of hard shell on this mammal's back protect its soft body inside. If the predator touches it just after it has rolled up, the armadillo suddenly snaps the bands together like a trap. Ouch! The animal's nose or paw gets a nasty nip that it will remember for a long time.

Three-banded armadillo

The hero shrew from West Africa well deserves this name. On the outside it looks like other shrews. On the inside, this tiny mammal has an unusually strong backbone. Its backbone is so strong that its small body can support a man standing on its back. If a person can't crush a hero shrew, could an animal possibly hurt it?

Strange but true

Sometimes an armadillo will run away from its enemy. If it needs to cross a river, it either walks along the bottom or blows itself up like a balloon and paddles across.

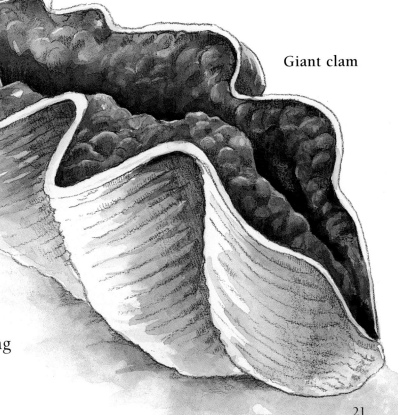

Hero shrew

Giant clam

Some clam shells can be pried open by a starfish or smashed by a sea otter or drilled by a sea snail. Not the giant clam. Its shell is too thick and heavy. In fact, the giant clam has the largest shell in the world. It weighs about as much as three adults and is about as long as a bathtub.

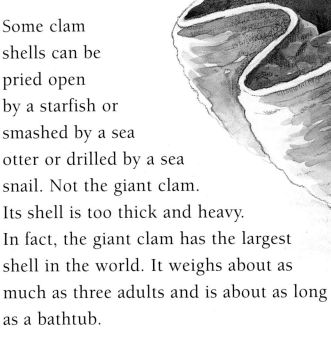

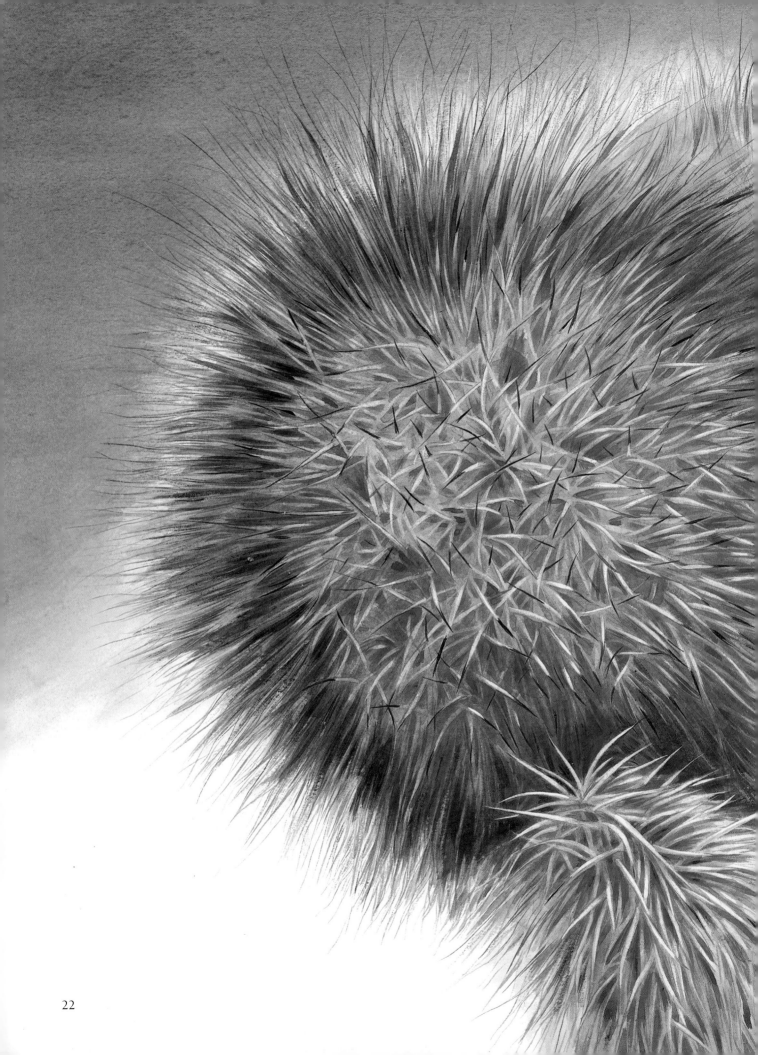

You can't hurt me

The North American porcupine's body is covered with about 30 000 quills. When the porcupine is threatened, it turns its back on its enemy. Then it lashes its tail wildly back and forth. If a fox or weasel is too close, it gets a snout full of quills. Can the fox pull them out? Not likely. The tip of each quill is covered with hooks, or barbs.

Warning, stay away!

Just as a red light tells you to stop, bright colors on animals warn predators to stop — and not eat them. If they do, they'll get very sick. Warning colors can be red or yellow or orange. They often form a pattern with black.

Even though the striped skunk hunts at night, its black and white marks are very clear. They mean "keep away." If a predator doesn't keep away, the skunk gives other warnings. It stamps its feet, arches its back and raises its tail. If the predator still doesn't get the hint, the skunk sprays it in the face. The spray is so strong that it blinds the predator for several hours.

Skunk

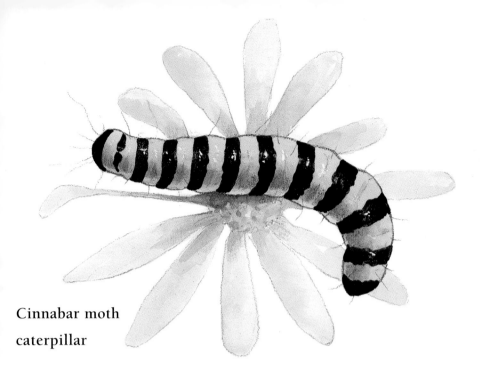

Cinnabar moth
caterpillar

A snake, bird or lizard wouldn't dare eat a cinnabar moth caterpillar. These animals know that if they did they would get very sick. The yellow and black stripes remind them of this. What makes this European caterpillar so poisonous? The ragwort plant that it eats has a poison in its leaves.

Strange but true

The Oriental fire-bellied toad has warning colors on its underside. When threatened, it twists its legs and arches its back to show its bright colors. These remind predators that the toad's skin contains a burning poison.

Ladybug

Depending on where it lives, a ladybug, or ladybird beetle, could have two, seven or twenty-two spots. The spots could be black on a red back, black on a yellow back, or red on a black back. No matter how many spots a ladybug has, birds, spiders and beetles don't bother it. They know that if they do, the ladybug's leg joints will give off a horrible-tasting liquid.

Warning, stay away!

These colorful poison-arrow frogs are easy to find in a South American rain forest. But they don't have to worry about being eaten. A bird or snake that tastes one immediately spits it out. Its skin is poisonous. The poison from one kind of poison-arrow frog can kill 50 people. No wonder animals usually stay clear of these frogs.

Let's stick together

Do you help your friends when they are in trouble? That's what animals do too. Some animals try to stay safe by living in groups. Others find a partner and the two of them help each other out. This is called symbiosis. Either way, they are safer from a predator than if they were alone.

Dolphins attacking a shark

Dolphins spend their whole lives in groups. When a shark threatens a baby dolphin, or calf, the group takes action. One or two dolphins swim in front of the shark to get its attention. As soon as the shark turns toward them, the other dolphins attack the shark from all sides. They hit the shark with their beaks until its gills are crushed and it drowns.

When an enemy breaks into a termite nest, soldier termites call for help. They can do this in two ways. They give off a scent that warns other termites of danger. They can also bang their heads on the walls of the nest. This sends vibrations through the nest which termites feel with their legs. When they get these messages, hundreds of termites rush to attack the invader.

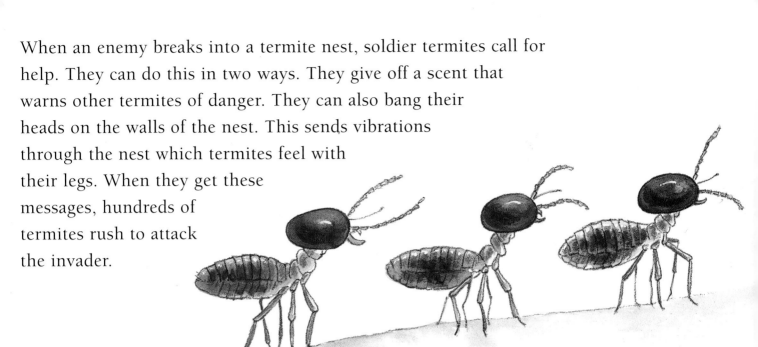

Soldier termites

Impalas and baboons

Groups of impalas and baboons often move around together on the plains. Impalas have excellent hearing and a keen sense of smell. Baboons have good eyesight. Together they keep watch for enemies. If they are attacked, the baboons are fierce fighters. This helps the impalas as well as the baboons.

Let's stick together

The hermit crab's partner is the sea anemone. The hermit crab lives inside a shell that has been cast off by another sea creature. The anemone lives on top of it. As the hermit crab looks for food along the seashore, the anemone gets a free ride. It also gets the leftovers from the crab's meals. In return, the anemone protects the crab with its fingerlike tentacles. The poisonous tentacles sting any animal that touches them.

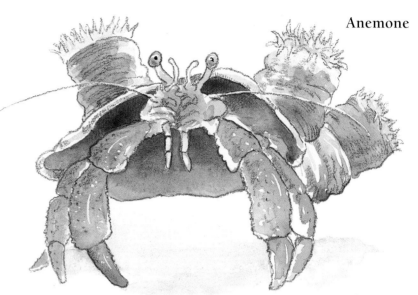

Anemone

Hermit crab

Oxpecker bird

The African buffalo has a personal alarm. It's the oxpecker bird. The oxpecker lives on the back of the buffalo. It eats the insects that burrow into the buffalo's hide. When the oxpecker senses danger, it screeches and flaps its wings. If the buffalo doesn't pay attention, the oxpecker uses its beak to rap the buffalo on the head. That usually gets the buffalo moving.

African buffalo

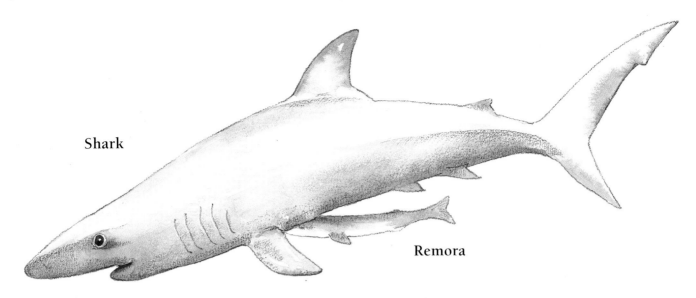

Shark

Remora

The remora is protected by sticking close to a shark. After all, who would attack a shark? The fish holds onto the shark with a large suction disc on its head. Wherever the shark swims, the remora goes with it, safe from enemies. In return, the remora cleans the shark's skin by eating the parasites that grow on it. It also eats the scraps of food the shark drops during its messy meals.

Strange but true

A little fish called Luther's goby and a blind shrimp are good partners. The shrimp digs a burrow for both to live in. When the goby guides the shrimp on feeding trips, the shrimp keeps its antennae in touch with the goby's tail. If there is danger, the goby wiggles its tail and the two of them hide in their burrow.

Shrimp

Luther's goby

Let's stick together

The clown fish is safe from enemies because it lives among the tentacles of a sea anemone. These tentacles are poisonous. Any fish that tries to catch a clown fish is stung to death by the anemone. It then becomes the anemone's dinner. Of course, the clown fish gets to share in the meal too. In exchange for protection, the clown fish chases away the anemone's enemies. It also keeps the anemone healthy by eating diseased parts.

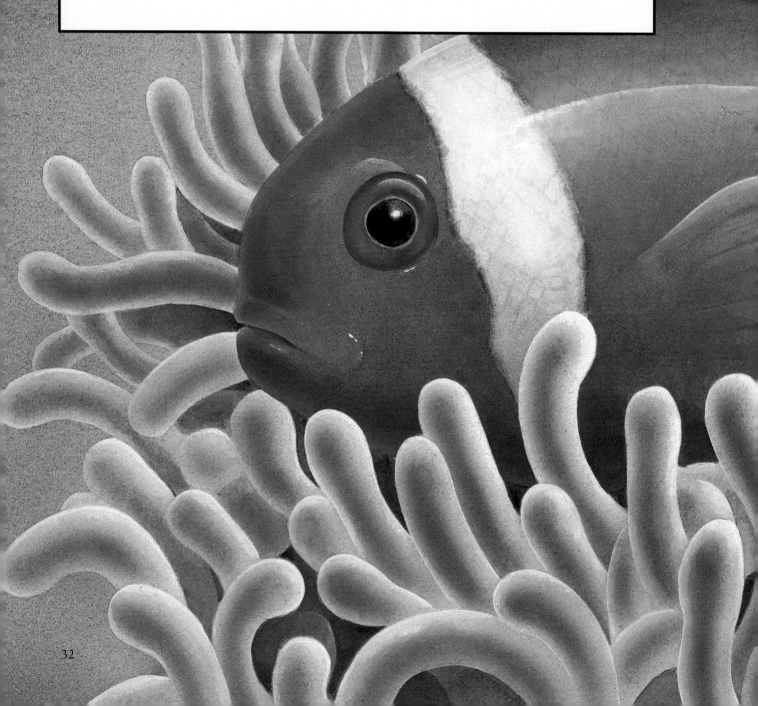

Playing tricks

Many animals save their lives by playing tricks on their predators. No one teaches them to do these tricks. It just comes naturally.

Baby killdeer stay safe because their mother puts on an act when an enemy approaches. The killdeer mother flies away from the nest, then lands and drags one wing as if it is broken. The predator follows because a hurt bird is easy to catch. When the mother feels the nest is safe, she flies away leaving the predator behind.

Killdeer

Hognose snake

Since most predators prefer to eat only freshly-killed prey, the hognose snake acts like it is dead. It rolls over and gives off a rotten smell as if it's been dead for several days. The snake's tongue hangs out and blood drips out of its open mouth. No wonder predators leave it alone.

Leopard gecko

Many lizards, like this Leopard gecko, have tails that break off when predators grab them. While the startled attacker watches the wriggling tail, the lizard has time to make a fast getaway. Amazingly, the lizard's tail grows back. But it's not as long or as straight as the original one.

Strange but true

Birds kill butterflies by attacking the head. But the hairstreak's head is hard to find. Hairstreaks have long fake antennae, which they wave about at the back of their wings. When a bird attacks these, the butterfly can usually escape.

Cuttlefish

A cuttlefish tries to blend in with its surroundings. When this doesn't work, it squirts a blue-black cloud into the water. A hungry shark attacks the inky blob, thinking it's the cuttlefish. Meanwhile, the cuttlefish quickly sneaks away.

Playing tricks

If the American opossum can't scare away its attacker, it "plays possum." The opossum tricks its enemy into thinking that it is dead. Suddenly, it falls over onto its side. Its tongue hangs out of its mouth and its eyes are half closed. Even if the predator pokes or bites it, the opossum doesn't move. It only moves again when it feels safe.

You can't catch me

Some animals are fast runners, fliers or swimmers. That's how they save their lives. But moving quickly is not always enough. Some animals have to outsmart their predators as well.

Pronghorn antelope

Pronghorn antelope can run fast over a long distance. But pronghorns don't just run away when they spot a wolf or coyote. They also give a warning signal by spreading out the long white hairs on their rumps. The large circles of hair reflect sunlight and can be seen from far away by other pronghorns. At the same time, the pronghorn gives off a strong scent which also sends a message that there are predators around.

Australian sugar-glider

It's hard for a predator to keep up with a sugar-glider. The Australian sugar-glider glides through the air from one tree to the next. It can travel as far as half a football field in a single glide. The sugar-glider has flaps of skin along the sides of its body connecting its hands and feet. When it glides, it stretches out the skin flaps and sails through the air. It steers with its fluffy tail.

When a red fox is being chased by a wolf or a lynx, it tries to hide its scent. It doesn't run in a straight line. It traces back over its own tracks. It runs through shallow water. It runs along the tops of fences and stone walls, and it even runs among cattle, pigs or deer. Once the predator loses the fox's scent, it can no longer chase the fox. The predator has been outfoxed!

Red fox

39

Index

COOK
IN A CLASS OF YOUR OWN

COOK
IN A CLASS OF YOUR OWN

with Richard Bertinet

Photography by
Jonathan Gregson

Kyle Books

For Sheila

ACKNOWLEDGMENTS
This book could not have been written without all of the customers at The Bertinet Kitchen who have, by their questions, given me the clearest guide as to what this book needed to include. Thank you to you all.

A huge thank you to Sheila Keating for her help both in starting and finishing this book, to my team at The Bertinet Kitchen, but especially Ben Peel, Jess Courtis, and Carrie Bell, for all their help and support; to Kyle, Sophie, and all at Kyle Cathie for their support; Jonathan Gregson, Tonia George, and Liz Belton for the beautiful photographs; Jenny Semple for the design; Charlotte Farmer for her fantastic drawings; Tim White and John Warwick for the DVD; to Jo (as always) for keeping me and the show on the road and to Jack, Tom, and Lola Maude for not minding too much when Daddy had to work through the family vacations.

Published in 2010 by Kyle Books,
an imprint of Kyle Cathie Ltd.
www.kylebooks.com

Distributed by National Book Network
4501 Forbes Blvd., Suite 200
Lanham, MD 20706
Phone: (800) 462-6420 Fax: (301) 429-5746
custserv@nbnbooks.com

Project editor: Sophie Allen
Designer: Jenny Semple
Photographer: Jonathan Gregson
Illustration on spine and endpapers: Charlotte Farmer
Food stylist: Tonia George
Props stylist: Liz Belton
Americanizer: Margaret Parrish
Copy editor: Catherine Ward
Proofreader: Ruth Baldwin
Production: Gemma John

ISBN: 978-1-906868-22-2

A cataloging-in-publication record for this title is available from the Library of Congress.

Color reproduction by Colourscan.
Printed and bound in Singapore by Star Standard

Contents

Introduction

I think there are three types of cook. Some people cook by instinct, giving recipes only a passing glance for inspiration. Others need to follow a recipe just once to feel confident enough to cook it again, adding their own twist or changing some of the ingredients. And then there are those who don't dare to try anything other than grilled cheese sandwiches unless they have a step-by-step recipe to follow religiously. Of course, you might have never cooked anything at all, so you don't yet know which category you fall into.

At the cooking school, our classes are made up of people of all ages and experience. As an ice-breaker at the beginning of each session I ask everyone to tell us a bit about themselves, and what, if anything, they can cook. Sometimes we have couples who come along together, and are a bit like Jack Sprat and his wife. One of them—usually the man—will be the "throw it in the pan, what the hell" type, who has decided (or his partner has decided for him) that it would be good to be not quite so hit-and-miss, and maybe get a grip on a few more dishes than the signature eggs and bacon. His or her partner is very often the opposite: needing precise weights, measures, and instructions every step of the way, but feeling stuck in a rut and wishing they could lighten up and experiment a bit more. I like to think that everyone takes away something valuable from our classes, whether it is first-time confidence, that "light bulb moment" when you see the quickest way to chop an onion or slice an apple, or a new sense of just having fun in the kitchen that revitalizes your cooking.

I asked Ben, one of the bright young chefs who worked with us at the school, what he thought people liked about cooking with us, and he said: "We give all the bits and pieces of tips and knowledge that often get left out of recipes. We don't just tell people how to shop for a list of ingredients, then whizz through the method and expect them to produce a dish without really knowing what they are doing or why they are doing it." That summed it up for me. In this book, just as if you were in the kitchen with me, I will talk you through each step of the recipe and, as well as looking at the big questions, such as "How do you joint a chicken?" I will answer all the little queries that come up whenever I cook with people, and are equally, if not more, important. Questions such as: "What are the best potatoes to use for making fries?" and "How can you tell when a sauce is the right consistency?" or "How do you check that a steak is cooked rare?"

We don't assume that everyone knows how to sear a piece of meat or understands what a reduction means—in fact, we avoid most "cheffy" terminology completely—and you won't find any ingredients lists that are as long as your arm. We don't even take it for granted that people know what a pinch of salt really is. It might seem ridiculous to ask someone who has been cooking for years to show me a pinch of salt, but usually people are amazed when they see what I call a pinch of salt. As a result, they may well be underseasoning, and their finished dish may not have the flavor it deserves. It seems like such a small thing, but correct seasoning is crucial if you want to maximize taste. "Check your seasoning" is something chefs say all the time—but what does that really mean?

So many people tell me that they have about 20 recipe books at home, but use only one. Well, I'd like this to be the one that you actually cook from. This is not a definitive textbook, but a collection of recipes that will show you a whole range of different techniques and ideas. Get to know each of them and you will be able to close the book and continue cooking with confidence, making your own variations according to the seasons and whatever you have in your pantry or fridge.

At The Bertinet Kitchen our motto is "Cooking, learning, eating." At the end of each class we always sit down together at a big table with a few bottles of wine and some bread from our bakery and eat the dishes we have cooked. It's our way of reminding everyone that this is what it is all about: not being overly ambitious, tortured and stressed, or panicking over fancy presentation, but enjoying cooking something simple, wholesome, and full of flavor that your friends and family will love to eat.

> "Get to know each of these recipes and you will be able to close the book and continue cooking with confidence."

Q&As explained...

When I'm teaching at The Bertinet Kitchen I find that similar questions crop up again and again when we are making particular dishes, so throughout the book I have included Questions and Answers and Step-by-Step techniques wherever they are most appropriate.

Obviously some of these apply to many different recipes, so this is a list of where each first appears. In addition, on each recipe, under the heading 'Bertinet Basics' you will find a note of which page to find the relevant Q&A's, Step-by-Steps and techniques that might be explained more fully in other recipes.

Of course, there is no substitute for actually being in the kitchen and seeing what is going on, which is why I have included a 30 minute DVD with this book, which shows you the complete Simple Chicken Pot recipe on page 116—a dish I have chosen because it includes a wealth of techniques, from securing your cutting board, dicing vegetables, and seasoning, to jointing a whole chicken and 'reducing' a sauce. You can also see me making Crème Brulee (page 173), French Apple Tart (page 189) and mayonnaise (page 68) discussing seasoning and much more. Wherever you see the **DVD** symbol below, the topic is also covered on the DVD.

Equipment and general techniques

Ingredients

Shop

I always find it strange when you walk into a supermarket and the first thing you see is fruits and vegetables. I know why: supermarkets want to give the impression of freshness, and fruits and vegetables look more attractive than raw meat to many people. But unless you cook only vegetable dishes, it goes against the way I think you should shop. The way I was brought up, shopping in the markets in France, you would never start with a carrot; you would look first at what meat or fish was good and then decide what to put with it. Enough has been said and written about buying fresh food, farmed and produced responsibly and with respect for animal welfare, so I don't need to add to it, except to say that I agree completely. However, I also know that such produce can sometimes be expensive, so it is worth trying to take an example from the way our grandparents' generation shopped and cooked: first, with specific meals in mind and second, with an eye on leftovers and making, say, a chicken stretch for maybe two or three meals—roast first, then soup, risotto, stir-fry, etc.—rather than buying pricey portions for one recipe only.

"Having everything in little bowls might seem like a very cheffy thing to do, but try it and see what a difference it makes!"

Prepare

One of the biggest differences between cooking in a professional kitchen and at home is the preparation. In a restaurant, as much advance work as possible is done in the morning, so that vegetables are chopped and in containers, sauces are made, fish is filleted; everything is organized and ready to go when the customers arrive and the actual cooking begins. And then, part of the ritual is to "clean down" whenever there is an opportunity, to give yourself a clean, uncluttered space to work. At home, how many times have you launched into a recipe, then realized you haven't chopped the carrots that should be going into the pan right now, someone hasn't put the whisk back in the right place, or it is in the dishwasher, your knife is blunt, or the knob of ginger you were convinced you had in the fridge has disappeared?

The first thing I do at home before I start cooking is to take 10 minutes or so to clear the kitchen and turn it into a place where I want to be. Psychologically, once I have picked up the kids' toys, school clothes, and all the bits and pieces that seem to accumulate around the kitchen table, emptied the dishwasher ready to receive used bowls and utensils, and cleared and cleaned my work surfaces, I'm in the right frame of mind and ready to immerse myself in cooking. Trust me, the extra time and effort you spend getting organized will definitely be worth it to avoid all that rushing around looking for things and getting stressed and confused.

$Q\&A...$

WHAT IS THE BEST WAY TO SHARPEN KNIVES?
A traditional whetstone gets knives very sharp; however, there is a bit of skill involved. Good cookware stores will show you how to use a whetstone before you buy one, but if you find the idea a bit daunting, you can buy good-quality electric sharpeners with ceramic wheels that are very effective and useful. Sharpening steels always look dramatic when you see chefs using them, but they really give an edge only to a sharp knife—they won't sharpen it if it is blunt.

You might think chopping, measuring, and having everything ready in little bowls on your work surface before you start cooking, along with whatever utensils you are going to need, is a very cheffy thing to do, but try it and see what a difference it makes to your life! Not only does it concentrate your mind on what you have, and what you are missing, but it will also make the actual cooking so much more relaxed.

If I am peeling and chopping a lot of vegetables, I always have a little "trash can" on the table: a basket, bowl, or box—anything to put all your waste into and keep the area around you litter-free and uncluttered.

Before I start chopping and slicing, I also secure my cutting board, either by putting a non-slip mat or a damp folded cloth or kitchen towel underneath it; that way, there is no danger of it moving around when you have a sharp knife in your hand. Position your board near the edge of your work surface, so the wrist and knuckles of your chopping hand are free. If the board is too far away you won't be able to wield the knife properly, especially if you are filleting fish.

Adjust

Don't necessarily think you can't make a dish just because you don't have one of the ingredients. Improvisation is the mother of invention.

Except in some of the dessert recipes, when specific quantities are sometimes needed to make something set, or a cake rise, in most cases it really doesn't matter if you don't stick to exact quantities. Whether you have a 2½lb or a 3lb chicken, whether you use one or two tablespoons of oil to fry a piece of fish, or if you add half a bottle of wine or

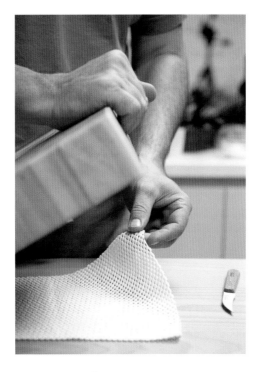

"Before I start chopping and slicing, I always secure my cutting board."

three-quarters to a casserole (see page 16), what matters is knowing how to tell when that chicken is cooked, making sure you don't crowd your pan so that your piece of fish browns properly, or being aware of how thick you want your casserole sauce to be. Enjoying cooking is about understanding and being in control of what you are doing, rather than just following a set of instructions to the letter.

Choose the right equipment

Tempting as cookware stores are, remember you don't actually need every gadget and gizmo they are offering. I would say you need three knives: a big chef's knife, a medium-sized slicing or utility knife, and a smaller paring knife—plus a filleting knife for fish, if you like. You will also need a good medium-sized whisk with seven wires (see page 178, Q&A), a peeler and corer, a wooden spoon, a spatula, a slotted spatula, and an offset spatula. Wooden utensils tend to absorb flavors, so it is worth having a duplicate set for delicate custards, etc.— rather than using a wooden spoon that has been regularly stirring garlic! And don't keep cracked or broken utensils, since they can be a health hazard. I always use a pair of tongs for turning big pieces of meat when they are browning in a pan. A Mandoline is also handy for slicing vegetables finely, or cutting them into "matchstick" pieces.

If you use plastic cutting boards, remember to replace them regularly, because scratch marks from your knives can create crevices that trap bacteria. Personally, I prefer wooden boards, and the advantage of wood is that it contains a natural antibacterial tannin—the important thing is not to submerge them in water, but to scrub them really well and make sure you dry them completely.

Q&A...

DO I NEED TO SPEND LOTS OF MONEY ON A GOOD PAN?

There are some beautiful pans in cookware stores, but don't be blinded by glitz; there is also a pan for every budget, if you are prepared to shop around. You can even find some very good value ones in supermarkets. Just make sure you avoid thin aluminum ones that will burn your food; instead, go for stainless steel pans with quite thick bases. Glass lids are handy for long cooking, since you can see what is going on in the pan without constantly having to take the lid off and change the temperature.

IS THERE A SPECIAL KIND OF STRING FOR KITCHEN USE?

Throughout the book I talk about "butcher's twine or string" (so-called because it used in the butchery trade) for tying herbs to make a bouquet garni, or trussing meat, etc. In cookware stores you might see it sold as cook's string: it is food-safe, made of rayon, and thin, very strong, and nonslippery.

Cook

Two important things often get overlooked: choosing the right pan and using the right heat.

THE RIGHT PAN

The size of pan you use makes a difference to the way you can cook certain things and how long it will take. If, for example, you want to brown a lot of pieces of meat, or fry some shrimp quickly, a wide, flat plan with a large surface area will get the job done much better than if you try to squash everything into a smaller pan, in which case the temperature drops. If, on the other hand, you are making something more delicate like a custard, it is best to use a smaller, deeper pan, so that you can control the heat and let it cook more slowly without boiling. It is lovely to have lots of pans, but you need only around five—put the rest on your birthday and Christmas lists. I would choose a big saucepan in which you can make stock or soup, cook a good-sized crab (see page 72) or use for pasta, which needs plenty of space for the boiling water to swirl around it. Then I would go for a two-handled sauté pan with a lid, about 10–12 inches in diameter, which you can use for anything from the chicken pot on page 116 to the risotto on page 102 or 104. Add to that a good nonstick frying pan and a medium and small saucepan, both with lids. A griddle pan for steaks and vegetables is also a great addition.

THE RIGHT BURNER

When you are cooking on the stove, choosing the right burner goes hand in hand with choosing the right pan. Most of us tend to use the same burner on the stove every time, out of habit, but stoves have different-sized burners for a reason, and using the best one for the job is like choosing a screwdriver when you are repairing something: you get the job done more quickly and better if you use the right size. If you have a large pan over a small flame it means that not all areas of the pan will heat evenly; if you have a small pan over a large flame, everything around the edge of the pan runs the risk of overcooking or burning, unless you stir constantly, because the heat will envelop it from underneath and around the sides.

THE RIGHT OIL

All cooking oils have a "smoke point" beyond which they tend to spoil and burn. While ordinary olive oil is fine for brief pan-frying of, say, a piece of fish, the finest extra-virgin olive oil is best kept just for sprinkling over dishes such as fish and vegetables at the end of cooking, when you really want to be able to taste it, or for dressings. There is a huge spectrum of flavors of virgin olive oil—from mild and fruity to dark green, peppery, and pungent—so choose carefully to avoid overpowering delicate dishes with too strong an oil.

Vegetable oil is fine for pan-frying, stir-frying, and deep-frying, but my favorite oil for cooking at high temperatures is canola, or rapeseed, oil. You can buy cold-pressed virgin canola, which is a "single" oil that has all its properties and goodness intact, but that can still be heated to a very high smoke point without deteriorating—and I also like its slightly nutty flavor in salad dressings.

KNOW YOUR OVEN

Short of actually showing up in your kitchen, there is no way I can know what kind of oven you have, where the hot spots are, whether you use a fan, whether you don't. Every oven behaves differently—don't I know it, setting up the ones in the cooking school! That is why writing recipes that you hope are foolproof is a nightmare. I am always wary of saying things like "cook in the oven for 20 minutes"—because in your oven it might take 15 or 25. So instead, don't take any cooking time too literally and check every five minutes the first few times you make a dish, until you get to know your oven. Be prepared to move things around from top to bottom, or turn dishes or pans around if you feel one side is cooking more quickly than the other, and, if necessary, adjust the cooking times and sometimes the temperatures slightly. By the way, a good oven thermometer might seem like a superfluous piece of gear, but, in fact, it is very useful for finding out what the temperature actually is in different parts of your oven.

"It's lovely to have lots of pans, but you only need around five."

Season

Beyond the planning and preparation, the other major difference between professional cooking and home cooking is in the seasoning. Salt has been slated as the big baddy in our food, and rightly so in terms of the hidden quantities of it in processed foods, such as some stock cubes, cereals, or cookies. But as a flavor enhancer, used carefully in home cooking with fresh ingredients, it is an important part of cooking. The problem is, the bad press has turned people away from salt so much that they are afraid to season, and then they think they can't cook, because their food is flavorless. The real baddy is processed "table salt" that is stripped of much of its goodness and often has chemicals added to make it flow freely, whereas natural sea or rock salt is full of minerals and has been valued for its vital role in regulating the body's functions since ancient times. I use a range of salts, from the *sel gris* of my native Brittany to the white crystals by Cornish Sea Salt Company. Wars have been fought over it and words formed from its name—for example, "salary," the Roman word for a payment in salt. And if you end up in the hospital, you are very likely to find yourself hooked up to a saline drip, a special solution of sodium chloride—salt, in other words—so it can't be all that bad!

Taste

If you take a little rock or sea salt on your finger and pop it on your tongue, you will taste something pleasant and flavorsome, unlike the harshness of processed salt—and because it has a distinctive flavor, you will need to use less of it in your cooking. I've tried to point out the most important stages at which to check your seasoning in each recipe, but the principle is always to taste as you go, season a little, wait for the salt to dissolve and disperse and have an effect, then taste again, rather than wait until the end of cooking, panic that there is not enough flavor in your dish and end up adding far more salt than you might have otherwise used.

A NOTE ABOUT WINE

If you look in your cupboard I bet you have odd wine glasses in all kinds of shapes and sizes—and you might be shocked to realize that some "large" wine glasses equate to about a third of a bottle, if not more. So it isn't particularly helpful to say "add a glass of wine." For the recipes in this book, I've tried to give quantities either in terms of how much of a bottle to use or cups to avoid any confusion, but do remember that these are only guidelines and don't feel you have to be rigid about them. The alcohol will evaporate if you are cooking over high heat, and what will be left is a rich, deep flavor. What is the worst that can happen if you put in a little extra? You will get more of the flavor of the wine. Just remember that you will need to cook it for a bit longer, if you are making a sauce that you want to reduce down and thicken. In something that is going to cook very slowly, such as a casserole, plenty of wine is a bonus, since it will all mellow out in the slow cooking. Sometimes in classes, just to prove the point, I stand by the casserole pan, talking to distract everybody, and all the time glugging in the wine. Eventually I say, "Tell me when!" and everyone realizes I have poured in half a bottle, then I'll say, "OK, it's Thursday, I think I'll add a bit more...." That said, don't go completely crazy and put in so much wine that you knock out the rest of the flavors. And don't feel you need to spend a fortune on cooking wine, just buy a bottle that is good enough to drink (see page 118). Of course, if you have a nice bottle open, pour yourself a little glass, too!

A NOTE ABOUT STOCKS AND SAUCES

I wanted this book to be as easy to use as possible, so that instead of constantly having to turn to a different page to find out how to make a stock or a sauce, each recipe, wherever possible, is completely self-contained. However, on page 200, I have included a very simple vegetable stock recipe, which can be adapted for fish, meat, or chicken and doesn't require hours of simmering. There are some quick all-purpose sauces (and vegetable dishes) there, too.

"Don't feel you have to be rigid about the quantity of wine, and if you have a nice bottle open, pour yourself a little glass, too!"

L'apéro

L'apéro is the French equivalent of the Italian antipasti. It is really just a collection of nibbles that you can put out in bowls or preserving jars with some good bread and have with drinks. It also makes for a nice, lazy weekend lunch that you can graze on and linger over for hours. You can make just one or two of these recipes, or all of them, and then add plates of cured hams, salami, cheese, and some dishes of olives or artichokes—whatever you like. If you want to serve these dishes as an appetizer and you are a bit behind in the kitchen, you don't have to get in a panic because everyone will be quite happy nibbling and talking.

I wanted to start the book with these recipes because they are easy to make, really tasty to eat, and they are all about relaxing and enjoying yourself. *L'apéro* for me really describes a way of living and eating, rather than any specific recipes, because every *département* in France has its variations, just like every region in Italy. In my native Brittany, you would probably see bowls of winkles with some local gray sea salt over the top, a jar of mayonnaise, and some bread; in Provence, there might be more of a Mediterranean feel, with anchovies and tapenade.

The recipes I have given here are for pesto, tapenade, chickpea and olive oil purée, oven-dried tomatoes, caramelized onions, and eggplant purée. At the end, I have included a very simple recipe for pork rillettes, the coarsely shredded confit of pork (or duck, rabbit, etc.) that you see in every delicatessen and supermarket in France. It is great to serve it as part of *l'apéro*. Everyone thinks it must be difficult to make, but, in fact, all you have to do is put all your ingredients in a pot on top of the stove and let them cook very gently for about 3–4 hours; then shred and place the meat in a jar.

You can find plenty of similar things in jars in the supermarket, but it is very satisfying to make something you might normally buy and find it tastes much better! Don't be afraid of making big quantities, since most of the purées and pastes will keep for about a week in the fridge, so you can bring them out again another day. You can also serve many of them in different ways: for example, with pasta, fish, or meat.

I started out as a baker and bread is a big part of my life, so the quality of the bread I put out with these little dishes is important. A sourdough or country loaf is perfect. You can toast the bread if you want to, especially if it is a day or so old. In France, we consider that bread that has become a little dry is made for toasting—once it has lost some moisture it will be crisper and better for the digestion than very fresh bread, which can be slightly doughy. We call bread that is going to be served with toppings in this way *tartine*, which is the equivalent of the Italian bruschetta. There is no mystery about it. You can either leave the toasted bread plain or brush it with some olive oil. For a bit of a kick, I sometimes rub it all over with a cut garlic clove as well, which breaks up and embeds itself into the bread, making it good and garlicky.

Rough eggplant purée

INGREDIENTS

Makes enough to fill 2 medium (8oz) preserving jars

2 medium eggplants
large sprig of thyme
1 garlic clove
sea salt and freshly ground
   black pepper
3 tablespoons olive oil
1 large shallot
1 tablespoon pine nuts
good slug of extra-virgin olive oil

PREPARATION

✳ Preheat your oven to 425°F. Cut the eggplants in half lengthwise and use a sharp knife to score the flesh in lines one way and then the other, to make a crisscross pattern.
✳ Pick the leaves of thyme from their stalks.
✳ Cut the clove of garlic in half and remove the green germ, if necessary.

METHOD

1 Season the eggplants and drizzle with 2 tablespoons of the olive oil.

2 Rub each half of eggplant with the cut edges of the garlic. It will disintegrate and disappear into the cuts in the eggplant to flavor it all the way through. Press the thyme leaves into the cuts, too.

3 Put the eggplant halves, cut-side up, on a baking sheet and place in the preheated oven for about 45 minutes, until they are soft and very black-looking. The point of cooking them for such a long time is to evaporate as much moisture as possible and concentrate the flavor.

4 Remove the eggplants from the oven, scoop out the flesh with a tablespoon, and put it into a colander (pieces of garlic and thyme, too) to drain off any remaining moisture.

5 Finely chop the shallot.

6 Turn out the drained eggplant flesh from the colander and roughly chop it.

7 Heat the remaining 1 tablespoon of olive oil in a pan, put in the shallot and pine nuts, and cook over very low heat for 2–3 minutes until the shallot is tender, but not colored.

8 Add the eggplant and cook for 2–3 minutes more. Take off the heat, add a good pour of extra-virgin olive oil, and stir well. Leave to cool.

Q &A...

HOW DO I STORE THE EGGPLANT PURÉE / CHICKPEA AND OLIVE OIL PURÉE?

If you are not using the purée immediately, you can put it into a clean preserving jar and keep it in the fridge for up to a week. Just spoon it in and make sure you pour a good layer of olive oil over the top to preserve it. If you take some out and then put the jar back in the refrigerator, add a bit more oil and wipe the sides of the jar to remove any paste that might turn moldy.

HOW ELSE CAN I USE THE EGGPLANT PURÉE?

This is good cold (or reheated over low heat in a pan) with fish. Or you could use it as a tasty sauce for pasta.

Chickpea and olive oil purée

PREPARATION

✳ If you are using dried chickpeas, soak them overnight in cold water and then cook them according to the instructions on page 86.

✳ If you are using canned chickpeas, drain them in a colander and rinse them well under cold running water, until all the cloying brine has been washed away and the chickpeas have separated out.

✳ Peel the garlic cloves, halve them, and remove the green germ, if necessary.

✳ Juice the lemon.

METHOD

1 Put the chickpeas and garlic into a blender and then use the pulse button to blend in short bursts until you have a reasonably smooth paste. The reason I always suggest using the pulse button is that I find people tend to put ingredients into food processors or blenders and process them to death, when actually what you might want is something a bit chunkier, with more character. If you use just short bursts, you are controlling the machine, rather than it controlling you. You can always process something a bit more, but you can never do it less!

2 The mixture of chickpeas and garlic will be quite stiff, so now add the lemon juice and pulse again. Next, begin to add the oil a little at a time (again, pulsing in short bursts before you add more) until you get to the consistency you like—you want to end up with a fairly loose, but not too runny, paste. You may not need all the oil, or you may want a little more, depending on how much the chickpeas absorb. The purée shouldn't need any salt and pepper because the garlic and lemon juice do the seasoning for you.

HOW CAN I VARY THE RECIPE?

If you would like a spicy version of this, you can add a chopped red chile to the chickpeas and garlic when you put them in the blender.

INGREDIENTS

Makes enough to fill 2 medium (8oz) preserving jars

1 cup dried chickpeas, or 1 x 15.5oz can
2 garlic cloves
1 lemon
about 1 cup extra-virgin olive oil

Q&A...

WHY DO YOU REMOVE THE GERM OF THE GARLIC?
The germ is the sprout in the center of each clove, which is quite small and pale when the garlic is young, but as the bulb grows older it becomes green and strong and bitter-tasting. The germ is the part that can make garlic indigestible. To remove it, halve the clove and then lift out the germ with the tip of a small sharp knife. This only applies to chopping garlic, not crushing the cloves.

Bertinet Basics

✳ **What is the best way to juice a lemon?** *See page 102*

Pesto

I like to add a little lemon juice to pesto to give some extra zing and freshness. You can also use walnuts instead of pine nuts, or arugula, cilantro, or a blend of herbs instead of basil. Pesto originates in Genoa in the Liguria region of Italy, where they traditionally make quite subtle, aromatic olive oil, which I prefer to a strong peppery, fruity one—the kind that is more typical of Tuscany—since the latter is a bit too aggressive.

INGREDIENTS

Makes enough to fill 2 medium (8oz) preserving jars

3 garlic cloves
1 cup Parmesan
1 lemon
¾ cup pine nuts
3–4 bunches of basil (you should have enough to fill the bowl of your food processor loosely)
about ¼ cup extra-virgin olive oil
sea salt

PREPARATION

* Peel the garlic, halve the cloves, and remove the green germs, if necessary.
* Grate the Parmesan.
* Halve the lemon and squeeze out the juice.

METHOD

1 The key to a good pesto is not to overwork the ingredients, otherwise the basil bruises and will start to turn black, and you will lose its fresh flavor. Traditionally, pesto was made using a mortar and pestle, and if you do want to do it this way, see the Q&A on the following page. I prefer to use a food processor, using the pulse button, as for the chickpea purée on page 23, so that you work it as little as possible and keep the pesto nice and coarse, but loose.

2 Put the pine nuts, garlic, and Parmesan into your machine and pulse for a few seconds, until you have a quite coarse paste. Add the basil and pulse again until the basil has all been chopped. Add the lemon juice and a little of the olive oil and pulse again. Keep adding oil to the mix, pulsing in bursts, until you have the texture you want. Taste and season with a little salt if you think it needs it—but remember that Parmesan is quite salty anyway.

Tapenade

I like to use Kalamata olives for this (see Q&A page 87), but you can use any good-quality black olives. The tuna and anchovies give a really deep "meaty" flavor, but if you want to make a vegetarian version you can leave them out and just add some more olives and capers instead.

INGREDIENTS

Makes enough to fill 2 medium (8oz) preserving jars

10oz black olives
3oz canned anchovy fillets, in oil
3oz canned tuna, in oil
5oz capers, in vinegar
½ lemon
5 tablespoons extra-virgin olive oil

PREPARATION

* Drain the olives, anchovies, tuna, and capers. If you are using Kalamata olives they will usually be in oil—if this is good-quality oil, use a few tablespoons in the tapenade in place of the olive oil.
* Pit the olives: with a small, sharp knife make three incisions in each olive from end to end—keep the cuts at equal distances—then pull away the three similar-sized segments from the pit, without tearing or bruising the fruit.
* Juice the lemon.

METHOD

Put the olives in a food processor and make good use of your pulse button to chop them roughly. Add the rest of the ingredients and keep pulsing in short bursts until you get a coarse paste. I like tapenade to be quite coarse, but some people prefer it smoother; in which case, just process it a little more. It really is up to you. You shouldn't need to add any salt because the anchovies should make it salty enough.

Q &A...

CAN I USE A MORTAR AND PESTLE INSTEAD OF A FOOD PROCESSOR?

Using a mortar and pestle is all about choosing the right kind of equipment and then crushing and grinding your ingredients, rather than just bashing them. There is no point in buying a small wooden or marble mortar (bowl) that is as smooth as a baby's bottom. It might look decorative, but what you need is a rough surface that is plenty big enough for your ingredients, so that you can crush them quickly and easily without overworking them. You can find big granite mortar and pestles relatively cheaply in Asian and Latino supermarkets.

HOW DO I STORE THE PESTO / TAPENADE?

They can be kept in the fridge, covered in a layer of olive oil, for a few days, or in a container in the freezer for several weeks. When you defrost them you may need to add a little olive oil to refresh them.

HOW ELSE CAN I USE THE PESTO?

Of course, you can use the pesto tossed through hot pasta, or drizzle a spoonful over grilled fish.

HOW ELSE CAN I USE THE TAPENADE?

To make a crunchy, golden topping for roast lamb. Prepare the tapenade without the tuna and combine it with bread-crumbs in a ratio of 2:1, i.e., to 4 tablespoons of tapenade add 2 of bread crumbs. Smear the mixture over your leg of lamb and roast in the oven in the normal way (see page 134). The anchovies and olives will infuse the lamb with a great flavor.

Oven-dried tomatoes

INGREDIENTS

Makes enough to fill 1 medium (8oz) preserving jar

1 container (9oz) cherry tomatoes
sea salt and freshly ground black
  pepper
1 teaspoon superfine sugar
few sprigs each of fresh thyme
  and rosemary

PREPARATION

✳ Preheat your oven to 225°F.

✳ Cut the tomatoes in half. I notice that most people seem to halve tomatoes by cutting them from top to bottom—i.e., starting at the point where the tomato was attached to the stalk—whereas I cut them the other way, through their "equator," if you like, since they look much neater when cut this way.

✳ A little tip: when you have cut the tomatoes in half, squeeze them slightly so some of their juice comes out. Removing a little bit of the moisture means they will dry out in the oven more quickly, which is useful, especially with the bigger cherry tomatoes.

METHOD

Lay the tomato halves on a baking sheet, skin-side down. Season and sprinkle with the sugar and herbs. Put in the preheated oven for 2 hours until they are dry, but still soft.

Q&A...

HOW DO I STORE THE OVEN-DRIED TOMATOES?

If you are not eating all of them immediately, leave the tomatoes to cool and then pack them into a clean preserving jar with enough good olive oil to cover them. Store in the fridge for 2–3 weeks.

HOW ELSE CAN I USE THE OVEN-DRIED TOMATOES?

For a quick, intensely tomato-flavored pasta sauce, process the contents of a jar of oven-dried tomatoes in olive oil in a food processor and stir into hot drained pasta.

HOW CAN I VARY THE RECIPE?

You can make a crusty, herby version to serve with grilled meat or fish by blending together some chopped basil and curly parsley, a couple of garlic cloves, a big handful of soft bread crumbs, and a little olive oil, and then pressing some of the mixture into each halved tomato before putting them in the oven at a higher temperature—around 350°F. For a more robust, Provençal filling, substitute some of the tapenade on page 24 for the herby bread crumb mixture.

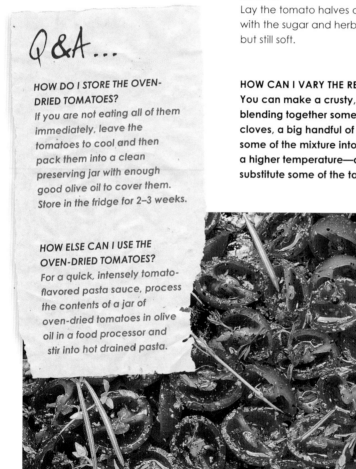

Caramelized onions

Onions are a fundamental part of the cooking of so many cultures, from Europe to Southeast Asia, because as they cook they lose their raw pungency and develop a depth of taste that also acts as a natural flavor enhancer, pulling together the ingredients in a dish. Every style of cooking treats them in a different manner: from quick stir-frying over high heat to this very, very slow, gentle method of cooking onions that owes more to the Indian way.

I find most people, when they come to my classes, are surprised at how long you can cook onions. The way we usually cook onions for the base of a casserole or a sauce tends to take 10 minutes or so, until they are just soft and transparent (that's if we don't put them on too high a heat and burn them, of course!). For many Indian dishes, however, you cook the onions for a much longer time before you start building up the rest of the flavors.

When onions are growing in the ground they store energy in the form of sugars, and so when you cook them really slowly like this, the sugars break down and eventually caramelize; the longer and slower onions are cooked, the sweeter they become. Even without the added sugar and balsamic vinegar, they would be sweet, but adding these just makes them more chutney-like.

PREPARATION
✳ Finely slice the onions.

METHOD
Put the sliced onions, with all the rest of the ingredients, into a big, heavy-bottomed pan over low heat. You want the onions to cook very, very slowly, so that they are soft and really sweet. So, rather than heating the oil and butter first, then adding your onions and running the risk of frying them too quickly and burning them, I find it helps to put everything in cold; then let the pan gradually come up to temperature. That way, you are much more in control. Once the oil and butter are hot, just keep everything ticking over very, very slowly, stirring regularly. First of all, the onions will start to soften and turn translucent and then they will gradually darken to take on a rich, caramel color—this could take anywhere from half an hour to an hour, so keep an eye on them, stirring every so often. Toward the end of the cooking time, they might start to catch a bit on the bottom of the pan, but don't worry, just add a little extra oil. The flavor of the onions really intensifies as they cook, so you shouldn't need to add any salt and pepper.

INGREDIENTS
Makes enough to fill 1 medium (8oz) preserving jar

6 medium onions
2 bay leaves
1 teaspoon good-quality *Herbes de Provence*
2 tablespoons dark soft brown sugar
1 tablespoon balsamic vinegar
8 tablespoons butter
4 tablespoons vegetable oil

Q&A...

HOW DO I STORE THE CARAMELIZED ONIONS?
You can keep the onions in a clean preserving jar in the fridge for about 2 weeks. Because they have been cooked with sugar and vinegar, which act as preservatives, you don't need to cover them with olive oil (as you did in the previous recipes).

Bertinet Basics

✳ **What is the best way to chop or slice an onion?** *See page 60*

Pork rillettes

The first part of the technique is making a confit, the age-old method in which meat is cooked very, very slowly, bathed in fat, so it stays very moist and tender, but has an added richness and completely different "fall-apart" texture from meat that has been cooked any other way. The most famous is duck confit, a French brasserie staple. Once cooked, the duck breasts or legs are kept preserved under a thick layer of fat that sets hard when cold, keeping the oxygen out so the meat doesn't spoil. You can buy confit in jars and cans in all French delis and supermarkets. When you want to eat it, you just have to reheat it at high temperature so that it heats through and the skin crisps up (see Bonus Recipe, page 29).

For rillettes, instead of keeping the meat in one piece, as for confit, once it is cooked you shred it into a very coarse pâté, season it with a little spice, and then preserve it in the same way with a layer of fat over the top, which will set hard. Traditionally, it is eaten just like pâté, with some tangy, vinegary cornichons (little gherkins) whose sharpness cuts through the sweet richness of the rillettes.

Some people cook the meat in the oven, but I prefer to do it in a big, heavy-bottomed pan on top of the stove. The thick base of the pan stops it from getting too hot, and it is easier to keep an eye on it—you don't want the meat to overcook or it will become chewy and won't shred properly.

It is a bit tricky to make small quantities of rillettes, since the meat is more likely to dry out as you cook it, so it is best to make plenty and keep some in the refrigerator—it will last for 1 month in preserving jars sealed with a layer of goose fat.

This recipe uses pork shoulder, but you could make it in exactly the same way using the equivalent weight of wild boar, rabbit meat, duck or goose breasts or legs instead. You need to use the pork belly, whatever other meat you have, since it contributes to the fat content and adds its own flavor.

What makes good pork rillettes is careful seasoning. I have made the addition of mixed spice optional. I like the warmth that a bit of added spice brings—but you already have nutmeg in there, so I suggest you taste the rillettes at the point of seasoning first, and see whether you feel they need something more.

INGREDIENTS

Makes enough to fill 4–5 medium (8oz) preserving jars

1lb pork belly
1lb pork shoulder, off the bone
2 garlic cloves
few sprigs of thyme and rosemary
   plus a couple of bay leaves, for the
   bouquet garni
about 10oz goose fat—you need
   enough to cover all the ingredients
   in your pan
1/3 cup dry white wine
5 black peppercorns
1/2 nutmeg, to taste
sea salt and freshly ground
   black pepper
pinch of ground mixed spice (optional—
   see introduction)

"I like the warmth that a bit of added spice brings."

PREPARATION

✳ You will need to make this 24 hours before serving so that the rillettes can chill and firm up in the fridge.
✳ Cut both batches of pork into strips, roughly 2 x ½in.
✳ Peel the garlic cloves and lightly crush with the back of a knife.
✳ Tie the herbs together with a piece of string to make your bouquet garni.

METHOD

1 Put the pork, goose fat, wine, garlic, bouquet garni, and peppercorns in a heavy-bottomed pan over very low heat for 3–4 hours. I mean really, really low heat. The surface of the fat should be just trembling, not actually bubbling. Experiment to find the best burner on your stovetop and if you are having difficulty keeping it low enough, raise the pan above the heat source with a trivet of some kind—one of those stands that are sold to balance woks would do the trick.

2 The way to test whether the meat is ready is to take out a little bit and press it between your finger and thumb. If it shreds easily, it is done.

3 Now drain off the fat, which you will need to keep. I'm saying this upfront because psychologically people think: "drain... over a sink..." and then all the precious fat is gone! So, yes, drain the contents of the pan through a colander, but put it over a bowl, so that you collect all the fat. Remove the garlic cloves and discard them.

4 Place the bowl of fat next to the part of the stovetop you have been using, so that it stays warm while you shred the meat. The easiest way is to use two forks and pull the meat into strands the way the Chinese shred Peking duck at your table in restaurants.

5 Stir the shredded meat into the bowl of warm goose fat and then grate in your nutmeg. Stir well and taste. Season with salt and pepper. You will need to salt it properly to bring out the flavors fully, but add just a little salt at first, and then wait for the crystals to dissolve well and penetrate the meat before tasting again to make sure you have seasoned enough. At this point, you can take a teaspoonful and mix it with a sprinkling of mixed spice, to see if you want to add it or not.

6 Ladle the mixture from the bowl into preserving jars, pressing down so that the fat rises to the top. You need a good thick covering of fat, which will turn solid to seal and preserve the rillettes. If not enough rises to the top, use what is left in the bowl to pour over the top. Chill in the fridge for at least 12 hours before serving. If you have any fat left over that you don't need, you can keep it in the fridge for when you make rillettes the next time.

Bonus recipe: How to make confit of duck

This is a great dish for when friends come over, because you can prepare it in advance, keep it in the fridge, and then simply heat it through. Traditional confit involves curing the meat first by salting it for a few hours. This is a quick version. Score the skin of 4 duck legs in a crisscross fashion, using the tip of a sharp knife, and then rub with some rough sea salt and freshly ground black pepper. The scoring of the skin will help the meat absorb the salt. Follow the method for rillettes, but don't use the pork belly. You might need some extra goose fat to make sure the duck legs are completely covered in the pan. When they are cooked, instead of shredding the meat, leave the legs whole. Store them with the herbs and peppercorns under the fat in a big jar or other sealed container. To reheat them, lift them out of their fat and fry quickly or put them on a baking sheet in a hot oven (400°F) for 12–15 minutes, until they are heated through and the skin is crispy.

Q&A...

HOW DO I STORE THE RILLETTES?
The sealed jars will keep in the fridge for 1 month.

WHY DO YOU KEEP THESE PASTES AND PURÉES IN A CLEAN JAR, NOT A STERILIZED JAR, AS COOKBOOKS OFTEN SAY?
Because you are keeping them in the fridge, for a relatively short time, it is fine to use clean jars—make sure they are scrupulously clean, though. It is only when you are storing preserves, such as jam or pickles, for a long time, not necessarily in the fridge, that you need to sterilize the jars first. If in doubt, put your jars through a dishwasher cycle and cool them before putting in your pastes and purées.

WHY DO YOU SOMETIMES CRUSH GARLIC RATHER THAN CHOP IT?
It depends on how much of a strong garlicky flavor you want. If you just peel and chop a garlic clove, the flavor won't disperse as well as if you crush the peeled garlic lightly with the back of a large knife. When you do this, it breaks down the cells, so you release more of the oil and flavor, and also you don't get big pieces of garlic in the mouth. Something I find myself doing increasingly is leaving the garlic cloves in their skins when I crush them. That way, you get the flavor into a dish, but the cloves stay intact and easily recognizable, so if people don't want to bite into a whole clove they can avoid them.

A big green salad

You might wonder why I am including a green salad in this book—doesn't everyone know how to make one? Well, I think what you put into a salad deserves as much thought as you would give to anything else you make. However, salads often suffer either from being boring—just some lettuce, tomato, and cucumber—or from being way too complicated. In the last decade or so, since they have become fashionable, they are often stuffed full of ingredients that are meant to be unusual or daring but don't necessarily add up to something you want to eat.

The green salad that I grew up with in France was as straightforward as could be: green leaves, tossed in oil and vinegar. It would be put on the table with the bread at the beginning of the meal, but it would usually be eaten with the cheese, as a refreshing palate cleanser, before dessert.

This green salad has a few more things in it, but still keeps the flavors simple and clean. If you want to test in advance what a combination of ingredients and leaves is going to taste like, cut some small pieces of asparagus, avocado, zucchini, whatever you are planning to put in, and roll them up inside a little stack of the different leaves and herbs you intend to use, take a bite, and see what you think.

A good salad shouldn't need more than four or five main ingredients, and it should have good color and texture—you don't want everything to be soft, or crunchy; try to get a good contrast of both.

When people in my classes ask about what ingredients go best with what, I say that the first thing to think about is what ingredients are in season, since you usually find that when things are ready for harvesting at the same time, they go together. Beyond that, a good guideline is to think of the flag of a country—say, Italy or Spain—and then include only produce that is typical from there. Rules are meant to be broken, of course, but what I am saying is don't go wildly mixing Moroccan spices with Italian buffalo mozzarella, or putting prosciutto with couscous, assuming that because you are mixing everything together in a salad bowl they will somehow taste good together. I'm not saying seemingly outlandish combinations can't be amazing: just think and taste before you plunge in.

This salad is inspired by being in England in the spring and summer. Maybe being French I am more aware of the way the two countries seem to have their own colors and light, but I am always struck by the beautiful mix of different greens, especially around Bath, where I live and work. There are some days when the sun comes out over fields that are lush because there has been a lot of rain, and the colors of the grass, the hedgerows, and the trees are so vivid they are just stunning. So different from the countryside of northern France, where I was brought up, or the colors of sun-baked fields and lavender around Provence, where we go on family vacations.

"A good salad shouldn't need more than four or five main ingredients."

It is that mix of greens that I have tried to capture in this salad, with its peas, asparagus, and beans—all of which sum up England in the spring and summer.

As I said, rules are meant to be broken, and I've also included avocado, which is grown only in tropical climates and is no way native to England. However, it has

Q&A...

DO YOU ALWAYS USE THE SAME RATIO OF VINEGAR AND OIL FOR VINAIGRETTE?

My guideline is always 1–2 parts vinegar to 3–4 of oil. Some people like more or less of each, but the one thing I would say is that the dressing is called vinaigrette for a reason. I know there is a fashion for using quite a high ratio of oil, but I think you should be able to taste the sharpness of the vinegar—this is what helps you digest the foods you are eating it with, which are usually richer: for example, meat, pasta, or cheese. To your mixture of oil and vinegar you can add anything you like: a little mustard, some chopped shallot, a squeeze of lemon juice, and soft herbs such as chives, parsley, mint, basil, or tarragon, chopped finely; even some roughly chopped tomatoes (skinned and deseeded first—see page 77 for an easy way to do this). I find that once I give people the basic formula they are happy to experiment.

INGREDIENTS

Makes enough for 4–6

1 large Romaine lettuce
big bunch of local asparagus
   in season
1lb peas in pods in season
7oz fine French beans
2 ripe avocados

FOR THE VINAIGRETTE
1 teaspoon Dijon mustard
2 tablespoons red wine vinegar
8 tablespoons olive oil
herbs (optional): basil, thyme, mint,
   parsley, chives, whatever you like
sea salt and freshly ground
   black pepper

pretty much been adopted in the country, and its flavor works really well with the other ingredients.

I've gone for crunchy, sweet Romaine lettuce, but you could also use baby spinach or pea shoots when they are in season. And you could add chopped parsley or mint. When asparagus is out of season you could also add some raw shaved fennel or grated zucchini (if you prefer, you can blanch the vegetables first, as in the recipe). The one thing I wouldn't put in is scallions, which I find too strong in a salad.

If I were you, I would also make up a much larger quantity of the vinaigrette than I have suggested here—just the oil, vinegar, mustard, and seasoning—and keep it in a bottle in the fridge. You can add whatever chopped herbs you like the next time you want to use it.

Of course, this salad doesn't have to stay green. If you want to bulk it up a bit, to make it into a main course, you could add some cooked chicken or chunks of cooked salad potatoes. I wouldn't add anything with too distinctive a flavor, though, such as smoked salmon.

I like it just as it is, with roast chicken and a bowlful of buttered new potatoes.

PREPARATION

✳ Cut up the lettuce, using the big green leaves as well as the heart. Wash well in plenty of running water and then dry, either in a kitchen towel or using a salad spinner. You don't want soggy lettuce, and any water clinging to the leaves will dilute your dressing.

✳ Provided your asparagus spears are fresh, if you bend them, they will snap about three quarters of the way down, just above the woodier part. Keep the top parts (i.e., the ends with the tips) for the salad. You can chop up the rest and put in the freezer for adding to stocks or soups (see page 200).

✳ Pod the peas. Trim the beans at the stalk end, but leave the pointed ends.

✳ Have ready a big bowl filled half full with cold water—preferably with some ice.

✳ Finely chop the herbs (if using) for the vinaigrette.

METHOD

1 First, make your vinaigrette. Put the mustard into a small bowl, add the vinegar and oil, and whisk together. Add the chopped herbs and season to taste.

2 Bring a pan of water to a boil and either put in the beans and cook for 2 minutes or put them into a steaming basket over the top and steam for the same length of time. You aren't cooking them, just taking that raw edge off them, so they should still be nice and crunchy. Lift them out of the water with a slotted spoon (keep the water for cooking the asparagus) and put them into your bowl of cold water. The cold stops them from cooking any further and also preserves that brilliant green color, which will fade if you let them cool down slowly.

3 Cook the asparagus in the same water, or steamer, as before—again, for just a couple of minutes, until the spears are just tender if you pierce the thickest part with the tip of a sharp knife. Add them to the beans in the cold water.

4 I like to use the fresh peas raw, but if you prefer, you can boil or steam them in the same way, for just a minute, and then add to the beans and asparagus in your bowl of cold water.

WHAT KIND OF VINEGAR IS IT BEST TO USE FOR VINAIGRETTE?

I almost always use red wine vinegar, because it has a nice mellowness and gives a rosy color to the dressing. I might use white wine vinegar if I want something a little more neutral, if I were using a strong herb like fresh tarragon and I wanted the flavor really to come through. Cider vinegar I use only occasionally, but it works nicely in a goat cheese salad. I wouldn't use a very expensive matured Balsamic vinegar in a vinaigrette. If you are going to pay a lot of money for a beautiful aged vinegar, just drizzle a little over some tomatoes to show it off at its best. If you do want that sweetness in your dressing, use a less expensive Balsamic vinegar.

WHAT KIND OF OIL SHOULD I USE?

Just as I wouldn't use my best Balsamic vinegar, I wouldn't use a very expensive extra-virgin olive oil either—keep that to sprinkle just as it is over grilled fish or use it all by itself over salad leaves (maybe with just a little sea salt or the tiniest squeeze of lemon).

The salads I was brought up on in Brittany were dressed with vegetable oil, vinegar, and mustard, and tasted fantastic. Olive oil wasn't used much in my part of France until years later. Now, of course, we are all aware of using good extra-virgin olive oil, not only for its flavor but also for its health-giving properties. Often, I will use half extra-virgin olive oil and half vegetable oil; lately though, I have been using rapeseed (canola) oil much more, since it makes a lovely dressing.

5 Drain your vegetables in a colander, while you prepare the avocados. Cut each one in half, then take the half with the pit and tap the pit firmly with the part of the knife blade near the handle so that it cuts into the pit and you can lift it out cleanly. Once the pits are out, cut each half of avocado lengthwise again, then you should be able to peel the skin easily from each quarter. Cut each quarter into slices, crosswise or lengthwise, as you like.

6 At the last minute, dress the salad: put the vinaigrette in the bottom of your serving bowl and then tumble in the leaves and vegetables and gently toss together really well. Take your time, making sure everything is well coated.

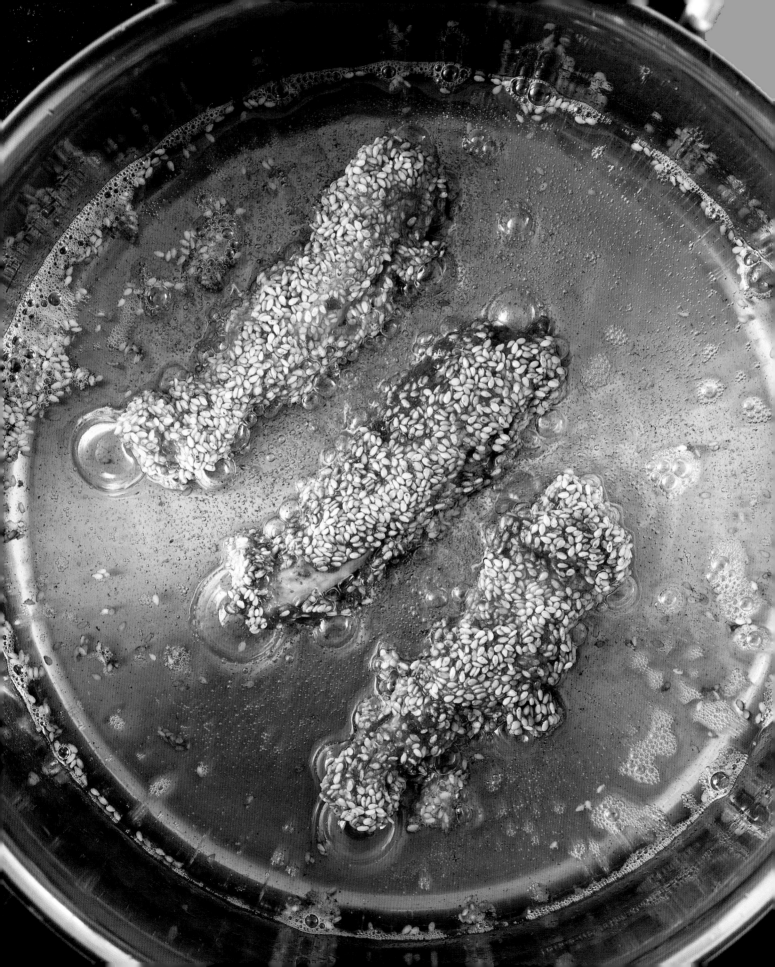

Crispy sesame chicken salad with raspberry beer dressing

This is a more substantial salad that could be an appetizer or lunch. It follows the same principles as the green salad (see page 30), in that what you are looking for is a good contrast of texture and flavor. In this case, the sesame seed batter gives a crispy crunch and the raspberry beer and fresh raspberries add a sweet and sour element.

The beer and sesame batter is an idea I picked up when I was cooking at a South African food festival many years ago. I started making the batter with raspberry beer because fruit beers are a favorite in my part of northern France. I also use beer in the dressing.

There is a long tradition of including fruit in salads, and as long as you don't overdo it, it can work really well—in this salad, there is only a scattering of raspberries, so you get just the occasional taste. It's lovely in summer with a glass of chilled raspberry beer or rosé.

The edible flowers are completely optional, but adding something like mint, pea, geranium, chive, or barage flowers is a very easy way of making a salad look a bit special; and each has its own flavor.

The choice of salad leaves is up to you. In French markets, you often see big boxes of *mesclun,* a mixture of all kinds of salad leaves. You pick what you want and put it into a bag. I've seen similar mixes of leaves at farmers' markets and gourmet groceries, but I guess most people pick up mixed bags of ready-to-eat leaves in the supermarket. I can't argue against these, except to say that if you can find loose ones you are avoiding excess packaging. These bagged salads have introduced all kinds of leaves to customers who once had a choice of only a few varieties of lettuce, and perhaps they have also encouraged some people to grow their own. After initial worries about what gases were being used in the bags, and whether the leaves were washed in chlorine, the fears seem to have settled down, and since most preprepared leaves are now washed in mineral water, there is no need to wash them again.

This is not a pinch of salt

...but this is!

I like the nuttiness of the canola oil in the dressing, which goes well with the sesame seeds and the spelt flour, but you can use a light olive oil if you prefer.

INGREDIENTS

For 4

1 large egg (preferably free-range)
$1/3$ cup raspberry beer (you will need
    some more for the dressing, below)
sea salt and freshly ground
    black pepper
$3/4$ cup fine spelt flour, plus extra for
    dusting the chicken (you can use
    all-purpose flour, but the spelt
    gives a nice nutty flavor)
$3/4$ cup sesame seeds
2 good-sized skinless chicken breasts
mixed salad leaves of your choice
canola oil (or vegetable oil),
    for frying
edible flowers (optional)
handful of fresh raspberries, to garnish

FOR THE DRESSING
1 tablespoon Dijon mustard
1 teaspoon good honey
2 tablespoons raspberry beer
2 tablespoons red wine vinegar
    (or raspberry vinegar, if you
    have some)
sea salt and freshly ground
    black pepper
6 tablespoons extra-virgin
    canola oil

**HOW CAN I VARY THIS RECIPE?
Sometimes I use cherry beer—
another favorite in my part of
France—and garnish the salad with a
few fresh cherries in season, rather
than with the raspberries.**

PREPARATION

✳ Make the batter: whisk the egg in a bowl with the beer and a pinch of salt.
Start to add the flour gradually, whisking well to prevent lumps. Once all the flour
has been incorporated, leave the batter to rest while you prepare the rest of
the ingredients.

✳ Pour the sesame seeds onto a plate and keep to one side.

✳ Slice horizontally through each breast of chicken (as if you were cutting
through the middle of a baguette to make a sandwich) so that you end up with
two pieces the same shape and thickness. Then cut each half into fine strips
lengthwise—you will probably get 10–12 thin strips per breast, depending on
its size.

✳ Put the strips into a bowl, season well with a good pinch of salt, and then
sprinkle on some spelt (or all-purpose) flour and toss well with the chicken, so that
the strips are coated. This dusting of flour will help the batter to cling to the
chicken—without it, the batter would just slide off the smooth surface of the meat.

✳ Wash and dry the salad leaves if they are loose or picked from the garden.

✳ To make the dressing, place all the ingredients in a clean jelly jar, put on the
lid and shake lightly. The more you shake it, the smoother your dressing will
become, but rather than completely amalgamating it, I like the dressing to be a
bit loose—you are going to drizzle it over the chicken and salad at the end,
rather than toss the salad with it, and so it will look more interesting if the vinegar
and oil are slightly separated; the vinegar will look a bit like oil slicks on water!
Sometimes, if I have a little mustard left in a pot, I make my dressing in that—
waste not, want not!

METHOD

1 Dip each strip of chicken into the batter and then into the sesame seeds.
   Coat well in the seeds.

2 In a big, heavy frying pan heat enough canola (or vegetable) oil to come to
   about ½ inch in depth. We tend to think of battered food as being deep-
   fried, which is true of, say, large pieces of fish in batter that need plenty of oil to
   cook properly, but for this recipe we are using thin strips of chicken, so it is fine to
   shallow fry them. The key is not to overcrowd your pan or you will bring down the
   temperature of the oil. This chicken is going to cool a little before you serve it
   anyway, so you can cook it in batches if you need to, allowing each piece a bit
   of space around it.

3 Once the oil is hot, but not smoking, put in the strips and cook for 2–3 minutes
   on each side, depending on their size, or until the batter is light golden and
   the sesame seeds whitish. The meat should be perfectly cooked through, but if
   you want to test it, take out one of the strips and cut in half to make sure.

4 Lift the strips out of the hot oil with a spatula and drain well on paper towels.
   Leave to cool slightly before assembling the salad.

5 To serve, arrange the leaves on plates, scatter the chicken strips on top,
   drizzle over the dressing, and garnish with a few edible flowers (if using) and a
   handful of raspberries.

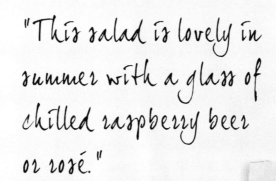

"This salad is lovely in summer with a glass of chilled raspberry beer or rosé."

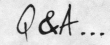

Q&A...

WHAT DO YOU MEAN BY "GOOD" HONEY?

There is a massive range of honey around. Cheap honey can be very sweet and not very distinctive-tasting because it is usually a blend of different honeys. However, in the same way as you have single estate wines and olive oils, you can also find honeys that come from bees that have collected nectar from a specific plant—heather, hawthorn, clover, etc.—that gives the honey a special flavor, aroma, and color. Even though some climates may not be suited to honey production, local honeys are often available in many regions. The advantage of buying from a local producer is that the honey will usually be less filtered than commercial honey, which is also heated—a process that often removes the pollen, much of the flavor, and also many of the health benefits. In France, pollen is a poplular ingredient added to many dishes—in the US, health-food stores sometimes stock it. Occasionlly, I sprinkle a little over this salad at the end; I like the flavor, and it is supposedly very good for you.

Bean and tomato salad with ginger, chile, and herbs

INGREDIENTS
For 2

1 shallot
small knob of fresh ginger
1 red or green chile, or more, to taste
2 fresh tomatoes or 1 x 14.5oz can
handful of cilantro or basil, or
   whatever herb you like
1–2 x 15.5oz cans mixed beans
½ lemon or lime
1 tablespoon red wine vinegar
good slug of extra-virgin olive oil
sea salt and freshly ground
   black pepper

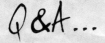

Q&A...

WHY USE SHALLOTS RATHER THAN ONIONS?
Shallots have a little more subtlety and sweetness—I would rather eat raw shallot than onion.

WHAT IS THE HOTTEST PART OF THE CHILE?
The membrane and the seeds. This is where the natural chemical capsaicin occurs; this gives the heat and the chile-rush of endorphins (the body's natural painkillers) that makes people love chile. If you don't want so much heat, run a teaspoon along the length of the halved chile and scoop out the seeds and membrane. Wash your hands well after you have touched chiles and before you touch your eyes or any sensitive parts of the body or they will sting and burn.

The point of this recipe is that it is pretty much a salad straight from the pantry. I first made it when I had a craving for carbohydrates that nothing in the fridge would really satisfy. Now it has become one of my favorite snacks or suppers. I have given the quantities for just two people, but I also often make a big bowlful of it in the summer if I am barbecuing tuna or meat (sometimes I even add a can of tuna). The quantities are very loose, so you can scale it up as you like.

There is something really nourishing about beans, and you can use whatever you like—cranberry beans, black-eyed peas, or lima beans—but the best is a mixture. You could add chickpeas, too. Of course, you could cook some dried beans (see below), but the idea is that you can put everything together really quickly—at a push you can do it in about 4 minutes, or during a commercial break on TV—so no excuses for phoning for takeout. There is no need to be snobbish about using canned beans, any more than canned tomatoes, which to an Italian are a valued staple when the local season for fresh tomatoes is finished. I have been known just to open a can of plum tomatoes and beans, drain (and rinse the beans), and mix them together with lots of good extra-virgin olive oil and black pepper: gorgeous—and healthy. I don't have any hang-ups about beans from a can, since I was brought up on canned cassoulet, the traditional dish of confit meat, sausages, and beans—it's a time-consuming business to make from scratch, and so, like every other family, I knew we would have cans and jars of good-quality cassoulet in the pantry.

If you do want to use dried beans, soak them in cold water overnight, then drain and rinse well. This will rehydrate them and plump them up so the cooking time will be shorter. Put them into a saucepan with enough cold water to cover, a couple of bay leaves, and a few peppercorns. Don't add salt, since this toughens the skin. Bring to a boil, and then turn down the heat to simmer. With a spoon, skim off any "scum" that rises to the surface—this white-gray froth is a result of proteins being released from the beans. Depending on the type and size, the beans will take around 45 minutes to an hour to cook. To check if they are ready, pop one in your mouth—it should be just tender.

PREPARATION
✳ Rinse the beans under cold water.
✳ Finely slice the shallot.
✳ Peel the ginger and finely slice.
✳ Finely slice the chile.
✳ Cut the tomatoes into quarters.
✳ Roughly chop the herbs.
✳ Squeeze the lemon or lime.

METHOD
Toss all the ingredients together and season well!

"There is no need to be snobbish about using canned beans."

Layered omelet

This is a quick and easy variation on the flat Spanish-style tortilla or Italian frittata. Instead of making one quite thick omelet, you make seven thin ones—one plain and six with different flavorings—that cook in no time. You then stack them up and cut through them all so each layer tastes different. It is a great dish to serve with drinks at a party or as a snack.

INGREDIENTS

For 6 as an appetizer or 24 party portions

FOR EACH OF THE 7 OMELETS
2 large eggs (preferably free-range)
1 teaspoon milk
sea salt and freshly ground black
    pepper
1 teaspoon vegetable oil

FOR THE FLAVORINGS
2 button mushrooms
½ zucchini
1 tomato
¼ cup grated Gruyère
4 tablespoons Parmesan
small handful of mixed herbs, e.g., a few
    leaves of fresh sage, rosemary,
    thyme, and oregano

Bertinet Basics

✳ **What is the best way to clean mushrooms?** *See page 57*

✳ **What is the best way to peel, deseed, and chop tomatoes?** *See page 77*

PREPARATION

✳ Organization is the key here, so get your own little production line going. Have seven little bowls or glasses ready in front of you, each containing 2 eggs, 1 teaspoon milk, and a few twists of salt and pepper. Behind all but the first (which is going to be plain) have a bowl or glass with each of the flavorings: finely diced mushrooms; finely diced zucchini; skinned, deseeded, and finely diced tomato; finely diced or grated Gruyère; finely grated Parmesan; and finely chopped herbs.

✳ Line a flat baking sheet with parchment paper, ready to stack the omelets on as you cook them.

METHOD

1 Heat 1 teaspoon of vegetable oil in a frying pan (about 8 inches in diameter) over medium heat. Ideally, use a nonstick omelet pan or a frying pan that you use regularly and know won't stick.

2 Quickly whisk your first set of eggs and milk with a fork and pour into the pan, lifting and tilting it so that the egg covers the whole of the base. Cook for about 1½ minutes until the egg looks just cooked on top, and then slide it gently out of the pan onto your parchment paper. Don't overcook it; you will be putting another omelet on top of it in a minute or so, and as you keep on adding layers the heat of each omelet will continue to cook the one beneath.

3 Put another teaspoon of oil into your pan. Whisk your second set of eggs and milk, and repeat, but this time as soon as you spread the eggs over the pan, scatter over your first filling—in this case, the mushrooms. Cook for 1½ minutes, as before, and then slide on top of the plain omelet.

4 Continue in this way until you have one plain and six different-flavored omelets sitting one on top of the other. Then put another sheet of parchment paper on top of the stack and press down gently. The oil in each omelet will help them all to stick together as one.

5 You can serve the layered omelet warm or cold. Either way, cut into big wedges, or smaller bite-sized squares. If you want to serve small squares at a party, skewer them with cocktail sticks so that people can pick them up easily.

Q&A...

WHAT IS THE BEST WAY TO CHOP HERBS?
With herbs, you are trying to keep the essential oils intact, thus preserving all the goodness and flavor, so use a very sharp knife (or a mezzaluna if you are comfortable using one). Alternatively, use scissors. Don't worry too much about how finely the herbs are chopped. The important thing is not to bruise them by using something blunt—when this happens, particularly with parsley or basil, you will see the leaves start to turn black. Always dry your herbs well after rinsing them and before chopping; otherwise, if they are damp, they will become mushy and difficult to chop or snip. And only chop/snip them at the last minute, so that you don't release their flavor too early.

WHY ADD MILK TO THE EGGS?
This is an old habit of mine— I think it makes the omelet lighter in taste and texture.

Bonus recipe: How to make a traditional French omelet

Remember, organization is everything, so if you are making a flavored omelet have your filling ready to go before you start: i.e., grate the cheese, chop the ham, mushrooms, etc. The key is not to put in too much filling, or you lose the flavor of the eggs—of course, as always, that flavor depends on good fresh eggs, so try to use free-range or organic eggs from a farm where the hens have been allowed to run around eating natural vegetation. This is what gives tasty, deep golden yolks. Don't season with salt too early or it will begin to break down the eggs and they will be more watery and won't fluff up as well.

Break 3 eggs per omelet into a bowl, add a teaspoon of milk, beat lightly with a fork, and then season with salt and pepper. Put a spoon of butter and a little vegetable oil into an 8in omelet pan or frying pan that won't stick and heat the pan over medium heat. When the butter stops "singing"—i.e., it is no longer sizzling, but hasn't started to turn brown—pour your eggs into the pan. Tilt and swivel your pan with one hand, drawing the eggs lightly into the center with a wooden spatula as they start to cook, and letting the rest of the egg spread out around the pan underneath. Continue doing this until you have a nice fluffy layer that is just set around the outside but still runny in the middle. At this point, you can sprinkle any filling you are using onto the omelet and, with the help of a spatula, fold the other half over the top. I like an omelet to be quite soft in the middle, so I slide it off right away onto my plate, but you can leave it for a minute longer if you prefer your egg firmer.

Mackerel in white wine and vinegar

Really fresh mackerel is one of the tastiest fish, it's cheap, and it's good for you. It is also very underrated. If you get a chance to do a bit of mackerel fishing with the kids on vacation, or manage to buy some from a local fisherman as he comes into the harbor, you won't believe the flavor of the fish when it has just been caught. The next best thing is to look for line-caught mackerel from small day boats or from a fishery that has been accredited by the Marine Stewardhip Council. All the fish comes from boats that work outside different harbors and coves throughout the season to conserve stocks.

Fish prepared this way—i.e., cooked very briefly and marinated in a vinegary solution—is known as *escabeche*, or *carpione* in Italy (where sometimes they fry the fish first). Here, the fish is cooked very briefly in hot vinegar and wine and then left to cool. Most countries have some similar way of "pickling" fish—think of the South American *ceviche*, in which you use citrus juice, usually lime, to "cook" the fish, with no heat, or Scandinavian or Jewish "soused" herrings or rollmops, as they are sometimes called, marinated in vinegar and often sugar.

If you have been into French delis and supermarkets and seen little flat cans of *maquereaux au vin blanc*—the kind that have tops you peel back with a ring pull—that is what I am talking about. When I was growing up, this dish was a classic in bistros all over town, as well as in our house. My grandfather used to go fishing for mackerel and my mother would have a big dish of this in the fridge, which we would enjoy with a green salad and new potatoes for lunch. Once it has chilled in the fridge, the cooking liquor becomes like a soft jelly around the fish, so it is a wonderful, easy thing to take with you on picnics.

There is chile in this, but it isn't meant to be massively hot; otherwise, the delicate flavor of the mackerel will be overpowered. The chile is there for a little background warmth, so I would use a medium-sized red chile (usually the smaller they are, the hotter they become)—but it is up to you.

Q &A...

HOW CAN YOU BE SURE YOU ARE BUYING FRESH FISH?

The golden rule, whenever you buy fish, is that if it is really fresh it will smell only of the sea. If it smells of fish, it is old already. The eyes shouldn't be dry and cloudy—they should be nice and shiny, and not sunken. And if you lift up the gills, they should be bright red underneath, not brown. As I always say, the best thing to do is try to build up a relationship with your fishmonger, if you have one locally, and keep asking questions about where your fish comes from and where it was caught. Even if you just want fillets, I would recommend you buy the whole fish and ask the fishmonger to fillet it in front of you—so you can watch and learn. That way you get more for your money!

"If the fish is really fresh it will smell only of the sea. If it smells of fish, it is already old."

Q&A...

WHY IS LINE-CAUGHT FISH BEST?
If a fish is caught with a rod and line it will usually be handled more carefully, and it will suffer less stress, so its texture will be better. However, line fishing doesn't necessarily mean fishermen sitting in boats with old-fashioned rods, hand-catching each fish; often, the lines are trailed behind boats, and they can catch other unwanted fish, too. The whole issue of fishing methods and sustainability is a tricky one and not that black and white. However, this method is better for the environment than trawling with big nets and disturbing the ocean bed and all the sea life it supports. Some line-caught fish are now tagged, so that you can trace each one back to the fisherman who caught it. A good guide is to look out for fish that are certified by the Marine Stewardhip Council, which works with the fishing industry and marine scientists and awards its blue checkmark to fisheries that meet its standards of sustainability and management.

"My grandfather used to go fishing and my mother would have a big dish of this in the fridge."

PREPARATION

✳ Preheat the oven to 400°F.

✳ If you are using whole mackerel, you will need to fillet them. You need a sharp, flexible knife, not a big chef's knife. Some people start at the back of the head. I find it easier, especially with mackerel, which are relatively small, to begin at the tail end. Start by making an incision at the tail end of the fish and cutting away from you. Edge your knife along the spine, really feeling where it is and keeping your knife in contact with it. The idea is to leave as little of the flesh on the bone as possible. As you work, lift up the tail end of the upper fillet with your free hand and move the blade gently backward and forward as you go—this gentle sawing movement will help you avoid ripping the flesh. Keep going gently, moving the hand that is holding the fillet farther upward toward the head to keep things steady, but, remember, the fish is fragile, so don't press the flesh too hard. Stop cutting just behind the gills. To finish off, cut around the back of the head so that the fillet comes away easily. Now, turn the fish over and repeat on the other side. Cut away the dark area from next to the rib cage.

✳ When you have removed all 8 fillets, wash them carefully and wipe off any excess water with paper towels.

✳ With most fish, I would say keep the bones to use for stock, but not mackerel, since it is too oily and it will make your stock greasy.

✳ Peel the carrot and cut into very thin slices, slightly at an angle, so that you get ovals, rather than rounds.

✳ Peel the onion and slice into rings. Slice the lemon into thin rounds.

✳ Slice the chile in half lengthwise and scoop out the membrane and seeds, which are the hottest part; discard.

✳ Tie all the herbs together in a bunch with butcher's twine to make a bouquet garni.

METHOD

1 Put the sliced onion, carrot, and lemon into a pan. Pour over the wine, water, and vinegar and put in the herbs, spices, chile, sugar, and salt. Stir well and bring to a boil, then turn down the heat and simmer very gently for 15 minutes, until the carrot slices are just tender.

2 Lay your mackerel fillets in an oven-proof dish. I like to alternate them so that you have one skin-side up, the next skin-side down, and so on—it just looks more attractive that way. Once the fillets are in, pour the hot cooking liquid, along with all the vegetables and spices, over the top. It should just cover the fish.

3 Put the dish onto the middle shelf of the preheated oven for just 2 minutes. Normally, I wouldn't be so precise about time, but for this dish, don't guess: set your oven timer. You don't want to cook the fish in the true sense of the word, but the hot vinegar, wine, and salt is curing it, and it will continue to do so as it cools down.

4 Leave the fish to cool in the hot liquid and then put it into the fridge to cure/ set for at least a couple of hours, and up to half a day. If you are not eating it immediately you can pot it in a clean preserving jar—just make sure the fish is submerged under the liquid—and store for up to a couple of weeks in the fridge.

INGREDIENTS

For 4

4 whole mackerel (or 8 mackerel fillets)
1 large carrot
1 medium onion
1 unwaxed lemon
1 medium red chile
few sprigs of thyme
1 bay leaf
bunch of curly parsley
½ bottle of dry white wine, ideally Muscadet
½ cup water
⅓ cup white wine vinegar
4 cloves
1 teaspoon black peppercorns
1 tablespoon sugar
1 tablespoon sea salt, preferably *sel gris* (see page 93)

Goat cheese, mozzarella, and red pepper "roulade"

A couple of techniques are involved in this recipe that will stand you in good stead for many other dishes, including skinning red peppers and then using them to make a "wrapper" for your cheese. I didn't actually want to call this a roulade, because it sounds so seventies, but that is what it is, so what can I do?

This recipe is inspired by Annick, a lovely lady who looks after our family house in France. We were talking about food one day and she told me she had just made a terrine with red peppers and goat cheese. Then she brought some for us to taste, and it was very good. This is my version, in which I have added some mozzarella to the goat cheese to give extra creaminess. I roll up the peppers around the cheese, chill it for 24 hours or so until it is firm, and then, instead of serving it cold, I slice it into rounds and pan-fry it, dusted in some corn flour (or meal) to give a nice crunch and golden color. All the flavors come together beautifully.

If you don't want to slice and fry it you can serve it cold, and it looks pretty impressive if you slice it at the table. I like to make a big roulade, which will feed lots of people. My view is that if you have gone to the trouble of skinning the peppers and rolling everything up, you might as well make plenty, because what you don't eat immediately you can keep in the fridge for up to a week. If you really don't want to make such a big quantity, just halve the ingredients.

I like to use the long, pointed Romano peppers in this roulade. These have a more individual, sweeter flavor than standard red peppers and you can find them easily in most greengrocers or supermarkets.

PREPARATION

✳ You need to assemble everything 24 hours before you want to eat it so that it can chill and firm up in the fridge.

✳ First, skin the peppers so that they are soft and pliable enough to wrap around the filling. If you have a gas stove, the easiest way to do this is to skewer each pepper whole with a fork and hold it over one of the burners, turning all the time until the skin softens, blackens, and blisters. (Alternatively, you can put them under the broiler or on the barbecue in summer.) When they are blackened, put them into a plastic freezer bag, tie a knot in it, and leave to stand for 15–30 minutes. The peppers will steam inside the bag and their skins will loosen. Open up the bag, hold each pepper by its stalk, and then wipe downward with a piece of paper towel. The skin should come off easily, but if you have a few little black bits left, don't worry—they will give a nice chargrilled look to your roulade.

✳ Now you can split each pepper in half lengthwise and take out the seeds and the stalk.

✳ Cut two pieces of plastic wrap, 20 x 12in, and lay them one on top of the other on your work surface.

✳ Tear the mozzarella into shreds.

INGREDIENTS
For 10–12

8–10 long Romano peppers
   (or about 12 large red peppers)
14oz buffalo mozzarella
1¼lb soft goat cheese
freshly ground black pepper
big bunch of basil leaves
about 4 tablespoons extra-virgin olive
   oil, plus a little extra to serve
salad leaves, such as peppery arugula,
   to serve
corn flour (or meal), for dusting
good olive oil or canola oil,
   for frying
balsamic vinegar (optional), to finish

"To roll up the roulade, take hold of the edges of the plastic wrap nearest to you (both layers) and lift upward and away from you."

METHOD

1 Mix the mozzarella with the goat cheese in a bowl. Season with lots of black pepper—you don't need salt because there should be enough saltiness in the two cheeses. Add the whole basil leaves and stir with a wooden spoon. Mix in about 4 tablespoons of extra-virgin olive oil and put in the fridge for 5–10 minutes.

2 Lay your peppers on the double layer of plastic wrap, with the side where the skin was facing downward. You want to arrange them so that the pointed ends and wider ends interlock and overlap very slightly, creating a solid layer with no gaps (see the picture sequence above).

3 Spoon your mixture of cheese down the center of the peppers. To roll up the roulade, take hold of the edges of the plastic wrap nearest to you (both layers) and lift upward and away from you. As you do so, your layer of peppers will start to roll over the cheese mixture. Continue to pull the plastic wrap upward

Q&A...

ARE RED PEPPERS SWEETER THAN GREEN?

There are many varieties of pepper, but in terms of the regular, bulbous ones you see in the grocery and supermarket, the different colors just tell you how ripe they were when they were picked. Green peppers are the most immature and are quite tangy and bitter-tasting, so I would use them when you want a bit of sharpness in a dish. Yellow and orange peppers are sweeter, and red peppers are sweeter still. Sometimes, though, red peppers can be a bit bland and disappointing, which is why I use the pointed Romano variety instead, which have much more flavor—they have become really popular, so you can find them in most supermarkets.

and also use your hands to help the pepper layer wrap around the cheese as tightly as possible. When it is completely rolled, tuck the plastic wrap you have been holding over the top and wrap it up tightly. If you wish, you can wrap it in an outer layer of foil, for extra protection, and twist the ends like a candy wrapper.

4 Put the roulade into the fridge for at least 24 hours. It will firm up nicely in that time, so you will be able to slice it easily.

5 When you are ready to serve, have your salad leaves ready (wash and dry them if they are loose or from the garden).

6 Keeping the roulade in its wrapping, slice into rounds about 1 inch thick with a very sharp knife. You could happily serve this dish as it is, cold, but my favorite way is to have it fried. Remove the plastic wrap. Sprinkle some corn flour (or meal) onto a plate and dust each slice in it. Heat a thin film of olive or canola oil in a large frying pan and fry for about 1 minute on each side, or until golden and crispy—be careful not to overheat the oil to the point of smoking or you will burn the coating of corn flour. The peppers and outer layer of cheese will be warm and melting, and the inside still cold.

7 Serve with your salad leaves and drizzle with some extra-virgin olive oil and a few drops of balsamic vinegar (if using).

Melon and mint chilled soup

This recipe is actually for three different soups: one made with a charentais melon (the French variety of a cantaloupe), one with a watermelon, and one with a honeydew, each of which has its own distinctive and refreshing taste. You can serve a selection in little glasses as an appetizer, with spoons, or hand them around on trays at parties for people to sip (you could even give them straws). The idea shows just how easy it can be to produce something that tastes and looks fantastic, and it will provide quite a talking point.

One thing I always miss is the smell of ripe melons in the French markets throughout the summer. The way to check if a melon is ripe is to press it slightly at the base. There should be a little give and a sweet-scented aroma. On the other hand, you don't want something that is past its best: you will be able to tell if it is overripe because it will have a fermented smell and will be very soft to the touch.

PREPARATION FOR ALL RECIPES
✳ Cut the melon into quarters and run a sharp knife close to the skin to remove it.
✳ Scrape out the seeds and cut the flesh into chunks.
✳ Squeeze the juice of the lime.

For 6 as an appetizer, or 12 for a party (3 mini glasses each)

INGREDIENTS
1 ripe Charentais melon
1 lime
2 teaspoons sugar
2 tablespoons white port
few basil leaves

Charentais melon soup

METHOD
Put the melon, lime juice, and sugar into a food processor and blend until smooth. Add the port and stir. Chill well in the fridge until really cold. Cut the basil leaves into shreds and scatter over the soup.

INGREDIENTS
½ small watermelon
1 lime
2 teaspoons sugar
couple of shots of vodka

Watermelon soup

METHOD
Put the melon, lime juice, and sugar into a food processor and blend until smooth. Add the vodka and stir. Chill well in the fridge until really cold.

Honeydew melon soup

This melon has a different kind of sweetness from the charentais, so I like to enhance it with honey, rather than sugar. I also offset it with a little more lime juice, and no alcohol—since I like the clean taste of the mint—but feel free to experiment.

INGREDIENTS
1 honeydew melon
1 lime
1 teaspoon honey
few mint leaves

METHOD
Put the melon, lime juice, and honey into a food processor and blend until smooth. Sometimes I like to add the mint at this point as well, so that you get little specks of it running through the soup—alternatively, you can keep it back, shred it finely, and scatter it over the top when you serve the soup. Chill well in the fridge until the soup is really cold.

Q&A...

HOW CAN YOU TELL IF A LIME CONTAINS A LOT OF JUICE?
Limes can sometimes be disappointingly dry. To find the juiciest, look for ones with darker green skins, which are more mature than yellowy-green-skinned ones, and choose thinner-skinned ones that feel heavy.

CAN YOU JUICE A LIME MORE EASILY IF YOU ROLL IT UNDER YOUR HAND FIRST?
Yes, this softens the lime and breaks up the membranes, releasing the juice. A few seconds in the microwave will also help.

Chicken, ginger, chile, and noodle soup

Mrs. B doesn't cook very often, but there are a few favorites that she turns out from time to time. This one usually makes an appearance after a period of overindulgence—perhaps in the new year or after we return from vacation. It is such a quick, easy soup that is also a perfect lesson in putting together flavors. The quantities are fairly loose because it really doesn't matter whether you have lots of noodles or bean sprouts, or just a handful, and the quantity of chile you put in is entirely up to you, too. It is also a great thing to make on a Monday night after you have had roast chicken on Sunday. You can boil up the carcass to make the stock (see page 201) and shred any leftover chicken meat into the soup. Alternatively, you could put in some shrimp rather than chicken. Preferably, use raw shrimp and add them with the rest of the ingredients. If you use cooked ones, add them only at the very last minute or they will overcook and become rubbery. To make it more of a meal, add some Chinese leaves or bok choi (chopped) just before you put in the noodles. People seem to love or hate cilantro—there is no in-between—which is why I suggest substituting Thai basil if you can find it and prefer it.

PREPARATION
✳ Shred the chicken.
✳ Split the chiles lengthwise and scoop out the membrane and seeds if you don't want the soup to be too hot.
✳ Peel the ginger and chop very finely.
✳ Remove the hard outer layers of the lemongrass, so you are left with the tender stem. Chop very finely.
✳ Finely slice the shallot.

METHOD
Heat up the stock in a large pan. Add the chicken (or shrimp), chiles, ginger, lemongrass, and bean sprouts and simmer for a couple of minutes. Add the noodles and continue to simmer for another 2–3 minutes until the noodles are just soft. Shred the cilantro or basil with a sharp knife, scatter it over the soup, and serve. Let everyone squeeze in their own lime juice.

Bertinet Basics

✳ **What is the hottest part of the chile?** *See page 38*
✳ **Do you need to make your own stock?** *See page 201*
✳ **What is the best way to chop or slice a shallot?** *See page 60*
✳ **How can you tell if a lime contains a lot of juice?** *See page 53*

INGREDIENTS
For 4–6

good handful of cooked
   chicken (or raw, peeled shrimp)
1–2 red or green chiles
small knob of fresh ginger
1 stick of lemongrass
1 shallot
1 quart chicken stock (or fish stock, if
   you are using shrimp, or 1 package
   miso soup dissolved in 1 quart water)
1 small bag of bean sprouts
1 package of thin, dried wheat noodles
   (or any other noodle of your choice—
   we sometimes have rice noodles
   or udon noodles)
handful of cilantro (or you can use
   Thai basil, if you can find it)
lime quarters, to serve

Q&A...

WHAT IS THE DIFFERENCE BETWEEN ORDINARY BASIL AND THAI BASIL?
There are lots of different varieties of basil, but the one that most of us are familiar with is sweet basil. Thai basil has a less smooth finish to its leaves, which are often tinged with purple, and has a very distinct aniseed flavor (sweet basil can sometimes be quite aniseedy, too, if the leaves are old). You might also see holy basil in Thai supermarkets, which has a very strong flavor and furry leaves. This is really meant for particular, long-cooked Thai dishes, so it isn't what you want for a light, refreshing soup like this one.

All-season pea and ham soup

In every season there is a soup to be made. This is a light one similar to the Italian minestrone. It is full of vegetables that are lightly cooked, the idea being that you keep all the color, flavor, and nutritional value of the ingredients. You can put in leeks, zucchini, fennel, whatever you like and whatever is available. In the winter, you can use rutabaga and frozen peas; in the spring, fresh peas and new potatoes. Whatever you use, just follow the simple principle of adding the hardest vegetables to the pan first.

I like to use the cooking water from the ham on page 125, together with some of the shredded meat, but you could use some good, thickly sliced bought ham.

INGREDIENTS

For 4–6

4 carrots
1 medium rutabaga
4 celery ribs
2 medium onions
2 garlic cloves
1 container mushrooms (about 7oz)
1½ quarts chicken stock (or ham stock, see page 125) or water
4 tablespoons olive oil
1 sprig of rosemary
1 sprig of thyme
1 bay leaf
sea salt and freshly ground black pepper
4 cups raw peas
good handful of chunky pieces of cooked ham
handful of fresh herbs of your choice, such as chervil or parsley

Bertinet Basics

✳ **What is the best way to chop or slice an onion?** *See page 60*

✳ **Why do you sometimes crush garlic rather than chop it?** *See page 29*

✳ **Do I need to make my own stock?** *See page 201*

PREPARATION

✳ Try to cut all the vegetables to the same size, since this will make the soup look more attractive. In the summer, I dice them very small, so that the soup looks light; in the winter, it is nice to have bigger chunks, to make it look more hearty and filling.
✳ Peel and dice the carrots and rutabaga (see page 118) and dice the celery.
✳ Peel and finely chop the onions.
✳ Leaving the garlic cloves in their skins, crush them lightly with the back of a large knife, just to release the oils, but don't chop them—that way people can avoid them in the finished soup if they want.
✳ Clean the mushrooms. Leave them whole if they are small or cut them in half.

METHOD

1 Pour your stock into a pan and heat through.

2 Put the oil, onions, garlic, rosemary, thyme, and bay into a separate, large, heavy-bottomed pan, add a pinch of salt and heat. The reason for heating everything up from cold is that I frequently see people getting the oil too hot and then putting in the onion and garlic and burning them, which results in a bitter taste in the finished soup.

3 As the onions and garlic begin to sizzle, just keep them cooking gently, stirring well for a few minutes.

4 The key to keeping the vegetables full of flavor, color, and with a little bite to them, rather than becoming mushy, is to put them in with the onions one at a time, starting with the hardest. After a couple of minutes, when the first one is partly cooked, you can add the next, and so on, finishing with the most delicate. In this case, add the rutabaga first, stir around for a couple of minutes, then add the carrots, then the celery, and, finally, the mushrooms.

5 Add the stock, peas, and ham and simmer for a few more minutes. Taste and season, if necessary—if you are using ham stock it may be quite salty anyway. If you feel the soup is oversalty, add a little boiling water to dilute it.

6 Chop the chervil, parsley, or whatever herb you are using and scatter over the top of the soup. Serve with lots of good bread.

Q&A...

WHAT IS THE BEST WAY TO CLEAN MUSHROOMS?

Simply wipe them with a brush or paper towel. Don't use water or the mushrooms will soak up the moisture, which will come out again in the pan when you fry them and make them soggy.

Sorrel soup

This is a different style of soup from the previous recipe—creamy, but still full of spring and summer flavors, thanks to the tangy, lemony sorrel. When sorrel is out of season you could make this soup with spinach instead. It is the kind of thing that you don't need a huge portion of: just a small cup makes a lovely appetizer. It also makes a good sauce, which I discovered almost by accident when I had a little left over. I served it with some grilled fish and it was great.

INGREDIENTS

For 4

½lb new potatoes
1 small shallot
6oz sorrel
2 cups light vegetable stock (see page 201) or water
3 tablespoons butter
sea salt and freshly ground black pepper
2 egg yolks (preferably free-range)
½ cup heavy cream or crème fraîche
drizzle of almond or walnut oil (optional), to serve

Bertinet Basics

✳ **What is the best way to chop or slice a shallot?** *See page 60*

✳ **Do I need to make my own stock?** *See page 201*

PREPARATION

✳ Scrub or peel the potatoes and cut into rough ½ inch cubes.
✳ Finely chop the shallot.
✳ Wash the sorrel and dry in a kitchen towel or salad spinner.
✳ Heat the stock (or water) on the stove ready to go.

METHOD

1 Put the butter in a large, heavy-bottomed pan over low heat and add the potatoes and shallot. Allow the butter to melt and let the vegetables cook very slowly without coloring for a good 10 minutes.

2 Put in the sorrel and stir until it wilts, then add your hot stock (or water). Taste and season as you think is necessary, then simmer very slowly until the potatoes are soft.

3 Don't let the soup boil, since too high a heat will cause it to lose its lovely fresh flavor.

4 While the soup is simmering, put the egg yolks and cream or crème fraîche into a bowl and whisk together.

5 When the potatoes are soft (after about 8 minutes), take the pan off the stove. If you have a handheld blender, use it to mix everything really well. Otherwise, put the soup into a blender, process, and pour it back into the pan.

6 Add the cream and egg mixture and stir it in well. Return to the heat and simmer gently without boiling for 4–5 minutes. The soup will thicken a little and the eggs and cream will give it an unctuous texture and flavor.

7 Taste again, to see if you need a little more salt or pepper. Now turn off the heat and allow the soup to cool down slightly so that it is almost at room temperature. If you serve the soup too hot, you won't be able to taste the delicate flavor of the sorrel properly. Serve in small cups, with a little nut oil swirled over the top (if using).

Q&A...

IS CRÈME FRAÎCHE A STRAIGHT SUBSTITUTE FOR CREAM?

Crème fraîche, which literally translates as fresh cream, is the French version of sour cream. It is made from cream that contains around 30 percent fat and has had a lactic culture added to it, to thicken and slightly ferment it, giving it a natural, quite delicate tang—a commercial process that mimics what would once have happened in dairies naturally. It has a more subtle flavor than sour cream, which is thinner and isn't stable enough to cook without splitting. I find crème fraîche lighter than cream and prefer it for some savory dishes. Incidentally, the reason for using heavy cream instead of light cream or half and half in cooking is that it won't split and thickens quickly.

WHY IS IT IMPORTANT TO SIMMER, RATHER THAN BOIL?

Think of simmering as the moment before an explosion. The surface of the liquid will break gently with occasional bubbles, before building up into the volcanic bubbling that signifies it has reached a full "rolling" boil. The point of simmering is that it is a more gentle form of cooking that can be drawn out over a longer time. If you continuously boil the liquid around pieces of meat, fish, vegetables, or legumes, after a while the outside of the meat or fish will overcook and become tough and dry, and the vegetables and legumes will break up, making the liquid

Step-by-step: Preparing onions

Most cooking starts with onions. Sometimes, you just want slices—for example, for the caramelized onions on page 27, for an onion tart, or to fry for topping a burger or hot dog. At other times, you want finely chopped or "diced" onion—i.e., you cut it up into small or larger squares, depending on your recipe. If you want the onions virtually to disappear, as in a risotto, you want to make your dice very small. If you are making a casserole, or something more rustic, they can be bigger.

Everyone has his own theory about how to stop yourself from crying when you chop onions. I was teaching a class of children once and one of them piped up with the idea that if you have half a lemon in your mouth when you chop onions, you won't cry. So we decided to try it out, and I had fifteen children with halved lemons in their mouths, chopping away and still crying their eyes out—but mostly with laughter!

Onions contain strong natural sulfurous chemicals that they draw from the soil and that give them their pungent smell. The one that makes us cry is called lacrimator (*lacrima* is Latin for tear), and this is released when you cut into the onion's cells. The chemicals seem to be concentrated mostly in the root, so if you leave this on until the end there is less risk of weeping. Leaving the root on while you slice or chop holds the onion together. I often see people cut onions in half and then cut both ends off right away, only to find that the onion falls apart when they come to chop it. It literally explodes all over the board, and the more they randomly try to chop it into pieces, the more crying juice is released.

What is the best way to chop or slice an onion?

Remember that there are no prizes for speed here, despite the way chefs often show off by whizzing along with their knives. Better to keep your fingers intact and work slowly until you get used to what you are doing. Chefs have different ways of slicing and chopping onions quickly and neatly. This is my way:

1 Leaving the skin on, cut the onion in half.

2 Take off the skin and any thicker outer discolored layers that come away with it—you can use these for stock—until you are left with a smooth, white, shiny surface. Put the halved onion flat-side down on your board with the root facing to your left (if you are right-handed). Always chop onions flat-side down, never rounded-side down, or they will roll and your knife might slip.

SLICING

3 If you are right-handed, hold the onion steady on top with the fingers of your left hand, and then make 1 (or, if the onion is large, 2) horizontal cut(s) from right to left, almost to the root but not actually through it.

4 Next, turn the onion so that the root is facing away from you. Working from right to left, make a series of vertical cuts each about ¼ inch apart. Each cut should go as close to the root as possible, without actually cutting through it.

5 At the end, you can slice off the root, slanting inward at the bottom, so you release all the slices.

CHOPPING, OR "DICING"

Follow steps 1–4, but don't slice off the root (step 5) because you want the onion still to be held together.

6 Turn the onion so that the root is on your left-hand side and hold the onion steady with the fingers of your left hand—the blade is going to come very close to them this time, so tuck the tips of your fingers in to protect them and bend your thumb out of the way behind your fingers. People often forget about their thumbs!

Working from right to left, make a series of vertical cuts, ¼ inch apart. Try to use the first knuckle of the middle finger that is holding your onion as a guide against which to glide your knife gently through the onion, moving your "holding" fingers backward continually as the blade comes close. As you cut, the onion will tumble into nice neat squares. (If you want larger dice, just space your vertical cuts farther apart.)

When you reach the root, discard it in your tabletop "trash can" (see getting organized in the kitchen, page 13).

Chopping Shallots

You can chop shallots in the same way. Very small ones can be a bit tricky, so try to use bigger shallots. Sometimes you will find that there are two individual sections, like twins in one shallot; in which case, treat them separately.

Smoked fish chowder

This really is a meal in a bowl, but it's very quick to put together, and with no seasonal ingredients you can make it with a clear conscience at any time of the year. We have a course at the cooking school called Desperate Housewives & Hapless Husbands, designed for people who feel clueless in the kitchen, and this is one of the recipes we include. It is so popular that people email us and write to us to say that they have made it time and time again at home afterward. It really is very difficult to ruin and is such a wonderful, classic combination of flavors that even if you brown the bacon too much, it will still taste great.

You can use whatever bacon you have in the fridge for this dish. If it is smoked, so much the better, because it will enhance the smokiness of the fish, but if it is unsmoked, don't worry. I think bacon is a very personal thing, so use whichever you prefer. What I would say, though, is try to find a good, traditional, dry-cured bacon. Mass-produced bacon is often pumped up with injections of water or brine, sometimes containing preservatives, in order to increase its weight, and when you fry it the liquid leaches out again into milky-white puddles.

As with all cooking, the key is to be organized. Don't put your butter in your pan and then start chopping everything up wildly. Or cut up a couple of things and leave the rest so you are in a panic when ingredients should be in the pan. It might seem pedantic to have everything ready to go in little bowls, but, trust me, it makes a recipe like this go like smooth sailing.

Note: You can make the chowder a day in advance, if you like. Keep it in the fridge and then reheat it gently. Serve in big hearty bowls, or in mugs as an appetizer.

INGREDIENTS
For 4–6

2 medium onions
9oz bacon or pancetta,
    smoked or unsmoked
1 container (about 8oz) button
    mushrooms
4 large potatoes
1 large (10oz) fillet of smoked
    haddock, skinned—preferably,
    traditionally smoked, undyed fish
½ bunch of curly parsley
large spoonful of butter
about 2 tablespoons olive oil
1 quart fish stock (or vegetable stock, or
    even water if you have no stock)
¾ cup heavy cream
sea salt and freshly ground
    black pepper

Bertinet Basics

✳ **What is the best way to slice or chop an onion?** *See page 60*

✳ **What is the best way to clean mushrooms?** *see page 57*

✳ **What is the best way to chop herbs?** *see page 41*

✳ **Why curly parsley?** *see page 99*

✳ **Do you need to make your own stock?** *See page 201*

PREPARATION
✳ Finely chop the onions.
✳ Using a pair of scissors, snip the bacon into strips about the width of your little finger.
✳ Clean and then halve or quarter the mushrooms.
✳ Peel the potatoes, and then cut them into rough ½ inch cubes.
✳ Cut the fish into big chunks, roughly 1 inch in size.
✳ Roughly chop the parsley.

METHOD

1 Melt the butter with the olive oil in a large, heavy-bottomed pan. Add the onions and bacon and cook gently over medium heat for about 4–5 minutes. The bacon will start to brown a little, but the onions should just be translucent. Add the potatoes and stir well; then add the mushrooms.

2 Stir well to coat all the ingredients in the oil and butter, and then add just enough stock to cover everything. Stir and bring to a low simmer for 8 minutes.

3 Add the cubed fish and cook very gently for another 5 minutes, just long enough to poach the fish, without overcooking it. Don't let the soup boil, otherwise the fish will disintegrate and the soup will look mushy and unappetizing. Add the cream and stir gently to heat through. Taste the soup at this point. The bacon and fish are quite salty anyway, so you may not need to add any more salt. Season with pepper, if you like, then put in the parsley and serve.

HOW IS PANCETTA DIFFERENT FROM BACON?

Pancetta and bacon strips are used in the same way; both are made from pork belly and can be smoked or unsmoked, but they are cured slightly differently. Pancetta is cured flat or rolled, usually with the addition of garlic and herbs as well as salt and pepper. Sometimes it is also rubbed beforehand with red wine. As a result, it has a more delicate, complex flavor than bacon, which is more simply dry-cured with salt and sometimes a little sugar, or wet-cured in brine (after which it might be smoked).

WHY DO YOU USE TRADITIONALLY SMOKED, UNDYED FISH?

Sometimes called "haddie" or "Finnan haddie" in the US, traditionally smoked or "cured" haddock is first brined (i.e., dipped in a saltwater solution) and then "cold-smoked" very gently for up to 20 hours, over the smoke produced by smoldering sawdust. In the oldest smokeries, this is drawn up tall chimneys, which gives a natural, pale creamy-golden color to the fish. Little traditional smoking happens these days, and most commercially smoked haddock is produced more quickly in computer-controlled heated kilns that have smoke wafted through them. Since the haddock doesn't change color naturally, food dye can be added to the brine, producing bright yellow fish. A backlash against food colorings has meant that you can now find undyed haddock more easily; however, unless you buy from a traditional smokery, it will usually have been smoked in the faster way, just without the coloring.

Crab,
langoustines,
and crayfish with
mayonnaise

Crab, langoustines, and crayfish with mayonnaise

When I am back in Brittany we have wonderful seafood, but in the restaurants I often see tourists watching shellfish platters being brought out to the locals and looking as if they would like to order the same thing, but aren't sure what to do when it arrives. There is a nervousness about cracking shells and eating with your fingers, but to me there is nothing more satisfying than a long, lazy lunch of a big crab and some langoustines or crayfish, a bowl of mayonnaise, some good crusty bread, and a bottle of rosé. It's my perfect meal; a kind of Breton tapas.

For me, the sad thing is that the British coastline is also full of fantastic seafood, and yet it is so undervalued there. When I was in Pembrokeshire, England, with the family a summer or so ago, I went down to the beach and bought four big crabs and a lobster straight out of the sea and the flavor was unbelievable. I looked at the coastline and thought that if this were Brittany, it would be lined with restaurants full of families tucking into platters of seafood.

I much prefer cracking a whole crab to ordering a dressed one, in which the meat has all been taken out for you and arranged in the shell. I find a dressed crab is too much of a good thing all at once. The whole point of cracking the shell, breaking the legs, and searching for the sweet meat yourself is that you eat slowly—I'm talking hours here—and you really appreciate every mouthful.

Langoustines (also known as Dublin Bay

Q&A...

HOW DO YOU CHOOSE GOOD LIVE SEAFOOD?

All seafood, like fish, should have a sweet, fresh smell of the sea that shows it is fresh—not a strong ammonia smell. There is no substitute for getting to know your fishmonger (however challenging it might be to find one) and asking a lot of questions about when and where the seafood was caught. With crab, always buy a live one if you are intending to cook it yourself, and cook it right away. Although crabs can be kept in the bottom of your fridge, covered in a damp cloth for a day or so, should they die, they need to be cooked immediately, because once the crab dies its flesh deteriorates quickly and can become toxic. Unless you are constantly putting your head in the fridge and checking up on it you can't be sure exactly when it died. Male cock crabs are the biggest—you can recognize them by their pointed tails, which are on the underside of the body at the back. Female hen crabs have rounded tails and tend to have more brown meat, depending on the season. Look for one that is lively, feels heavy (since this means that it will be nice and meaty), and is moving all its legs and claws, with no damage to any of them. If you want to buy one precooked, a good fishmonger will cook them every day. Don't be afraid to ask: crab that has been cooked 3 days before will have dry, flavorless meat: you'll be put off for good.

"prawns," Norway lobster, and scampi) and crayfish both belong to the lobster family. Langoustines have long claws and slim tails, which means that there is relatively little meat, but what there is is very sweet. In the sixties, the big fashion was to coat the tails in bread crumbs, deep-fry them, and call them scampi—all the rage with french fries in a basket at the local pub. Crayfish—also known as crawfish or crawdads, depending on where you are—are freshwater versions of lobsters (which are sea creatures). The UK has its native white claw crayfish; however, many rivers have recently become overrun with the bigger, aggressive American signal crayfish, which was introduced and farmed for the restaurant business in the seventies. Some of them escaped and have been reproducing at a massive rate, causing all kinds of havoc in the river environment and threatening their native crayfish population—so much so that safe-haven lakes are now being set up to protect local species. In the US, the signal crayfish, native to the Pacific Northwest, has invaded California waters throughout the state, pushing out native species there as well. If there is an upside to all of this, it is that there are plenty of signal crayfish on sale, and it is our duty to eat them and keep the population down! In the US, however, even though signal crayfish abound, the red swamp or Louisiana "crawfish" is still the most popular and the most widely available type of crayfish. Crayfish are some of the few shellfish you can readily find sold live, although you can also buy them cooked and out of their shells. Use them when you might otherwise use shrimp: for example, in a seafood cocktail, with avocado and crisp lettuce and shrimp cocktail sauce—retro heaven!

Live langoustines are best, there's no doubt, but, unfortunately, since they are fished in the North Sea and Bay of Biscay, they are virtually impossible to find live in North America and are, for practial purposes, only sold frozen. Still, make sure you use the best quality you can, since their flesh can take on a limp and cottony texture if they are not frozen when fresh—not a pleasant sensation at all. That really means buying them from either a good fish market or a high-quality gourmet grocer. A good fishmonger will be more than happy to advise you if you call up and say, "I'm making a seafood platter for the first time. Can you help?"

Note: the shells of crab, crayfish, and langoustine all make great stock (see page 201), so once you've finished your shellfish platter, don't throw them away.

Mayonnaise

When I am taking classes at the school I find that mayonnaise is something everyone wants to be able to make, but is scared of trying—either because they think it is too difficult, or because they are worried about raw eggs. However, provided your eggs are good quality and fresh, there should be no problem. Also, when you add your mustard, which contains vinegar, and your lemon juice, to a certain extent the acidity they provide acts as a natural preservative and stops bacteria from growing. The key, though, is to make only enough mayonnaise to go with whatever you are eating, and throw away any that is left over—especially don't leave it sitting around outside on a hot day and then put it back in the fridge. I also use mayonnaise as a perfect opportunity to teach people how to taste and season properly, since there is such an obvious boost to the flavor once you start to add salt.

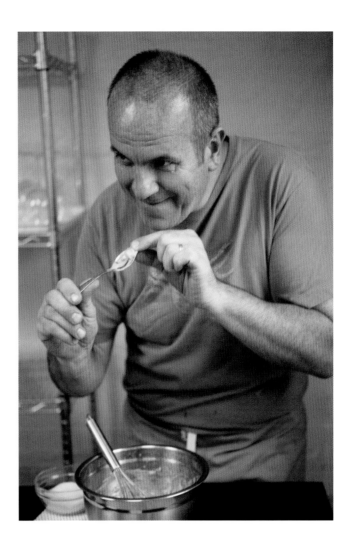

If you haven't made mayonnaise before, your benchmark is probably a storebought jarred product with a vinegary flavor. Good homemade mayonnaise is unbelievably different and you will be kicking yourself that you haven't made it before.

I learned how to make mayonnaise from my mother, who would make it whenever we had seafood. She used peanut oil, which was fashionable then, and the texture was always shiny and silky, and really unctuous—like a thick, yellow custard. Mayonnaise was considered something fantastic that you could conjure from very simple, relatively cheap ingredients. In other words, you would never use your best olive oil because it would be too pungent and you would be doing battle with it when you tried to season it. It is better to go for something more mellow. The more I use it, the more I like the flavor, color, and texture of extra-virgin canola oil for mayonnaise, and there is something right about making mayonnaise using an oil that hails from the local countryside, rather than from olives that don't grow there.

Many mayonnaise recipes use vinegar. I prefer to add vinegar by way of mustard, and then give a little extra sharpness with lemon juice. Also, some recipes suggest adding a little salt to the egg yolks at the beginning to help them thicken—but I don't think it's necessary.

Every cook and chef has his or her own way of making mayonnaise—not that the technique varies dramatically, but there will be little tricks or habits, a variation in quantities, or some additional flavorings that people develop. You might, for example, find you prefer it made with English mustard instead of French. This is my way, but as you get more confident you will probably develop your own way.

Once you have made your mayonnaise you can add other ingredients, but for serving with seafood I like to leave the mayonnaise plain, or just add some garlic (then the mayonnaise is known as aioli). What I quite often do is make my mayonnaise, then divide it into two bowls and flavor one with garlic, so people have the choice.

"I learned how to make mayonnaise from my mother, who would make it whenever we had seafood."

Step-by-step: Making mayonnaise

INGREDIENTS
For 2–4

6 tablespoons canola or light vegetable oil
¾ cup light olive oil
½ lemon
2 garlic cloves (optional)
2 large egg yolks (preferably free-range)
1 large teaspoon smooth Dijon mustard
sea salt and freshly ground pepper (I like black, but if you don't want to see the spots, use white)

Bertinet Basics

✳ **Why do you remove the germ of the garlic?** *See page 23*

✳ **Why do you sometimes crush garlic rather than chop it?** *See page 29*

✳ **What is the best way to juice a lemon?** *See page 102*

PREPARATION
Even after decades of mayonnaise making I often wish I had three hands—one to hold the bowl steady (especially tricky if it has a rounded base), one to pour in the oil, and one to whisk all at the same time. So here are a couple of tips to make the process of mixing easier:

✳ The way to get around keeping the bowl steady is to wrap a cloth around it, and then wedge it into a heavy saucepan so that it is a tight fit and stays in place.

✳ Then, I suggest you measure your oils into the kind of cheap squeeze bottles you can buy from all kitchen stores these days. They are light and easy to hold and you'll find it much easier to squeeze out the tiny quantity of oil needed as you start to add it to the eggs. I can judge the quantity of oil straight from the bottle, controlling the flow with my thumb over the top, but if you've never done it before you'll find a big bottle of oil heavy and cumbersome. A squeeze bottle makes life much easier.

✳ Squeeze the juice from the lemon half (you can cut the other one in half again and put it in finger bowls of warm water for people to use).

✳ Peel the garlic (if using) and remove the green germ, if necessary. Chop, then crush and grind the cloves to a paste using the flat edge of a big kitchen knife.

METHOD

1 Put your egg yolks in a wide bowl that will give you space to mix properly, and then whisk in the mustard. When they are well blended, start dribbling in the vegetable oil first, very slowly: literally, a drop at a time to begin with. The mayonnaise will start to thicken as you whisk, and as it does so, you can increase the oil to a gentle stream. Once all the vegetable oil is incorporated, start adding the olive oil. Keep whisking all the time—you don't have to whisk frantically, just keep a slow, gentle rhythm and stop when you have the consistency of thick custard. It doesn't matter if you haven't used up all of your olive oil. Remember that the more oil you add, the thicker the mayonnaise will get—not thinner, as people sometimes think.

2 Provided you add your oil slowly and patiently at the start, the mayonnaise shouldn't split (i.e., become curdled-looking, because the oil and egg haven't amalgamated properly). However, if it should start to separate early on, you can usually rescue the mayonnaise by whisking in a tablespoon of boiling water. This should bring everything back together and you can continue to add your oil dribble by dribble.

3 If you are still having a problem, I would whisk another egg yolk in a fresh, wide bowl, with half a teaspoon of mustard, and then slowly whisk in the split mayonnaise, bit by bit. It should then all come together.

4 Now you need to season your mayonnaise. Unseasoned mayonnaise tastes incredibly bland—in my classes, when I get people to taste it, they hate it! So, add your pepper first, which will give a bit of warmth, then start adding salt, a little at a time, mixing it into the mayonnaise and waiting until it dissolves before you taste. You will notice a dramatic difference in flavor as you add more salt. When you hit the point where you feel happy with the salt, add some more pepper, if you like. When you get the seasoning right, it will be like a light bulb going on in your head. It isn't easy to explain, but instead of different ingredients being identifiable, they will all taste like a whole, with no dominant taste of oil or egg, and nothing harsh on the tongue or the back of the throat—just a rounded, full flavor! Now you can whisk in the lemon juice.

5 At this point, as I mentioned, I often divide the mayonnaise and add garlic to one bowl only, leaving the other plain. I then put out both bowls with the seafood and let people decide which they prefer. The reason for leaving the garlic until the end is that if you put it in before you season with salt and pepper the taste of the garlic will dominate and stop you from judging your seasoning properly. When you add the garlic, do it little by little, stirring in well, until it is as subtle or as punchy as you want it.

Q&A...

WHY DO YOU USE A MIXTURE OF OILS FOR MAYONNAISE?

As always with oils, it comes down to personal taste. I find a mayonnaise made entirely with olive oil, particularly if it is a rich green, full-bodied, fruity one, can be too strong or bitter, so much so that it will be impossible to season your mayonnaise properly. Also, mayonnaise made only with extra-virgin olive oil can sometimes separate an hour or so after you make it—it will look like custard that has split—because of the nature of the oil.

Sometimes I use entirely extra-virgin canola oil, which has a golden color and a slightly nutty taste and is as silky as extra-virgin olive oil. But I also like to use a combination of light extra-virgin olive oil and good vegetable oil, which gives a more soft, rounded flavor—I find that you need a little extra-virgin olive oil, especially if you are adding garlic. Taste your oil first; if it tastes pungent from the bottle, it will taste pungent in your mayonnaise. You could also make the mayonnaise with canola, nut, or vegetable oil, and then whisk in a few drops of avocado oil at the end, which gives a slightly different flavor and a beautiful tinge of green.

WHAT OTHER FLAVORS CAN YOU ADD TO MAYONNAISE?

Once you have seasoned your mayonnaise properly, you can use it as a base for herbs, chopped watercress, or a few strands of saffron.

The Shellfish

Cooks and animal welfare campaigners all have differing views on whether crustaceans feel pain in the same way as we do, and whether or not you should kill them before they go into the water. The kindest way to approach dispatching them is to put them into the freezer for 45 minutes to an hour first, so they go to sleep and are desensitized.

The alternative school of thought is that you should kill lobsters and crayfish by slicing them through the head between the eyes, and for crab, turn it on its back and pierce it through the nerve centers with a screwdriver or a skewer: one of these is marked by a small hole under the pointed flap toward the back of the shell; the other is shown as a shallow depression just behind the eyes. Personally, I don't go along with this, because I think people are nervous about doing it correctly and find it distressing. I can't think of anything worse, for all concerned, than chasing around a lively crustacean with a sharp knife or a screwdriver, wondering what will happen if you miss the target. Also, you lose the juices from the crab by piercing it in this way. So I prefer to take the shellfish from the freezer and plunge it straight into rapidly boiling water—no hesitation, straight in, lid on. I know that it can seem quite scary to put a live crab or a crayfish into boiling water, even if it is in a comatose state, but whatever sense of pain it has will be dulled and the heat of the water will kill it quickly.

The most important thing is to have a big pan capable of holding lots of water, and to salt it very well. If you don't salt the water enough, seafood can be really bland and disappointing, and no amount of seasoning once it is cooked can regain the flavor.

Fishermen traditionally boil up crabs in a pot of seawater. Atlantic seawater has around ¾–1oz salt per quart and I find that if you reproduce the salty conditions of the seawater that the crab is used to, the meat will be really sweet. (Incidentally, the composition of Atlantic saltwater is also perfect for bread baking—Nature is very clever!)

I have seen people try to add sweetness by putting ingredients such as carrots in the cooking water, but I don't believe in overcomplicating flavors. I would stick with the age-old fishing-community tradition of just salt, with a bay leaf and peppercorns to give the slightest spiciness.

Of course, the kind of salt you use is crucial. It should be grains of good sea salt, not harsh, processed table salt, which will make the seafood horribly salty.

"I prefer to take the shellfish from the freezer and plunge it straight into rapidly boiling water—no hesitation, straight in, lid on."

INGREDIENTS

For 4 (Just don't invite me!)

1 large (1¼–1½lb) live Dungeness
    crab (preferably a male)
12 live crayfish
12 langoustines, preferably live;
    if not, very fresh
½ cup sea salt, preferably *sel gris*
2–3 bay leaves
1 teaspoon black peppercorns

PREPARATION

✳ About 45 minutes to an hour before you want to start cooking, put your crab in the freezer, along with the crayfish. If you have live langoustines, put them in the freezer about 30 minutes beforehand.

✳ You will need to boil the shellfish in 5 quarts of water, so, although it might sound obvious, make sure your pan is wide enough to take the crab and big enough to hold all the water before you start. Depthwise, it should be big enough to take 4 crabs one on top of each other—even though you are cooking only one. This is important because if the crab and its legs and claws aren't submerged completely in boiling water it could take longer to die.

METHOD

1   Cook the crab first. Add the sea salt, bay leaves, and peppercorns to 5 quarts of water in your pan and bring to a boil; ½ cup might sound like a lot of salt, but, as I have explained, what you are trying to do is re-create the ratio of salt in seawater (see page 70).

2   The water needs to be boiling really hard—with big, rolling bubbles. At this point, take your crab from the freezer and put it into the pan immediately. Put the lid on to bring the water back to a boil as quickly as possible.

3   From this point, keep it boiling for 15 minutes. Then turn off the heat and leave the crab to sit in the water for another 10–15 minutes. When it is cooked, its shell will turn dark red.

4   Take the crab out of the water and leave it to drain and cool in a colander.

5   You can use the same water to cook your crayfish. Bring it back to a boil, drop in the crayfish, straight from the freezer, and put the lid back on. The secret is not to overcrowd them—if necessary, boil them in batches—or they won't have the space for the boiling water to wrap around them and cook them properly. When the water comes back up to a boil, cook the crayfish for 2–3 minutes if they are small, a little bit longer if they are larger. When they are cooked they will turn dark red. Lift out your crayfish and leave them to drain in a colander.

6   Bring the pan of water back to a boil and cook your langoustines in the same way: lid on, back to a boil, and then cook them for 2–4 minutes according to size, until the color of the shells changes to a dark orange. If you are feeling unsure, take one out and pull off the head. If the color inside the head is orange, it is ready; if it is blackish green and slimy, it needs a little longer.

7   Let all the seafood cool down fully before you eat it.

8   Enjoy with the mayonnaise, lots of good bread, a good bottle of white or rosé, and a big green salad if you like—and make sure you put out finger bowls and plenty of paper napkins (you don't want seafood juices all over your best table linen).

Cracking crab

Lay the crab on its back and break off the claws and legs. Then, with your thumbs at the bottom of the body, push them upward to lever it out. If it doesn't come out easily, insert a flat kitchen knife into the base and use it to help push out the body.

Inside the shell will be juice and brown meat, as well as the stomach sac and the feathery "dead mens' fingers." Take these last two out and throw them away, then you can scoop out the tasty brown meat.

Cut the body section that you levered out in half vertically, then you can go through all the little crevices, picking out all the sweet white meat with a toothpick.

To keep from spraying splinters of shells when you crack the claws, fold a clean kitchen towel over them, then use a hammer or the back of a big kitchen knife to break the shell. Now you can pick out the white meat. Do the same with the legs, and scoop out whatever meat you can, again, using a toothpick.

Shelling langoustines and crayfish

Break the heads off (top left), then squeeze the edges of the shell together all the way along the spine to break it (middle) then you can open out the shell like a book and the meat should slide out in one piece.

Bertinet Basics

✳ **What is sel gris?** *See page 93*

Q&A...

WHAT RED WINE GOES WITH SEAFOOD?
It's amazing how frequently I am asked this. People often prefer to drink red wine, but can't find one that works with seafood prepared in this way. That is probably for a good reason, because only a very light red, like a Beaujolais, really works with a seafood platter, and then it needs to be served chilled. Anything more butch, such as a Cabernet Sauvignon or Merlot, and the taste of the seafood is altered by the wine and vice versa. This doesn't apply to seafood that has been barbecued or fast-cooked, since this will have taken on a different flavor—especially if it has been cooked with spice or ginger—nor does it apply to shellfish in a stew or sauce, although I find red wine with moules marinières a bizarre choice. For crab and seafood cooked simply and served with mayonnaise, I think you can't beat a light, refreshing white wine, such as a Muscadet, or a Provençal rosé— which for me is the most amazing match, as you are complementing the sweet, delicate flavor of the crustaceans without dominating it.

14

Shrimp flamed with tomato and brandy

When we go to Provence on vacation this is one of my favorite dishes to make. We visit the market and buy the big Mediterranean shrimp that the Spanish call *gambas*, the ones that look almost see-through when they are raw, but have greeny, blue, or brown markings on them. If you can't find these in the US, any variety of fresh jumbo shimp will do. Shrimp are loosely divided into cold-water and warm-water varieties, with those living in cold waters usually smaller, but often more succulent than their warm-water cousins, so it really is a matter of taste as to which you prefer to use. I cook them in their shells in a big frying pan with tomatoes and Cognac, and then we just put the pan in the middle of the table with a bowl of garlic mayonnaise (see page 68) and a basket of bread for mopping up the garlicky juices and everyone tucks in.

As with the crab and shellfish in the preceding recipe, the beauty of this dish is eating it with your fingers—peeling the shrimp, dipping them in garlicky mayonnaise, taking a sip of wine, breaking off a piece of baguette... the very fact that you have to take the shells off the shrimp slows you down, makes you eat in a more leisurely way, so you never feel uncomfortably full.

When I teach this recipe at the school, part of its purpose is to show people how to flame safely, without being scared.

Whenever you add wine or spirits to a dish—for example, wine to a sauce or casserole—it is important to burn off the alcohol, which can be harsh tasting, so you just leave behind the beautiful, concentrated flavor. Usually you do this by starting over high heat, so that most of the alcohol evaporates, and then you let it simmer slowly to remove even more of the alcohol and concentrate the flavor further.

Standard wines and beers don't contain enough alcohol to set alight, but spirits like brandy, whiskey, or rum do, so if you are cooking on gas you can add the alcohol to your pan, tilt it toward the flame, and the alcohol will vaporize and burst into a flame that will turn blue and then burn itself out. Don't worry, the rest of the food in the pan doesn't turn to a cinder because the flame is only concentrated on the alcohol. It is the same principle as pouring brandy over your crepes and setting a match to it. The difference is that most of us feel in control when we do that, whereas the first time you flame alcohol in a pan it can take you by surprise if you are not prepared. I hate it when I see TV chefs creating massive flames for effect, because what you want is something small and contained.

Not every stove is suitable for flaming—if you have an overhead broiler or a low extraction fan, don't try it, or you will blacken them! And, of course, you don't have to flame this dish at all, although, if you don't burn off the alcohol, the brandy may taste a little more harsh.

I add a couple of tablespoons of ketchup to the sauce to give it a bit of sweetness. There's no need to be snobbish about ketchup; it's a great thing, with pretty pure ingredients in it. For centuries, cooks have known that if you add a little sugar to tomatoes when you cook them, you bring out the sweetness, and by adding ketchup, which contains sugar, you are doing the same thing, plus putting in some rich tomato flavor at the same time.

Bertinet Basics

✳ **Why use shallots rather than onions?** *See page 38*

✳ **What is the best way to chop or slice a shallot?** *See page 60*

✳ **What is the best way to juice a lemon?** *See page 102*

INGREDIENTS

For 4 as an appetizer,
or 2 as a main course

1 large shallot
2 garlic cloves
2 large tomatoes
1 lemon
about 2 tablespoons light olive oil
16–20 big raw shrimp, shells still on
2 tablespoons ketchup
about 6 tablespoons brandy or Cognac
large sprig of tarragon
½ cup white wine
handful of curly parsley
sea salt and freshly ground
    black pepper

PREPARATION

✳ Finely chop the shallot.
✳ Leave the skin on the garlic cloves, but crush them with the flat edge of a large knife. This releases the flavor of the garlic, but allows you to avoid actually eating it, if you don't want to, because the cloves are easy to take out.
✳ Peel, deseed, and dice the tomatoes (see next page).
✳ Squeeze the juice from the lemon.

METHOD

1 Heat the oil in a big sauté pan with handles, or a deep frying pan, over medium heat. You need this type of pan, since if you have a deeper pot, the alcohol will be too far away from the flame when you add it in step 2. When the oil is really hot but not smoking, add the shrimp, shallot, garlic, and ketchup. Stir them around well, and then add the tomatoes.

2 Now we come to the flaming. If you don't want the brandy or Cognac to flame, just take your pan off the heat and then pour in the alcohol and stir it in. Once it is absorbed into the sauce you can put the pan back on the heat.

3 If you do want to flame it, and if you are using a gas stove, keep the pan on the heat and pour the brandy or Cognac into one part of the pan near the edge and tilt the pan toward the flame. It will flame and then die down quickly. If you are nervous, you can add the brandy a tablespoon at a time and the flames will be much smaller. If you are using an electric stove, pour the alcohol into one part of the pan, as before, and use a match—preferably a long barbecue match—to set it alight.

4 Once the alcohol is flamed, add the tarragon, lemon juice, and wine. Turn up the heat and let it bubble up, to burn off some of the alcohol in the wine, and then turn the heat down to low and let everything simmer for 5–6 minutes, depending on the size of your shrimp. The shrimp will change color when cooked. If you want to test whether they are ready, take one out and pull off the head. If the color inside the head is orange, it is ready; if it is black/green and slimy, it needs a little longer.

5 While the shrimp are cooking, quickly chop your parsley and stir it in. If you like, you can finish with a twist of black pepper and some sea salt, but there should be plenty of flavor in the sauce.

HOW CAN I VARY THIS RECIPE?

You could add a pinch of saffron threads to the sauce (with the wine) to heighten the flavors. The sauce goes well with any kind of shellfish or fish, so instead of shrimp you could substitute pieces of squid, langoustines, pieces of monkfish, or any similar chunky white fish—cook them in exactly the same way.

Q &A...

WHY DO RECIPES USUALLY WANT YOU TO "DICE" VEGETABLES TO A CERTAIN SIZE?

This isn't just a cheffy affectation. Cutting a fruit or vegetable into equal-sized cubes means that all the pieces will cook evenly. If you chop everything up randomly in different sizes, you will often find some pieces end up over-cooked, some virtually raw. If you want a vegetable to virtually disappear, say, into the sauce of a slow-cooked casserole, then it is best to dice it very small. If you want identifiable pieces in the finished dish, make your dice larger. On page 118, I show you how to dice carrots. You can use the same technique for most other vegetables. See page 60 for chopping onions and shallots.

Step-by-step: Preparing tomatoes

1 Instead of pouring boiling water over the tomatoes to remove the skins in the way recipes usually suggest, simply cut the tomatoes into quarters.

2 Scoop out the seeds with a small paring knife.

3 Put the quarters, flesh-side down, on some paper towels.

4 Then, on a cutting board, flatten them with your index finger and you should easily be able to slice your knife between the flesh and the skin.

5 Now you can lift the flesh off rather than pulling the skins off.

6 Pat the pieces dry to stop them from oozing juice.

7 Slice each piece lengthwise into strips.

8 Slice again crosswise to make dice.

Mussels in the bag with ginger, chile, and lemongrass

I grew up eating mussels—in my region of France *moules frites* are as popular as fish and chips in England. In our house we would have a big pot of *moules marinières* (see bonus recipe), two pounds of mussels each every other week, and I can still remember the buttery-winey-parsley smell as they were spooned out of the pan. I love mussels every way: with clams in pasta sauces, in fish pies, and with flavors such as chile, lemongrass, and coconut milk, as in this recipe.

There are excellent mussels in North America—most of them cultivated in the Upper Mississippi River region or along the southeastern coast—and Prince Edward Island mussels are world-renowned. But I find there is often a nervousness about cooking and eating them, not to mention preparing them in the first place—should the shells be open or shut? In the classes, though, when we make a mussel dish together and get over that fear, almost everyone says that they wish they had cooked them long before, because they realize what they have been missing. Part of the problem is that mussels are often served badly. I can't understand restaurants that precook them and heat them up when customers come in—the mussels just become dry and tough, and there is no excuse, because they are so quick to prepare (I think of them as fast food) and the sad thing is that some customers may never try them again.

In this recipe they are cooked *en papillote*, which is just the French way of saying "in the bag." Cooking fish and shellfish in a paper bag has become fashionable, but it has long been considered an easy way of combining seafood and flavorings, while protecting the fish from direct heat and keeping everything moist and tasty as it steams gently inside the paper.

Mussels are found naturally in clusters in coastal waters, but most these days are cultivated. While fish farming has its critics, mussel farming pretty much mimics the way mussels grow naturally in the wild. The young seed or "spat" attaches itself by its beard to ropes suspended by rafts, instead of to rocks, the seabed, submerged jetties, or the hulls of boats: anything it can cling on to. Because of this, the Marine Conservation Society approves, in terms of preserving stocks and respecting the environment.

By the way, you don't want to get caught eating mussels with a knife and fork like a tourist—the proper way is to spear your first mussel with a fork, and then use the empty shell like pincers to snap the rest of the mussels from their shells and pop them straight into your mouth.

Q&A...

IS IT TRUE THAT YOU SHOULD EAT MUSSELS ONLY WHEN THERE IS AN "R" IN THE MONTH?

It used to be said of wild mussels that you should avoid them in the warm months, from May to August, none of which has an "r" in its name. This is for two reasons: first, from around April they reproduce and spend less time building up their weight, so they tend to be a bit smaller and weaker, and not so plump and flavorful. And second, some people think there is more chance of them becoming contaminated in the summer. Mussels are filter feeders—they pump seawater in and out on average at about a quart an hour, taking oxygen and whatever plankton and organisms they need. During the summer months, when the water is warm, there is more chance of bacteria being active and contaminating the water. Since most mussels are now cultivated, they are available all year round and once harvested they are held in purification tanks for 48 hours to remove any bacteria.

INGREDIENTS

For 4 as an appetizer,
or 2 as an entrée

2 red and/or green bird's-eye chiles
large thumb of fresh root ginger
2 garlic cloves
1 stick of lemongrass
about 4lb fresh mussels
2 x 14.5oz cans coconut milk
4 lime leaves
handful of fresh cilantro

PREPARATION

✳ Preheat the oven to 375°F.
✳ Have ready a big square of parchment paper.
✳ Finely slice the chiles. You can remove the seeds and membrane if you want to, but, personally, I like some real chile heat in this.
✳ Peel and finely chop the ginger. Peel and crush the garlic.
✳ Split the lemongrass lengthwise and remove the woody outer layers. Finely chop the tender inside stem.
✳ Clean the mussels very well under running water to get rid of any sand and grit. Remove any beards from the shells (using your fingers or a knife) and throw away any mussels that are broken. If any shells are wide open, throw them away. If they are just slightly ajar, tap them and they should close. If not, throw them away, because this shows that they are dead or dying.

METHOD

1 Put the coconut milk in a pan with the chile, ginger, garlic, lemongrass, and lime leaves. Warm gently over low heat—don't let it boil.

2 Put the square of parchment paper inside a roasting pan. Put the cleaned mussels into the center of the square of parchment paper. Spoon the coconut milk together with all the flavorings over the top and quickly gather up the sides of the paper to make a "money bag." Tie firmly with butcher's twine. Put into the oven for 20–25 minutes.

3 Meanwhile, finely chop the cilantro.

4 Bring the roasting pan to the table, open the pouch, and scatter in the cilantro. Stir everything around and serve—make sure you discard any of the mussels that haven't opened.

Bertinet Basics

✳ **Which is the hottest part of the chile?** *See page 38*

✳ **Why do you sometimes crush garlic rather than chop it?** *See page 29*

Bonus recipe:
How to make *moules marinières*

The best, classic *moules marinières* (mussels in white wine) recipe is the simplest and most pure. What you want is to taste the salty, minerally mussels in the lightest mixture of wine, juices, and herbs. If people are nervous about mussels, I always say to try the sauce on its own first: once you get that taste of the sea, flavored with wine and butter, you'll be hooked. The secret to the sauce is to cook your onion and shallots in the butter and wine before you put in your mussels; if you put everything into the pan at the same time your onion and shallots will still be raw; 4lb mussels will serve four as an appetizer, two as an entrée.

Put 4oz salted butter in a big pan that has two handles over medium heat with a large onion and two large shallots, both finely chopped, and a couple of garlic cloves (skins removed and crushed). Allow the onion and shallot to soften, and then add half a bottle of white wine such as Muscadet. Bring to a boil, season with black pepper, and then turn down the heat to simmer for 5 minutes. Put in the mussels, cover with a lid, and turn up the heat until the mussels on top are open (this means they should all be open as the heat rises from the bottom of the pan). Sprinkle a big bunch of chopped curly parsley onto one side of the pan, and, holding both handles, tilt the pan away from you slightly and using your wrists lift it up and down, slowly and rhythmically, so that the mussels from the bottom jump up to the top (imagine salad being tossed in a bowl)—it sounds like a slow handclap. Now you are ready to go. Discard any mussels that haven't opened, ladle the rest into deep plates or bowls, and spoon the sauce over the top. Put out plenty of good crusty bread to mop up all the juices.

Q & A...

ARE BIGGER MUSSELS BETTER AND WHY ARE SOME ORANGE-COLORED?
Some mussels are creamy in color, some orange. One theory is that the orange ones are female, and the pale ones are either immature females or males. They can also vary a lot in size. Mussels mature after a year and are usually harvested at about 3 years— although they can live for 15 years or more and can grow really big. Their size depends on how much plankton is around for them to eat, and the time of year; they are generally smaller in the breeding season. I like nice plump orange ones, but white ones are just as flavorful. I don't think it matters whether the mussel is 1 inch or 2½—the most important thing is that they are not overcooked, dry, and rubbery.

Pan-fried fish with chickpeas, olives, and mint

The key to this dish is searing the fish so that the skin is crisp and golden and the flesh is just cooked, and then adding the simple but very fresh and instant flavors of olive, mint, and lemon right at the end—this way they stay vibrant, fragrant, and full of flavor, and you get the full impact of their color. Each of these three ingredients would alter and deteriorate in flavor, fragrance, and color if you were to add them too early and let them "stew."

I like to use gurnard—often called sea robin in the US—but you can use whatever you like—from freshwater fish such as trout, to flat fish like sole, or something more expensive, such as sea bass. Monkfish also makes a great alternative. If you fillet the fish yourself (see page 44, but start by cutting off the fin with a pair of scissors) or your fishmonger does it for you, keep the head and bones to make your own light stock. Place the fish trimmings in a pan with a bay leaf and some peppercorns, plus enough water to cover, bring to a simmer and cook over low heat for 10–15 minutes before straining through a fine strainer.

Mint, I find, is a herb that people often have growing in their gardens, but don't always know what to do with. In this recipe, it gives a lovely fresh edge to the flavors of the fish and chickpeas.

If you are using dried chickpeas—and this is by far the more economical way—the trick is to soak them overnight first. If they have been stored for some time, chickpeas can get a bit dry and wizened, but the long soaking softens the skins and means they will need less cooking time to become tender. You can prepare them in advance if you like: just drain and rinse them after cooking and keep them in a plastic container. Alternatively, you can use a can of chickpeas instead, but make sure you rinse them really well to get rid of the sludgy brine.

I always cook more dried chickpeas than I need (I would probably double the quantity in this recipe), and then I can use the rest for other dishes later in the week. You can use them for the bean and tomato salad on page 38, or for the purée on page 23.

If you want to make the dish more visually appealing and you have the time, once the chickpeas are cooked, take a clean kitchen towel or a sheet of paper towel and gently rub off the skins to reveal the golden shade underneath. Instead of zesting the lemon with a grater, you can use a julienne cutter (or a Mandoline slicer), which will produce longer, more elegant strips that make a bigger impact on the look of the finished dish.

Note: When you buy Kalamata olives, they will usually be in oil. Don't pour it out—either use it to cook the fish, or keep it to add to salad dressings.

Bertinet Basics

✳ **What is the best way to juice a lemon?** *See page 102*

✳ **What is the best way to chop herbs?** *See page 41*

✳ **Do I need to make my own stock?** *See page 201*

Q&A...

WHY GURNARD?
I like to use gurnard because it is flavorful, sustainable, fairly cheap, and often overlooked. It's a fish I've been using since the early nineties, when I was working as a chef in Hampshire, England, so I am always surprised when it is written about as if it were a new discovery. It is a strange-looking fish with a big, bony head—of the various varieties, the three that you are most likely to see are the bright red gurnard, the "tub" gurnard, which is the biggest, and the gray gurnard. They are all firm-fleshed fish, not dissimilar to monkfish. In France, we call them *grondin,* from the verb *gronder,* which means to growl, because the fish "talk" to each other when they are swimming, making a growling noise. In the US, they are known as sea robins because of their large, winglike pectoral fins.

DO I NEED A NONSTICK PAN?
I find a thick-based, nonstick pan is best for cooking fish (a thin one can easily get too hot and you run the risk of burning the fish). When buying a new pan, it is best to go to a good kitchenware store where someone knowledgeable can advise you.

Q&A...

HOW DO THE WEIGHTS OF DRIED, COOKED, AND CANNED CHICKPEAS AND BEANS COMPARE?
When you buy cans of chickpeas, check the drained weight that also appears on the label—you will find that a can of around 15.5oz gives just over half that once drained. This is roughly equivalent to 4oz of dried beans, which will swell to around double their weight once soaked in water.

INGREDIENTS
For 4

about 4oz dried chickpeas (or 15.5oz canned chickpeas)
a couple of bay leaves
a few black peppercorns
4oz Kalamata olives (or similar)
2 lemons
¾ cup light fish or vegetable stock (see introduction)
4 boneless fillets of gurnard (or fish of your choice), about 5–7oz each
2 tablespoons light olive oil, vegetable oil, or canola oil (or the oil from the Kalamata olives)
sea salt and freshly ground black pepper
bunch of mint

PREPARATION
✳ If you are using dried chickpeas, soak them overnight in cold water. Drain them in a colander and rinse them under cold running water. Put them in a pan with enough cold water to cover. As with any legumes, I don't use salt in the cooking water because it toughens their skins. (You can season the chickpeas with salt, if you like, once they are cooked.) Drop the bay leaves and peppercorns into the water, bring to a boil, and then turn the heat down to simmer. You will see some "scum" rising to the top of the pan from time to time, particularly at the beginning of cooking. Just skim it off with a spoon. The chickpeas will take around 45 minutes to an hour, maybe a little more, to become tender. (It is difficult to be too specific about the cooking time because it will depend on how old and dry the chickpeas are.)
✳ Once they are tender, drain the chickpeas through a colander and rinse them well under the cold faucet to remove any remaining scum. Take out the peppercorns and bay leaves and put the chickpeas to one side. If you are using canned chickpeas, drain them in a colander and rinse them to remove the brine.
✳ Pit the olives: with a small, sharp knife make three incisions in each olive from end to end—keep the cuts at equal distances—and then pull away the three similar-sized segments from the pit.
✳ Zest the lemons with a grater or julienne cutter, but don't go below the yellow skin into the white pith because this is more bitter-tasting.
✳ Cut the lemons in half and squeeze out the juice.

"You can use anything from freshwater fish such as trout, to flat fish like sole, or something more expensive, such as sea bass."

METHOD

1 Pour the stock into a saucepan and bring up to simmering point. Add the chickpeas and allow them to heat through very gently, over very low heat, while you cook the fish—the stock doesn't even need to simmer now, or the chickpeas will soak up the liquid too quickly. Just before you cook the fish, stir in half of the lemon juice and half of the lemon zest.

2 Heat your frying pan, but make sure it isn't hot to the point of smoking because you don't want to burn the fish. If the fillets are thick, score the skin of each one quickly with a sharp knife. This helps them cook faster and will also release the tightness in the skin to stop the fillets from curling. Rub each fillet with oil and season lightly. The salt will help to prevent the skin from sticking to the pan.

3 Put the four fillets of fish into the hot pan, skin-side down. Now the important thing is not to move the fillets for about a minute, or a minute and a half. Just leave them alone. Don't try to push or mess around with them, or the skin will stick and tear. If they are thick fillets they may take a little longer, even if you have scored them, but once you see the edges and corners of the skin start to turn golden brown and the first layer of flesh above it turn opaque, it is time to turn them over. Now that the skin has crisped and browned you will be able to turn them easily.

4 Cook the fillets for just about a minute or so on the other side—again, if they are thick fillets they might need a little longer. When the flesh has turned opaque almost up to the top, take the pan off the heat. Remember that the fish will continue to cook for a little bit longer when the pan first comes off the heat.

5 Roughly chop the mint. Add the rest of the lemon juice and zest to the chickpeas, then the olive segments, and, finally, the mint. Taste and season, and then spoon the chickpeas and their broth into four deep plates right away. Place a fillet of fish on top. If you like, you can scatter the top of each fillet with a few flakes of sea salt.

HOW CAN I VARY THIS RECIPE?
You could make the dish substituting chicken breasts for fish; I have also served it with a slice of grilled eggplant on top as a vegetarian alternative. In both cases, use vegetable stock.

Q&A...

WHY KALAMATA OLIVES?
I have learned through our classes that lots of people think they hate olives, usually because the first one they tried was nasty: either hard, bitter, or flabby. So I encourage them to try again and the variety that seems to win people over is the Kalamata, which is quite fruity and slightly "sweeter" than other varieties. Not only that, but it also looks quite beautiful: a deep, purply eggplant color. Although it is classed as a black olive, most naturally "black" olives are really more purple or brown. The shiny jet ones you see sometimes on pizzas are actually green olives that have been turned black through a process of oxygenation. So look for genuinely "black" olives, such as Kalamata or Niçoise, which I also love. If you prefer green olives, they are fine, too.

When buying olives, the thing to do is to taste them first whenever possible. If you buy loose olives from a farmers' market, for example, you can usually try each variety before you buy. If you buy olives in brine, rinse them before using. If they are in olive oil, they are fine as they are.

WHY DO YOU OIL THE FISH, RATHER THAN THE PAN?
Throughout this book I have suggested you stick to the same technique of getting your dry pan hot first, and then oiling your fish or meat before putting it in, as opposed to heating the oil in the pan. I find this is the best way to avoid burning your oil and making it smoky, which will give it a bitter flavor and also burn your fish or meat.

Fish with herb and mustard glaze and cucumber

Bertinet Basics

✳ **What is the best way to chop herbs?** *See page 41*

✳ **What is the best way to juice a lemon?** *See page 102*

✳ **What is a pinch of salt?** *See page 35*

Not everyone likes the smell of fish frying, especially when you have invited people over to eat and the smell seems to fill the house. So this is a great, easy way to cook fish in the oven—a combination of baking, poaching, and steaming that you can use for anything from pollack to salmon. Try pollack; it's a great fish—I've been a fan of it for years, and I don't understand why in some instances it is rebranded as colin (the French name) to see if this will encourage people to use it.

Smearing the fish with a glaze protects it from direct heat in the oven, so that it stays nice and moist on the inside, while the glaze on top bubbles and browns to create a crust. I also pour a mixture of olive oil and white wine into the roasting pan to stop the fish from sticking and keep it moist. These mix with the fish juices in the oven to make a little sauce to spoon around the fish when you serve it.

The glaze is made in exactly the same way as mayonnaise, but with lots of herbs added and an extra egg yolk to give it more color.

The herbs I usually use are chervil, parsley, tarragon, thyme, and basil—a lot of parsley and slightly less of the rest—but this is really up to you. You don't have to use all the herbs if you don't want to, or you could vary them, but whatever combination you use, you just need to end up with a good handful of chopped herbs, since they are a prominent part of the glaze.

I like to serve the fish with some cucumber that has simply been tossed in salt, pepper, and lemon juice. It is really refreshing against the richness of the glaze. And a big bowl of new potatoes.

Note: The pieces of fish can be topped with the glaze and put in the fridge in advance, so all you have to do is put them in the oven for 10 minutes when you are ready.

"The herbs I usually use are chervil, parsley, tarragon, thyme, and basil."

INGREDIENTS
For 4

large sprig of thyme
small bunch of chervil
large bunch of curly parsley
small sprig of tarragon
a few basil leaves
½ lemon
3 egg yolks (preferably free-range)
1 large teaspoon smooth Dijon or
    English mustard
6 tablespoons canola or light
    vegetable oil, plus 3–4 tablespoons
    olive oil for cooking the fish
¾ cup olive oil
sea salt and freshly ground
    black pepper
3–4 tablespoons white wine
4 thick skinless fillets of pollack (or
    cod, halibut, turbot, salmon, trout,
    sole, etc.), about 5–7oz each

FOR THE CUCUMBER
1 cucumber
few drops of lemon juice
sea salt and freshly ground
    black pepper

PREPARATION
✳ Pick the thyme leaves from their stems and chop them roughly, along with the rest of the herbs.
✳ Squeeze the juice from the lemon half.
✳ Preheat the oven to 400°F.

METHOD

1 For the glaze, put your egg yolks in a wide bowl that will give you space to whisk properly, and then whisk in the mustard. When they are well blended, start dribbling in the canola or vegetable oil very slowly, a drop at a time at first, whisking constantly. As the glaze starts to thicken, you can increase the oil to a gentle stream. Once all the oil is incorporated, start adding the ¾ cup olive oil. Keep whisking all the time and stop when it has reached the consistency of thick custard. It doesn't matter if you haven't used up all your olive oil. As with mayonnaise, remember that the more oil you add, the thicker the glaze will get—not thinner. Season as for mayonnaise (see page 68), first with pepper, then adding a little salt, mixing it in well and then tasting, before adding more. Then season to taste with pepper, and squeeze in a few drops of lemon juice—just enough to give a little sharpness.

2 Finally, stir in your mixed herbs. If you leave the herbs until last you can make sure you have seasoned the glaze as you would like, otherwise the flavor of the herbs will dominate and make it more difficult for you to judge how much salt and pepper to add.

3 Now for the fish. Pour the white wine and 3–4 tablespoons olive oil into a large roasting pan, season with salt and pepper, and put in your pieces of fish. Because you have seasoned the wine and oil you don't need to season your fish—also, the glaze you are about to top them with should be well seasoned. Using an offset spatula, spread some glaze very roughly over the top of each piece of fish (on the side where the skin would have been). The depth of the glaze should be about the same as the thickness of the fish. Don't neaten it up on the top—it should be nice and uneven, like the rough topping on a shepherd's pie or fish pie, so that there are little peaks and bumps that will brown more than others.

4 Put the pan in the oven and bake the fish for 8–10 minutes, until the glaze is golden brown.

5 While the fish is baking, prepare the cucumber. If you have a Mandoline slicer with a julienne attachment, or a julienne slicer ("julienne" is just a term for vegetables cut like matchsticks), shred the flesh lengthwise, so that it looks like spaghetti. Keep shredding until you get to the soft, seedy inside. Discard this, since it is too floppy. If you don't have a Mandoline or julienne slicer, use a vegetable peeler to cut the cucumber into long, slightly wider ribbons, and then, if you, like you can cut them into thin strips with a sharp knife.

6 Put a few drops of lemon juice in a bowl with a good pinch of salt and some pepper, and then toss the cucumber in it so that it is lightly seasoned.

7 When the fish is ready, lift it out onto plates with a spatula. Spoon around some of the juices from the pan, and serve with a nest of cucumber on the side.

Whole fish with seaweed

I find that people often associate cooking and eating whole fish with being on vacation. They have fond memories of a favorite seafood restaurant where the fish was cooked in front of them on a barbecue or grill, but somehow when they get back home the thought of cooking a whole fish themselves seems scary, so it is back to fillets. It's a shame, because cooking fish whole on the bone is a great thing to do. You can ask your fishmonger, even if you are buying at a supermarket counter, to scale, gut, and clean the fish for you, so there is nothing complicated required.

I like the idea of cooking the fish in the oven on a bed of salt and seaweed, because it feels as if it is in its natural environment. You don't actually eat the seaweed—not because it isn't edible, it's just that it would be very salty—but the flavors come through into the fish as it cooks. This "bedding" also protects the fish from direct heat, so the inside stays nice and moist—especially so, since you are also stuffing it with juicy slices of lemon and herbs.

Think of the way the fish is prepared for the oven as a prototype for any whole fish. You could use sea bass, gurnard, trout, or monkfish. I like to use bream—there are three main species—black, red, and gilt head bream—which are all similar and really flavorful. It is a relatively inexpensive fish, so if you are uncertain about cooking whole fish, this is a good place to start, rather than with an expensive sea bass.

The seaweed I usually use is the purply-brown carrageen, or Irish moss—its correct name is *Chondrus crispus*—although it is not readily available in the United States. By all means, ask your fishmonger for fresh edible seaweed, but the chances are you will have to do as I do and buy it dried, then soak it for about 5 minutes before you start.

Q&A...

WHAT IS SEL GRIS?

This is the unprocessed, coarse, wet, gray sea salt that is harvested from the Guérande salt marshes in my native Brittany, so, of course, I like it! Salt has been harvested here since the 9th century using the old methods. The Atlantic tide flows through a network of pools until it becomes more and more concentrated and forms crystals. The coarser gray crystals form at the bottom of the salt "pans" and are raked up to the surface by salt workers called paludiers who pile them into pyramids to dry in the sun. This salt is full of flavor and especially minerals from the clay soil at the bottom of the marshes, which is what gives it its gray color. When I was an apprentice baker, it was so much a part of our lives. We used it to melt the snow and ice when we arrived at the bakery door early in the morning, as well as dissolving it in water to make the bread. Another salt, the finer fleur de sel, which means "flower of salt," forms on the surface of the ponds, in pinkish crystals that turn a pristine white when they are collected and dried in the sun. While the gray salt tends to be used in cooking, the fleur de sel is more for sprinkling over finished dishes. Because the gray salt is quite moist it is tricky to grind in most salt grinders, so if you want to make it finer for seasoning, it is best to use a mortar and pestle.

INGREDIENTS
For 2

1 lemon
few good handfuls of edible seaweed,
    such as carrageen moss or
    Japanese seaweed (see page 207
for stockists)
1 x 1–1¼lb whole bream (or sea
    bass, gurnard, trout, or monkfish),
    scaled and gutted
handful of thyme sprigs
sea salt, preferably *sel gris*, and freshly
    ground black pepper
about 1 tablespoon olive oil

PREPARATION
✳ Cut the lemon into slices.
✳ Preheat the oven to 375°F.

METHOD

1 If you are using dried seaweed, soak it in water for about 5 minutes to rehydrate it, then drain it in a colander.

2 If your fishmonger hasn't trimmed the fins of the fish, do this with a sharp pair of scissors. With a sharp knife, make two slashes in the skin of the fish parallel to each other, on each side. This helps the heat to penetrate the fish better and so it will cook more evenly. Push a few sprigs of thyme into each slash.

3 Season the fish inside and out with salt and pepper, and then push the lemon slices and any remaining sprigs of thyme into the cavity.

4 Scatter about 1 tablespoon of sea salt in a layer in an oven-proof dish, then put in the seaweed and carefully lift the fish on top. Sprinkle the top of the fish with olive oil.

5 Put the dish into the oven for 25 minutes. As the fish cooks the skin will become a little crispy. To test that it is cooked through, take a sharp knife and insert it into the fish, at its fattest part, toward the bone. The flesh should slightly come away from the bone.

6 To serve, take the whole dish to the table. Starting at the head end, and with a rounded table knife, make a cut behind the gills and slide the knife gently under the flesh along the central bone. The fish will just lift off in one fillet. Now you can turn the fish over and do the same thing again, to take off the other fillet.

HOW CAN I VARY THIS RECIPE?
Instead of salt and seaweed, you could sit your fish on a bed of finely sliced fennel, and then sprinkle it with a little Pernod as well as the olive oil, since Pernod and fennel both share an aniseed flavor. Alternatively, you could cut some cooked new potatoes in half and lay the fish on these. The cavity can be filled with tomato instead of lemon slices, and you can vary the herbs. Those that go particularly well with fish include: parsley, chervil, lemon thyme, basil, and oregano. I also use tarragon, although some people don't like the flavor with fish.

"I like cooking the fish on a bed of salt and seaweed because it feels as if it is in its natural environment."

Fish and seafood pie

There are two techniques here: poaching fish and making a classic white (Béchamel) sauce—well, maybe three, because you also have to make good mashed potatoes, of course!

I love my mashed potatoes—but they come with a warning: yes, you did read the quantity of butter correctly! I put two sticks into 2 pounds of potatoes. Well, I come from Brittany, what do you expect? I was brought up on good, salted butter and great seafood, and so buttery mashed potatoes on a fish pie is the ultimate for me. Not to be recommended every day, of course, but a real treat: creamy and beautiful. If you are throwing up your hands in horror, I completely understand, and you can use skimmed milk, and crème fraîche rather than the butter—but, please, don't use some kind of low-fat spread instead, since it won't taste the same. I know recipes sometimes say to add hot milk to mashed potatoes, to stop them from turning gray, but I have never done this and have never had a problem—maybe it has to do with the quantity of butter! Of course, you can heat the milk if you like—but whatever you heat it in just means more dishes to do.

There must be thousands of different recipes for fish pie, but after you have made it once, you can vary it with whatever fish and seafood you like best.

I love the taste of nutmeg, so I like to add some to the sauce. Fish pie is a comforting dish and nutmeg is one of the most comforting spices—it always reminds me of roaring fires in winter and of Christmas: mulled wine and Christmas cake.

You could replace some of the potatoes with parsnips, if you like, to give a little sweetness to the dish.

I prefer not to sprinkle the potatoes with cheese before putting them in the oven. The Italians have an unwritten law (which they don't always stick to) that fish and cheese don't mix, and in this case I tend to agree. It is just a matter of taste, so, if you like, you can grate some Gruyère or Emmental over the top. I usually serve fish pie with a big green salad, made with some bitter leaves like frisée and dressed with a nice sharp vinaigrette to cut through the richness and creaminess of the pie.

INGREDIENTS
For 6–8

½ bunch of dill
½ bunch of curly parsley
1¾ cups milk (I use whole milk)
1 bay leaf
few peppercorns
14oz skinless white fish, such as
   haddock, cod, or monkfish
7oz skinless salmon or trout
2oz good unsalted butter
6 tablespoons all-purpose flour
6 tablespoons white wine
sea salt and freshly ground black
   pepper
about ¼ nutmeg, to taste
   (optional)
7oz cooked, peeled shrimp

FOR THE MASHED POTATOES
2lb Maris Piper potatoes
   (or other floury potato, such as
   the Russet Burbank)
8oz good salted or unsalted butter
(see introduction)
3 tablespoons whole milk

PREPARATION
✳ Preheat the oven to 400°F.
✳ Scrub the potatoes, but leave the skins on.
✳ Roughly chop the dill and parsley.

METHOD

1 Cook the potatoes in their skins in boiling salted water until they are tender—
i.e., a knife pierces through easily. This will take about 20–30 minutes,
depending on their size.

2 In the meantime, bring the 1¾ cup milk to a simmer with the bay leaf and
peppercorns in a large sauté pan or frying pan big enough to hold the fish.
Put in the pieces of fish and poach for 1 minute only, then take them out with a
slotted spoon and keep to one side. You are not cooking the fish at this point, just
starting it off, sealing in the juices quickly. If it looks slightly pink in the middle, it
doesn't matter.

3 Pour the poaching milk through a strainer into a heat-proof pitcher, which will
take out the peppercorns and bay leaf. Keep the pitcher of milk to one side.

4 Now you are ready to make your Béchamel sauce. Melt the 2oz butter in a
small, heavy-bottomed saucepan over medium heat. When it is bubbling
gently, sprinkle in the flour and whisk it quickly, so there are no lumps. When all the
butter is well mixed, begin to add the wine a little bit at a time, still whisking. This is
my secret weapon! Adding wine at this point breaks down the butter and flour
and so, when you start to add the milk, the sauce will all come together much
more easily. And it also adds flavor.

5 Once the wine has been absorbed, start adding the poaching milk,
again, little by little, whisking constantly until all the milk has been
incorporated. Bring to a boil, and then turn down to simmer and cook for
2 minutes, stirring all the time.

6 Take the pan off the heat and season the sauce to taste with salt and
pepper. It might taste bland at first, so add salt and pepper bit by bit,
and then, if you like, grate in some nutmeg. The taste will start to come alive in
your mouth, until you reach a point where the sauce feels rounded and
balanced: you can't taste wine, milk, or flour, because everything has come
together as one.

7 Drain the potatoes and leave them in the colander to cool for a few
minutes. As they steam, they will dry out. Once they are cool enough to
handle, peel them and place them back in the pan. Mash them with the 8oz
butter and 3 tablespoons milk, adding the milk a little at a time so that you end
up with a solid mash, not a wet purée. Taste and season.

8 Break the pieces of poached fish that you have set to one side into large
chunks. Carefully mix them into the Béchamel sauce, together with the dill
and parsley. Add the shrimp. Pile into a big oven-proof dish and then spoon the
potatoes on top—it is easiest to do this in little dollops, joining them together by
roughing them up with a fork. Make sure the potatoes completely cover the top,

Q&A...

WHAT SHOULD I DO IF THE SAUCE IS LUMPY?

If you add your wine and then your milk really slowly and make sure each addition is well mixed before you add the next—as if you were making mayonnaise—it shouldn't be lumpy, but if you do have a problem, just rub it through a strainer into a clean pan.

WHICH POTATO MASHER SHOULD I USE?

Of course, you can use whatever you feel most comfortable with. In France, we always used a mouli—a little mill with a handle—but I find a ricer the easiest, since all you have to do is put in the potatoes and squeeze, and it gives you great, even mashed potatoes. My mother had never seen one until she came to the UK and watched me use one, and she immediately said: "I want one!"

WHY CURLY PARSLEY?

I cook with curly parsley, rather than the fashionable flat-leaf parsley, because I feel the curly variety has more flavor. I keep flat-leaf parsley for garnishing dishes and for using in salads.

SHOULD I USE WAXY OR FLOURY POTATOES?

While waxy potatoes like new or red potatoes are best boiled for salads, and some people prefer more floury ones like Russets for baking and roasting, for mashed potatoes it's a question of taste. If you can find them, Maris Piper are a good "in-between" potato.

and leave them nice and rough because the peaks will brown and make the dish more attractive.

9 Put into the oven for about 20 minutes. Don't be afraid to let the top get nice and brown and crusty, since you want the texture to contrast with the softness of the fish and the creaminess of the sauce. If the top isn't as crisp as you would like, you could put the dish under a hot broiler for a few minutes at the end.

10 The big thing with fish pie is not to serve it too hot, otherwise you just burn your mouth and don't appreciate all the flavors. I happily leave it to stand for half an hour before serving.

"I love the flavor of this risotto. It is a real spring/summer dish, very fragrant and refreshing."

20

Lemon and thyme risotto

I actually think that making a risotto is easier than boiling rice in water. There is an idea that risotto is complicated, because you need to stand over the pan and stir, but think about it: if you are watching it all the time, you have much less chance of ruining it, whereas when rice is boiling, it's easy to forget the time and then it turns to rice pudding.

I love the flavor of this risotto. It is a real spring/summer dish, very fragrant and refreshing. It can be a meal in itself, or you can serve it alongside meat or fish. The basic technique of making a risotto always remains the same, but there are several different ways of finishing it. The classic way is to beat in butter and Parmesan, but I have seen chefs use olive oil, mascarpone—I even saw one French chef use *Brie de Meaux*. The principle is that you want something creamy but quite neutral-tasting, to bind all the ingredients together at the end. The combination I use here of egg and Parmesan is rather like that of carbonara (see page 109), except that it is tangy with lemon.

I picked up a good tip from Giorgio Locatelli when he took an Italian cooking class at the school, which is that you don't have to rush to serve your risotto. Rice retains a lot of heat, so you can relax about finishing it off. It should be creamy and slightly soupy, so if you think it is too stodgy at the end you can just add some more hot stock until you are happy with the consistency.

There are three main varieties of rice used for risotto: Vialone Nano, Carnaroli, and Arborio. Italians usually have their own favorite, often depending on which region they come from or what kind of risotto they are making. I would say it is up to you… experiment and see which you prefer.

Bertinet Basics

✳ *Do I need to make my own stock?*
See page 201

✳ *What is the best way to chop or slice an onion? See page 60*

Q&A…

WHAT IS THE BEST WAY TO JUICE A LEMON?

If you want lemons for juicing, look for heavy fruit with smooth, finely grained skins, rather than thicker, more bumpy-skinned ones. Bear in mind, though, that thinner-skinned ones will be harder to zest—and there will be less of the zest. Choose really yellow lemons: if they have green streaks, they are not fully ripe and their flavor will be more acidic.

If you want only a squeeze of juice, instead of cutting the lemon in half, just prick the skin with a knife and squeeze. If you are juicing a half lemon, there is any number of gadgets you can use. The ones I have are the metal squeezers that you open out; you put in a lemon half and then close up the squeezer and press out the juice. I have different-sized ones for oranges, limes, and grapefruits. It really doesn't matter what kind you go for. The important thing is that it is practical and easy to keep clean—otherwise you won't use it!

PREPARATION

✳ Chop the onion into small dice—you want the onion to disappear into the risotto, so don't make the pieces too big.

✳ Put the egg yolks in a bowl.

✳ Grate the Parmesan.

✳ Zest the lemons and squeeze the juice. Reserve a few strips of lemon zest for the garnish.

✳ Pick the thyme leaves from their stalks, but leave a couple of sprigs whole for the garnish.

✳ Put your pan of stock onto the stove, bring to a boil, and then turn down to a simmer.

METHOD

1 Your risotto should take no more than 20–25 minutes from start to finish. Put the butter, oil, onion, and a pinch of salt into a wide pan over medium heat. Cook the onion very gently for about 4–5 minutes, until soft but not colored. It is really important with a risotto not to brown and burn your onion. This is a delicately flavored dish and the bitterness of burned onion will flavor the whole thing, so keep it in the center of the pan, rather than spreading it out—that way, it runs less risk of catching. Putting it into a cold pan, without heating the oil first, also helps.

2 When the onion is soft, add the rice, and stir very well to coat every grain. The pan will be getting quite hot and dry now, so add your white wine, sprinkling it in carefully in a clockwise direction around the pan—this evenly distributes the wine and helps it to reduce and evaporate more quickly. Add half of the lemon juice and half of the zest and cook for 1 minute. Keep stirring gently. You will hear the wine "singing" as some of it reduces in the pan. This will probably take about 2 minutes, and then the rice will look dry again.

3 Now you are ready to add your hot stock, a ladleful at a time. After every ladleful, stir well, really scraping the bottom of the pan, until the stock has almost disappeared into the rice. Then add another ladleful, keeping the rice moist all the time—don't let it get dry in between ladlefuls. After about 15 minutes of adding stock and stirring in this way, start to taste—be careful, since the rice will be very hot. The rice needs to be tender, but still have some bite to it.

4 When you feel that it is almost there, take the pan off the heat.

5 Quickly mix the cheese, thyme, and the remaining lemon juice and zest into your bowl of egg yolks, and then beat this into your rice as energetically as you can. The risotto should be nice and relaxed and creamy. If it feels a bit too thick, whisk in a little more hot stock. Taste at the end, and season if you need to. However, remember that if you are using store-bought stock it may be very salty anyway, as is the Parmesan, so you may not need much salt.

6 Spoon into wide bowls and garnish with the reserved lemon zest and thyme.

INGREDIENTS

For 4

1 large onion
2 egg yolks (preferably free-range)
3oz Parmesan
2 lemons
bunch of fresh thyme
1½ quarts vegetable stock
4 tablespoons butter
1 tablespoon olive oil
sea salt and freshly ground
   black pepper
14oz risotto rice
¼ bottle white wine

Q&A...

WHY BUY UNWAXED LEMONS?

Lemons, as well as oranges and limes, have naturally waxy skins to keep them juicy and moist inside, but these tend to deteriorate after harvesting. Many growers, therefore, seal the skins with a protective coating of wax to extend their life and make them look more attractive. Although it is edible, the feel of a waxed lemon always reminds me of a car that has just been through valet service! If you are juicing the lemon, it doesn't matter, but if you want to use the skin (or zest), buy unwaxed lemons. If you can't find any, scrub the skin under hot water with a brush or paper towel. I never feel that all the wax comes off when you do this—but it should get rid of the hard outer layer.

21

Whole spelt and squash "risotto"

Spelt literally brings me back down to earth. Because it has such an amazing heritage, it always makes me think of all the places it has grown, since biblical times. Part of the wheat family, it was out of favor for a long time because farmers preferred faster-growing, modern varieties of wheat, but now it is becoming popular again. I love the slightly nutty flavor, and I use the flour to make bread, as well as substituting the whole grain for rice in "risotto." The technique here is the same as in the recipe on page 102, but spelt has a slightly different texture and is quite a bit more filling, so I normally serve a small portion as a starter, or as an accompaniment to meat or fish. Obviously, if you want to serve a larger portion as a main course on its own, just double the quantities.

I have been a big champion of English spelt, especially the organic grain from Sharpham Park in Glastonbury and Bacheldre Mill in Wales, but recently I have discovered some beautiful spelt grown and milled in Denmark. The owners of Skaertoft Mill came over to one of my bread classes and brought me some of the wonderful flour that they produce. They set up their own breadmaking school back home, using my technique, and when they invited me over to see what they were doing, they showed me the old bakehouse with its oven that had been out of use for about a hundred years. I thought they should restore it and hold a bread festival, which they have done. So I had the privilege of taking some of the classes at their school during their first festival, teaching young Danish chefs about bread using this ancient oven and their amazing spelt. In the United States, spelt was introduced to the country by Swiss immigrants and today is grown mostly in eastern Ohio; never a commonly used grain in the US, it has experienced a slight increase in popularity in recent years.

I use canola oil rather than olive oil in this recipe because its nuttiness goes well with the spelt, and I tend to use shallot rather than onion because it is slightly sweeter, which works well with the sweetness of the squash. Also, you get a slight pinky-wine color in a shallot, which looks good. Red onions are an alternative, but if you don't have red, white are fine.

Q &A...

CAN YOU USE PUMPKIN INSTEAD OF SQUASH?

You can, although I always think of the big orange pumpkins as being better for carving faces out of at Halloween than for eating. Their flesh is often more watery than that of the smaller winter squashes, which tend to have more dense, slightly sweeter flesh. There are hundreds of varieties of squash, many, many more than we ever see in the supermarkets. In France, in the late summer, you find basketfuls of locally grown ones in every color, with stripes and spots, ridged and smooth. Some of them are funnily shaped and when you cut them open, depending on the variety, they might be seedy, soft-fleshed, stringy, or quite solid. Now that there is more interest in the UK and US, you can find some interesting ones in farmers' markets with fantastic names like "Sweet Dumpling" and "Pink Banana." The varieties you are most likely to come across in the supermarket are onion squash, acorn, gem, and spaghetti squash. Some can be quite bland, but the butternut has a distinctive nutty flavor and compact flesh that is a beautiful orange color, so no wonder it is the most popular.

PREPARATION

* Preheat the oven to 400°F.
* Steam the beets with the skin on (or boil) until your knife slides in but there is still a bit of resistance (roughly 20–30 minutes). Cut each one into quarters.
* Cut the squash into ½ inch dice (there is no need to peel it first) and scrape off the seeds (see Note below). Put the squash and the beet quarters into separate baking dishes and drizzle each with the olive oil, season with salt and pepper, and put a sprig of rosemary and thyme on top. Roast in the oven for 25–30 minutes, or until tender. Keep to one side.
* Finely dice the shallots. Grate the Parmesan. Cut the butter into cubes, but keep it cold.
* Put your pan of stock onto the stove, bring to a boil, and then turn it down to a simmer.

METHOD

1 Put the oil, shallots, and a pinch of salt into a wide pan over medium heat and cook the shallots very gently for about 4–5 minutes, or until soft but not colored. As explained in the recipe on page 103, if you keep the shallots in the center of the pan, you run less risk of burning them than if you spread them out. Also, if you start with cold oil, it is harder to burn the shallots.

2 When the shallots are soft, add the spelt and stir very well to coat every grain. As the pan becomes hot and dry, add your white wine, sprinkling it in around the pan in a clockwise direction to help it reduce and evaporate more quickly. Keep stirring gently. You will hear the wine "singing" as some of it reduces in the pan. After about 2 minutes, the grains will look dry again.

3 Now you can start adding your hot stock, a ladleful at a time. After every ladleful, stir well, really scraping the bottom of the pan until the stock has almost disappeared into the spelt. Then add your next ladleful, keeping the spelt moist all the time—don't let it dry out between ladlefuls. After about 15 minutes of adding stock and stirring, start to taste—be careful, because the grains will be very hot. Spelt will feel slightly different in texture from rice, but it should be comfortably soft in the mouth, yet still have a little bite to it.

4 When you feel that it is almost there, take the pan off the heat.

5 Beat in the butter—you really need to get some energy into it—and then beat in the mascarpone and Parmesan. The risotto should be nice and creamy now and quite loose. If it feels a bit too sticky, just beat in a little bit more hot stock. Taste and season, if necessary—remember that if you are using store-bought stock it may be salty, as is the Parmesan, and you have already seasoned your squash and beets.

6 Serve with your roasted squash and beet.

Note: You can roast the squash seeds separately, if you wish, to serve as a garnish or a healthy snack. Wash and dry them well, toss them in a little olive oil and sea salt, and roast them on a baking sheet in the oven until golden.

INGREDIENTS

For 4 as an appetizer or side

2 medium raw beets
1 small squash, preferably butternut, skin on
a little light olive oil or canola oil, for roasting the squash
sea salt and freshly ground black pepper
2 sprigs of rosemary
2 sprigs of thyme
2 large shallots
2oz Parmesan
4 tablespoons cold butter
1¾ cups vegetable or chicken stock
1 tablespoon canola oil
1½ cups spelt grain (pearled spelt)
½ cup white wine
2 generous tablespoons mascarpone

Bertinet Basics

* Do I need to make my own stock? *See page 201*

* What is the best way to slice or chop a shallot? *See page 60*

Q&A...

WHAT IS MASCARPONE?
Like ricotta, mascarpone isn't what you would call a true "cheese," even though it is often called mascarpone cheese. It is made from cream that has been heated and had an acid added to it, which makes it thicken and separates out the whey. It is then put inside a cloth and hung up so that the whey drains off to leave a thick, creamy "cheese."

"Spaghetti carbonara is my
idea of a 'happy meal.'"

Spaghetti carbonara

To all the Italians out there: I know that a true, authentic carbonara is made just with pasta, pancetta (actually, originally it was cured pork jowl, known as *guanciale*)**, eggs, and cheese. Heavy cream isn't something that features in traditional Italian cooking, but this is the americanized version that has taken over in many restaurants in the US.**

Sometimes, when people come to my classes they are surprised that I teach recipes made with dried pasta. There seems to be a bit of confusion about pasta, that somehow fresh pasta is superior to dried, whereas in Italy, they are seen as completely different. Of course, I love to teach people to make fresh pasta for things like ravioli, but this dish would never be made with fresh pasta, because you want that bite, known as *al dente*, that you can get only with good dried pasta. At the school, we use Di Cecco or Barilla. Spaghetti carbonara is one of the quickest, simplest, and most satisfying meals you can make—this is my idea of a "happy meal." Some people prefer to make it with pecorino cheese instead of Parmesan—it's up to you.

PREPARATION

✳ Bring a big pan of water to a rolling boil, with a tablespoon of salt, ready for the pasta.
✳ If you are using pancetta or bacon, cut it into strips or cubes.
✳ Grate the Parmesan.
✳ In a bowl, mix together the egg yolks, cream, and Parmesan. Season with black pepper, if you like.

METHOD

1 When the water is boiling fast, put in the spaghetti, curling the strands around the pan and under the water with a fork. Bring back up to a boil and stir the strands again with your fork to separate them. Cook at a rolling boil for about 6 minutes, and then start to test the pasta. You want it to be just *al dente*—i.e., it should be tender, but just have a little bite to it, rather than be completely soft.

2 While the pasta is cooking, get a frying pan hot over medium heat. Put in the lardons or pieces of pancetta or bacon and let them fry quickly in their own fat, until browned. Lift out and drain on paper towels.

3 When the pasta is cooked, drain off the water really quickly through a colander, and then immediately tip the pasta back into the pan, so it still retains quite a lot of moisture. Put the pan on very low heat, add the fried lardons, pancetta, or bacon and the egg, cream, and cheese mixture, and toss through for 30 seconds to 1 minute. The starchiness (from the pasta) of the moisture in the pan, together with this very brief cooking, will make the cream thicken just a little and give a glossy coating to the pasta—otherwise, the sauce would just slide off. The pasta and sauce should come together as one, not be separate entities. Don't leave the pan on the stove for any longer than a minute, or the eggs will start to scramble.

INGREDIENTS

For 4–6

sea salt and freshly ground
   black pepper
9oz pancetta, lardons, or bacon
4oz Parmesan, plus extra for serving
8 egg yolks (preferably free-range)
2 cups heavy cream
1¼lb dried spaghetti

Bertinet Basics

How is pancetta different from bacon? *See page 63*

Q&A...

DO YOU NEED TO PUT OIL IN THE WATER WHEN YOU COOK PASTA?
Some people suggest putting in a drop or two of oil to stop the strands of pasta from sticking together in the pan, but there really is no need, and most Italians wouldn't dream of doing it, since it means the sauce slides off the pasta. The secret is to use the biggest pan you have, with plenty of rapidly boiling water, to give the pasta lots of space to tumble around in without getting bunched up. Make sure you stir it well with a fork at the beginning to help keep the strands or pieces separate.

Penne with arugula, crème fraîche, smoked salmon, and tomatoes

This is another very quick dish that was first made for me by Richard Guest, now head chef at the famous Castle Hotel in Taunton, England, when we worked together at Maison Novelli in London. It was something he rustled up for the staff, using leftover pieces of salmon. The idea is to get used to making a sauce in the same time as it takes the pasta to cook, which is something most Italians do without thinking when it comes to making a quick supper.

It is a dish to make with trimmings of smoked fish, rather than prime slices. Most smokehouses sell the pieces that get left over when they trim the sides of salmon into slices—you can either buy them direct or from the supermarket. Wild salmon has become an endangered species and fish farms can be controversial. Ever since its farming took off in the seventies, salmon has become devalued to the point where we sometimes forget smoked salmon is actually fish. A bit like the strawberry, it has lost its preciousness and become just a commodity, because it is always there. When I grew up, smoked salmon was something you only had at Christmas or New Year, and you looked forward to it. I think we should go back to treating ourselves occasionally to a whole side of smoked salmon, or some good-quality slices, and really appreciating it—and making use of the trimmings, which would otherwise be wasted, for recipes like this one.

INGREDIENTS

For 4–6

sea salt and freshly ground
    black pepper
1¼lb dried penne
1 tablespoon olive oil
about 8oz cherry tomatoes
about 9oz smoked salmon trimmings
6 tablespoons dry white wine
1¾ cups crème fraîche
about 4oz arugula

PREPARATION

✳ Bring a big pan of water to a rolling boil, with a tablespoon of salt.

METHOD

1 When the water is at a rolling boil, put in the penne. After about 6 minutes, start to test the pasta to see whether it is done. As for the spaghetti in the recipe on page 109, it should be tender but just have a bite to it, rather than be completely soft.

2 While the pasta is cooking, heat the oil in a large pan over medium heat—it should be big enough for you to add the cooked penne shortly.

3 When the oil is hot but not smoking, put in the whole tomatoes and stir well. Add the smoked salmon trimmings and stir again, but not too vigorously because the idea is to try to keep the tomatoes intact. Pour in the white wine and let it bubble up in the pan to evaporate some of the alcohol.

4 Add the crème fraîche and stir again. After about 2–3 minutes, the sauce will start to thicken.

5 By now the pasta should be about ready. Check and then drain it quickly through a colander—you don't want to remove all the moisture because the starch in it will help bind the pasta and sauce together.

6 Quickly pour the pasta into the pan containing your sauce. Add the arugula, taste, and season with salt and pepper, and then toss everything together.

Q&A...

WHICH IS BETTER: WILD OR FARMED SMOKED SALMON?

Connoisseurs prefer the flavor and texture of the wild fish because its incredible journey along the river makes it very athletic and firm. But we have fished too much of it, and most smokeries now have to use some, if not all, farmed salmon. Some farms (essentially massive cages located in the sea) have had bad press, with horror stories about their use of chemicals and the pollution of the seas—especially when they are located alongside routes that wild salmon take. Also, you have to catch a huge amount of small fish to get enough fish oil to feed the farmed salmon. Of course, it is impossible to police conditions in the oceans, but do try to buy from a farm that isn't cramming as many fish as possible into a small space. Organic farms focus on sustainability and the welfare of the fish.

Cape Malay vegetable curry

I discovered these flavors when I went out to the South Africa Gourmet Festival in Cape Town in 1996, when I was cooking with Jean-Christophe Novelli. He was demonstrating some dishes at a local cooking school where we met the cook and writer Cass Abrahams, who is the guru of Cape Malay cooking. The original Malay "slaves" were skilled workers brought over from outposts in India, Malaysia, and Indonesia to this part of Africa by the Dutch, who had secured the monopoly of the Spice Islands and had set up the Dutch East India Company. Many of them worked as cooks to the rich merchants on the Cape, and although over the generations they have intermarried in the "rainbow" society of South Africa, they have kept their cooking traditions going, passing recipes down through families. Today, Cape Malay cooking is considered a big part of the food culture in and around Cape Town.

This vegetable curry reminds me of a kind of African-Indian ratatouille. In a typical Cape Malay meal, as in an Indian meal, it would be one of lots of dishes on the table at once, such as bredie (stew), bobotie (a dish of baked ground beef with golden raisins and almonds), rice, sweet and sour salads, and sambals, which are like salsas. What I enjoy about Cape Malay cooking is the subtle way the spices are blended without the finished result being overly hot.

Growing up in Brittany, I didn't really encounter spice until I came to Britain. However, over the years, and being lucky enough to work alongside chefs such as Atul Kochhar of Benares, India, at the cooking school, I have discovered the difference between freshly ground, well-sourced spices, and ones that have been sitting in the pantry for years, losing their flavor and color. Even peppercorns differ from country to country and region to region, according to the essential oils they contain and how they are grown. Try to buy your spices from a good supplier, and, if possible, buy whole spices—for example, cumin and coriander—which will keep for much longer than ground ones. When you come to use them, simply heat them gently in a dry pan until they release their aroma, and then grind them in a coffee grinder, or in a mortar and pestle, and sift them to a fine powder. If you prefer to buy ready-ground spices, make sure you keep them in an airtight container away from light and heat. Use them within 3–6 months or they will lose their magic.

Serve this curry with rice and a little sambal of tomato and cucumber. Peel a cucumber, take out the seeds, and grate it. Sprinkle with salt and leave for 10 minutes, then squeeze it out and pat dry with paper towels. Add 1 large chopped tomato, 2 chopped green chiles, and a good handful of chopped cilantro, then toss with a mixture of 4 tablespoons of vinegar to 2 of sugar.

Note: If you like, you can triple or quadruple the quantities of garlic, chile, and ginger in the curry paste and freeze some for next time. Just make sure you double up the freezer bag or the smell will fill your freezer.

Q & A ...

WHAT ARE CURRY LEAVES?
These come from a tree that grows in parts of India, the Himalayas, Thailand, and Sri Lanka; they have a quite delicate, spicy, lemony flavor. You can find them in Asian supermarkets.

WHAT IS THE DIFFERENCE BETWEEN CASSIA AND CINNAMON?
The two are interchangeable, since they are both made from the dried bark of different species of laurel—cinnamon originally comes from Sri Lanka, and cassia from Myanmar. They have the same kind of flavor and aroma; however, cassia is more intense, whereas cinnamon is slightly warmer and sweeter.

INGREDIENTS

For 4–6

1 large white onion
1 large red onion
1 eggplant
2 zucchini
2 red bell peppers
6 large red tomatoes (or 3 x 14.5oz cans plum tomatoes)
large "thumb" of fresh ginger
4–6 garlic cloves
1–2 green chiles
about 2 tablespoons light vegetable oil
3 cardamom pods
1 large stick of cassia (or cinnamon)
3 curry leaves
1 heaping teaspoon ground cumin seeds
1 heaping teaspoon ground coriander seeds
1 heaping teaspoon garam masala
½ teaspoon ground turmeric
sprig of cilantro, to garnish

PREPARATION

✱ Slice the onions (the addition of red onion adds a little extra color and sweetness). Chop the eggplant, zucchini, and red bell peppers into similar-sized pieces (about 1 inch), so that they cook evenly—don't be too precious about it, because this is a rustic dish.
✱ Roughly chop the tomatoes. (If you are using canned tomatoes, drain them through a strainer, reserving the juice.)
✱ Peel and roughly chop the ginger and garlic.
✱ Pound the ginger, garlic, and whole chile(s) in a mortar and pestle, or using the end of a rolling pin, to form a paste. (Alternatively, pulse in a blender.) This is the traditional way of preparing these ingredients, and when they are smooth like this they are absorbed more easily into the curry.

METHOD

1 Heat the oil in a pan and cook the onions very gently with the cardamom pods, cassia (or cinnamon), and curry leaves. Stir until the onions are soft, and then add the eggplant and garlic/ginger/chile paste.

2 Stir the paste in well, and then add the zucchini and red peppers. Now add the rest of the spices and stir well again. Next, add the tomatoes. (If you are using a can, keep back most of the liquid for now, since you don't want the curry to be too "wet"—in theory, there will be enough moisture in all of the vegetables to soften the curry, but if it starts to dry out, you can add some more of the juice later.)

3 Put the lid on the pan to keep all the moisture inside, and cook very slowly on low heat for 1 hour, checking regularly to make sure it isn't getting too dry. If the curry does start to dry out, add either some of your reserved tomato juice or a little water. Garnish with the cilantro.

HOW CAN I VARY THE RECIPE?

This particular curry has no meat in it, but you can include some chicken pieces if you wish—for example, legs, wings, and/or breasts (cut these in half). Heat a little vegetable oil in a frying pan or sauté pan, season the chicken pieces, and brown them on all sides, as for the simple chicken pot on page 116. Make up the curry in the usual way, adding the browned chicken at the same time as the eggplant.

"What I enjoy about Cape Malay cooking is the subtle way the spices are blended without being overly hot."

Simple chicken pot

This is exactly what it says, a simple one-pot dish that is good with rice or mashed potatoes. You can use it as a blueprint for any slow-cooked meat or vegetable dish.

I like the term "one-pot" because it sums up what it is without getting into a debate about whether a dish like this should correctly be called a casserole or a stew. What is the difference? To be honest, I don't think there is an exact definition of either. After all, they contain the same basic ingredients: meat or fish, vegetables, probably herbs, and liquid. Everyone will tell you something different: that a casserole involves browning the meat rather than putting it into the pot raw with vegetables and liquid; or that a casserole is cooked in the oven, rather than on the stove—or vice versa; or I've heard it said that a casserole involves light meat, whereas a stew is a heartier, red meat dish. So let's just stick with the idea of one-pot—a big, heavy-bottomed pan that you bring to the table and everyone helps themselves from. It's the kind of dish that is about sharing and feeling happy and comforted.

In classes, I like to show people how to cut up a whole chicken (see page 120), since you get so much more flavor from meat left on the bone, and there is no waste. However, if you don't feel confident enough to do this right away, cook this dish a few times first using chicken thighs, breasts on the bone, and legs, so that you get the hang of it, and then move on to jointing a chicken later. If you do joint your own chicken, you can use the bones, together with the vegetable trimmings, to make the stock, rather than buying it.

The cream in this dish is entirely optional. You can leave it out if you wish, or use crème fraîche if you want the creaminess, with less fat.

INGREDIENTS
For 4–6

1 corn-fed or other good-quality chicken (or 2 breasts on the bone, cut in half crosswise, 2 legs, and 2 thighs)
1 large onion
4 shallots
2 carrots
2 celery ribs
14oz button mushrooms
2 garlic cloves
1 sprig each of thyme and rosemary
1 bay leaf
bunch of parsley
small bunch of tarragon
1 quart chicken stock (or use the vegetable and chicken trimmings to make your own, see page 201)
sea salt and black pepper, plus a few black peppercorns for the stock (if making your own)
about 4 tablespoons olive oil or canola oil
½ bottle red wine
½ cup crème fraîche or heavy cream (optional)

Bertinet Basics

✳ **What is the best way to slice or chop an onion?** *See page 60*

✳ **What is the best way to clean mushrooms?** *See page 57*

✳ **Why do you sometimes crush garlic rather than chop it?**
See page 29

✳ **What is the best way to chop herbs?** *See page 41*

PREPARATION

✳ If you are using a whole chicken, cut it into 8 portions leaving the breast on the bone (see page 120).

✳ If you like, instead of using ready-made stock, you can use the leftover chicken bones to make a quick and easy stock of your own. Chop the bones and the neck (if you still have the giblets), and put them in a large pan. Pour in about 1½ quarts water, add the peppercorns, and all your vegetable trimmings as you prepare them. Bring to a boil, skim any scum from the surface, and then turn down the heat to simmer for about 30 minutes while you continue with your preparation and brown your chicken and vegetables. You should have around a quart of stock by the time you need it.

✳ Peel the onion and roughly chop. Peel the shallots.

✳ Peel the carrots and dice about ½ inch thick (see page 118).

✳ Cut the celery into chunks about 1 inch thick.

✳ Wipe the mushrooms. Quarter them if small; slice them if large.

✳ Don't peel the garlic, but just crush the cloves with the side of a knife.

✳ Make a bouquet garni by tying the thyme, rosemary, and bay leaf together with a length of butcher's twine.

✳ Take the leaves from the parsley and tarragon and set aside for later. Chop the stalks and put them into the stock pot.

✳ Heat your quart of stock (if you are using a bought one) in a pan.

✳ Season the chicken, rubbing well into the meat, just before you are ready to start cooking it. If you season it too early, the salt will draw out the moisture and the chicken will be drier and tougher.

Use this technique of slicing, cutting into batons, and then into dice for most vegetables...

Peel the carrots, then slice downward.

Gather a few slices together, one on top of the other.

Slice lengthwise into batons.

Slice the batons into dice.

Q&A...

WHY USE ONIONS AND SHALLOTS?

It is something I have always done when making this dish. Onions are at the base of almost every savory recipe because they are natural flavor enhancers that bind different tastes together. Shallots have a little more sweetness, which is why I like to use them in slow-cooked sauces; and often for quickly cooked sauces, I will use chopped shallot instead of onion.

WHAT KIND OF WINE SHOULD I USE?

One of the questions I am always asked in classes is whether you should use good wine or cheap wine, and whether the style of the wine makes any real difference. I would say don't spend more than 5 or 10 dollars if you are buying a new bottle: but buy something you would happily drink. Obviously, if you have any unfinished bottles that you have popped the cork back in, use those. As for the style, yes, a dish made with a big, fruity, oaky New World wine will taste different from one made with a more subtle European one. I tend to avoid oaky wines because they can easily overpower the rest of the ingredients. In winter, I might use a richer, fruitier Cabernet/Bordeaux style of wine; in summer, my instinct will be telling me to go for something lighter.

METHOD

1 Put your baking dish or large pan onto high heat—don't put any oil into it at this point. When it is hot, rub 2 tablespoons of the oil over the chicken and put the pieces into the pan. When you put them in, think of the pan as a clock face. Start at 12 o'clock, put in your first piece, skin-side down, and then put in the rest of the pieces clockwise around the pan, finishing in the middle. Then, when you are ready to turn them over, go back to 12 o'clock again. It might sound pedantic, but if you keep to this sequence, the chicken pieces will be evenly browned, rather than if you just flip them over at random.

2 Once all the chicken pieces are in the pan, leave them alone and don't be tempted to fiddle with them for a good couple of minutes. In classes, we talk a lot about not fussing—i.e., not pushing things around in a pan just for the sake of it, especially when you are browning meat, because all you do is cool down the pan and stop everything from cooking correctly.

3 The point of browning meat like this is not to cook it, but to seal in the juices and give it a nice color, so it doesn't look flabby and unappetizing in the finished dish. Here, you are aiming for a nice golden-brown color.

4 When the pieces are golden brown on the underside, turn them over in your clockwise sequence and brown the other side. Lift onto a plate with tongs.

5 Take the pan off the heat and, if necessary, wipe the inside quickly with some paper towels, just to remove the excess grease. Put the pan back over medium heat and put in the onions, whole shallots, garlic, celery, and carrots, stirring well to make sure they don't burn. Add the the bouquet garni and cook for 2–3 minutes.

6 Now you are ready to add the wine. As before, what I do is start at 12 o'clock and then drizzle the wine in slowly around the pan clockwise, ending in the middle as I did with the chicken—again, this is about keeping the heat in the pan. If you pour all the wine in at once, it will cool down, and you will have to wait while everything comes back up to temperature.

7 Let the wine come to a boil, because you want to reduce the liquid slightly and burn off the alcohol. You will know when it has reduced enough because it will look different. At the beginning, the bubbles will be big and sparse, and then, as the liquid reduces down and starts to thicken, the bubbles will become tiny and you will see a bit of a tide mark around the edge of the pan—as if the sea has gone down and the vegetables are poking out like rocks.

8 Pour in your hot stock slowly (if you are using your own, strain it into the pan through a fine strainer) and bring to a boil. Return the chicken to the pan, turn the heat down to a simmer, put on the lid, and cook gently for 20–25 minutes. Because the pan has been kept hot all the time, you can transfer it to a small burner and it will bubble away nicely. After around 20 minutes, place the lid slightly ajar, and then continue cooking for another 20 minutes.

9 The way to test if the meat is ready is to remove a piece from the pan. First, take off the lid and turn it over to use as a plate. Take out a piece of chicken thigh, put it on top and, with a wooden spoon, press down on it. If the meat comes away from the bone easily, it is done; if it is still quite tight, put the lid back on and cook for another 5–10 minutes before testing again. As soon as the chicken is cooked, don't leave it any longer, since you still have to add the crème fraîche or cream (if using) and mushrooms, so the chicken will have another 5–10 minutes' cooking time. While you won't damage the flavor, you don't want to cook this casserole for so long that the meat is virtually falling off the bones, because a pot full of exposed bones isn't very appetizing.

10 So, when the chicken is just done, take out the bouquet garni. Add the crème fraîche or cream (if using) and cook on low heat for another 5 minutes. Your sauce should be nice and creamy.

11 Meanwhile, quickly fry the mushrooms in the remaining 2 tablespoons of oil in a separate frying pan, seasoning lightly. I prefer to sauté mushrooms separately because you get a lovely nutty flavor, which will stay intact in the finished dish. If you add them with the rest of the vegetables, they will just disappear; if you add them raw at the end, they will be a bit flabby and less tasty.

12 Add the sautéed mushrooms to the pot and simmer for another 5 minutes. If you have seasoned your chicken and mushrooms correctly, you probably won't need to add any more salt and pepper at this stage, but taste and check. Rest the dish for up to 20 minutes—the sauce will naturally thicken a bit. Chop the parsley and tarragon leaves, and sprinkle them in at the last minute to give the dish an added zing.

Note: If you want to serve the chicken on plates rather than from the pot, and you like a smoother sauce, take out the chicken and most of the vegetables at the end of their cooking time using a slotted spoon, and arrange on your plates. Turn up the heat and let the liquid reduce, as before. Once it has thickened, strain it through a nylon strainer and spoon a little over the chicken.

Bertinet Basics

✳ **Why is it important to simmer, rather than boil?** *See page 59*

Q&A...

WHAT SHOULD I LOOK FOR WHEN BUYING A CHICKEN?

There have been enough high-profile campaigns by chefs, highlighting good versus bad chickens, for everyone, hopefully, to have gotten the message. I know that you have to buy what you can afford, and a free-range or organic chicken is expensive, but you have to ask yourself what kind of sad life a cheap chicken has led. It comes down to respect for the animal, which is why it is worth eating chicken a little less often, and appreciating it more. Instead of buying two breasts in packages, buy the whole chicken and make it last longer—a good chicken can provide several meals, and stock.

Welfare isn't the only issue: a chicken that has been slowly grown and roamed freely will have much better flavor and texture, and its properly formed bones will give you great, gelatinous stock. Use a good local butcher who can tell you where he buys his chickens, or farmers' markets and supermarkets that sell them from named farms that put welfare at the top of their list.

WHY PUT THE LID AJAR FOR THE LAST PART OF COOKING?

When I am cooking a one-pot dish I find it works best to leave the lid on to begin with to keep everything moist and help the meat to become tender. I put the lid ajar toward the end of the cooking time to allow the liquid to evaporate slightly—this will thicken the sauce and intensify the flavor. You can take the lid off if you need to thicken the sauce more quickly.

Step-by-step: Jointing a chicken

"When you see the chicken standing upright, you start to understand its anatomy."

We tend to get very lazy about buying chicken. How much do you pay for two breasts of free-range or organic chicken in the supermarket? For the same price, you can buy the whole chicken and use the bones to make stock or a quick soup. Every time you cut up a chicken, keep the bits of backbone and wing, which are full of gelatinous goodness, and put them in a bag in the freezer until you have enough to boil up. Just 30 minutes of boiling chicken bones in water will give you a lovely flavor—strain it, and you will have a clear soup, into which you can drop some dried noodles, to cook for a couple of minutes, and maybe some finely chopped ginger and chile.

I always stand whole chickens up on their legs in front of people in classes, so they can be reminded that chicken isn't just something that comes in pieces in plastic trays. It makes people cringe sometimes when I do it, but I think we have to remember that a chicken is a creature that was running around not so long ago and give a bit of respect back to it. That way, we might think more about buying a good free-range or organic one that has lived a natural life, rather than one that has been squashed into a packed hen house. Also, when you see the chicken standing upright, you start to understand its anatomy. You can familiarize yourself with the connection between the legs, the breasts, and the wings, and see where the joints are, so that when you portion it up, it will make sense.

1–2 The first thing to do is lay the chicken, breast-side down, on your board and cut down each side of the backbone, either with a sharp knife or a pair of kitchen shears. Remove the backbone (you can keep it and chop it up for stock).

3–4 Now, open the chicken out like a book. This is known as "spatchcock"—a chicken opened out and flattened like this is great for putting on the barbecue because it cooks much more quickly. Next, cut right through the breastbone so that the chicken is in two halves.

5–6 Take the first breast and pull the leg outward a little—you should be able to feel the seam joining the leg to the breast. Make a cut along here, separating the leg from the breast. Do the same with the other half of the chicken.

7 Cut each breast in half crosswise.

8 Finally, take the wings off the breasts. The wing is in 3 sections: imagine it like your arm. The tip is equivalent to your hand, then there is the forearm, with a joint equivalent to your elbow and then, closest to the breast, is the thicker part that is equivalent to your biceps. Cut off the tip (the "hand" part) and keep it for stock, then cut the rest of the wing off at the "elbow," leaving the last bit attached to the breast.

9 Next, you need to attend to the legs. Feel each leg first so you can find the joint. Cut straight through the joint on each leg to separate the drumsticks from the thighs.

Now you should have 10 pieces: 2 thighs, 2 drumsticks, 4 pieces of breast, and 2 pieces of wing.

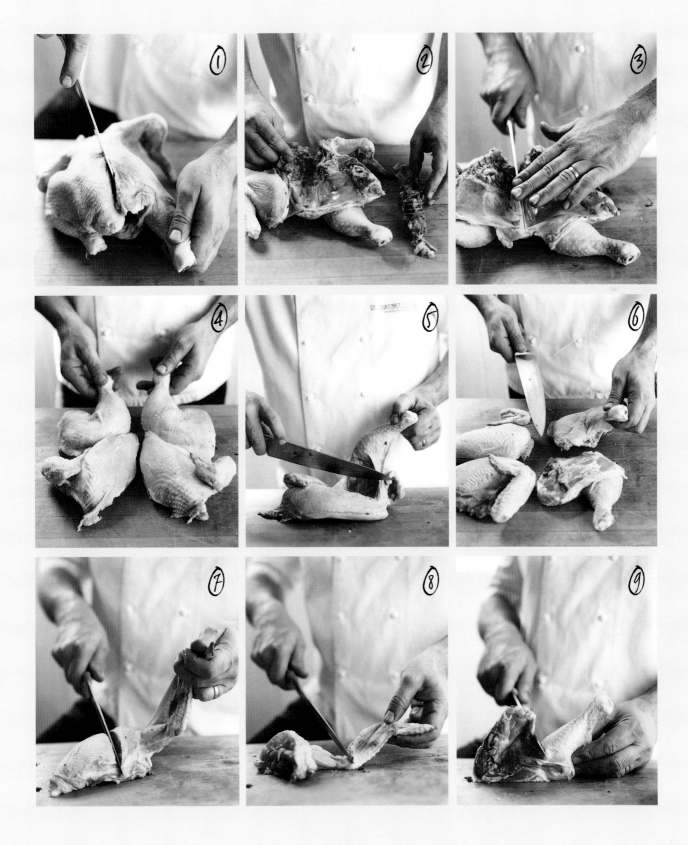

Chicken with fennel and herbs

This is all about baking a whole meal in one dish, which you can bring from the oven to the table. The meat sits on top of the vegetables, and the spices, herbs, and juices infuse their flavors into each other. You don't need to make a sauce: it is all self-generated, and you can put everything together in 10–15 minutes.

I love the aniseedy flavor of fennel, which rounds out beautifully when it is cooked slowly. The star anise has its own slight aniseedy flavor, which picks up the taste of the fennel. If you don't have any, but you have a bottle of Pastis or Pernod, you could add a couple of tablespoons of that instead. Of course, if you don't like the flavor of fennel, you could use leeks or red onions in its place.

INGREDIENTS
For 4–6

9 tablespoons butter
1 corn-fed or other good-quality
  chicken (or 2 breasts, cut in half
  crosswise, 2 drumsticks,
  2 thighs, and 2 wings)
2 large fennel bulbs
4 large tomatoes
4 garlic cloves
16–20 small new potatoes
few sprigs of chervil
few sprigs of curly parsley
few sprigs of rosemary
few sprigs of thyme
sea salt and freshly ground
  black pepper
1 large or 2 small unwaxed lemons
2 whole star anise (preferably) or 1
  heaping teaspoon ground star anise
½ cup dry white wine
6 tablespoons olive oil

Bertinet Basics

✳ **What should I look for when buying a chicken?** *See page 119*

✳ **Why do you sometimes crush garlic rather than chop it?** *See page 29*

✳ **What is the best way to chop herbs?** *See page 41*

✳ **Why buy unwaxed lemons?** *See page 103*

PREPARATION
✳ Preheat the oven to 400°F.
✳ Take the butter out of the fridge to let it soften.
✳ If you have bought a whole chicken, joint it into 10 pieces (see page 120) so you end up with 4 breast pieces (on the bone), 2 drumsticks, 2 thighs, and 2 wings.
✳ Cut the fennel bulbs in half lengthwise to give 2 identical halves (as if you had opened out the fennel like a book) and cut each piece lengthwise into 4.
✳ Halve the tomatoes.
✳ Crush the garlic cloves with the back of a knife.
✳ Wash the potatoes.
✳ Finely chop the chervil and parsley; leave the rosemary and thyme sprigs whole.

METHOD

1 Layer the tomatoes, cut-side up, in a very big roasting pan. Lay the fennel on top, followed by the garlic cloves and a few sprigs of rosemary and thyme. Put into the oven for about 20–30 minutes to start them cooking.

2 If the butter isn't soft enough, bash it with a rolling pin! Mix all of the chopped herbs into it.

3 Put the chicken pieces into a bowl and season with salt and pepper. Add the herb butter and really massage it well into the chicken.

4 Take the roasting pan out of the oven and put the chicken pieces on top of the vegetables. Cut the lemon(s) in half and squeeze the juice over. Tuck the squeezed halves in among the chicken.

5 If using whole star anise, crush them in a mortar and pestle (or use the end of a rolling pin to crush them on a cutting board). Sprinkle the star anise over the chicken and put the potatoes on top, so that they can brown.

6 Pour over the wine and olive oil and put in the oven for 30–45 minutes. Halfway through, take the pan out and turn the chicken over. The potatoes will tumble underneath, but that is fine. At the end of the cooking time, check that the largest piece of chicken breast and the biggest thigh are cooked by inserting a sharp knife into the meat. The juices should run clear.

Q &A ...

ARE WILD FENNEL AND BULB FENNEL THE SAME THING?

Although they belong to the same family, bulb fennel (sometimes called Florence fennel) is very different from wild fennel, which is the feathery herb. Although many people call it wild fennel, it is also cultivated—not only for its fronds but also for its seeds, which are used particularly in Asian cooking. Bulb fennel has similar fronds, which are often still attached when you buy the bulb. You can use the fronds in the same way as the herb, but their flavor isn't quite as strong. Both the bulb fennel and the herb have a distinct aniseed flavor—if you shave the bulb into salads it is quite strong, but if you cook it slowly, as in this recipe, it mellows, and it works wonderfully with chicken or fish. Once cooked, it also makes a good purée—just blend it in a food processor and then stir in a little bit of cream.

HOW CAN I VARY THIS RECIPE?

You could do it in exactly the same way, but substitute the chicken with a big fish, such as a sea bass, cleaned and scaled; rub it inside and out with the herb butter before putting it into the oven (for 20–35 minutes). Instead of star anise, you could use a sprinkling of ras el-hanout (North African spice mixture), paprika, or chile.

"There is something about the combination of ham, sweetness and spice that always makes me think of the Christmas season."

Roasted ham hock with maple syrup and spice glaze and roasted vegetables,

27

This is a great way to feed people on a quite cheap joint of meat. I always remember when I came over to England the first time, sitting in a pub and seeing a whole ham hock come out—for one person. It looked so amazing. Of course, there is a big bone in there, but there is so much beautiful melting meat around it—it is cooking the ham on the bone that keeps it so moist. The ham hock is the pig equivalent of the lamb shank, which became so fashionable a decade or so ago, and I think it is every bit as good.

Don't throw away the cooking water after you have simmered the hocks. It breaks my heart to see all that wonderful stock going to waste because people don't realize it can be used like chicken stock. It can be a bit salty sometimes, but taste it, and if it is too salty just dilute the stock with water. You can then freeze it for using in soups, etc.

I like to boil the ham first and then brush it with a maple syrup and spice glaze and finish it in the oven. There is something about the combination of ham, sweetness, and spice that always makes me think of the Christmas season. Any ham left over is good cold, or you could shred it and use it with the stock for a soup (see page 56), or even a risotto.

Everyone likes roasted vegetables—especially children, who wouldn't otherwise be wild about carrots or parsnips. They love the caramelized sweetness and crispiness of the tails of parsnips, and the edges of the carrots that catch around the outside of the pan. It's the plain-boiled-potato-versus-fries syndrome: once you create a bit of texture, "boring" vegetables are transformed—but they don't have to be deep-fried!

Q&A...

WHAT IS MAPLE SYRUP, AND COULD I USE SOMETHING ELSE? Maple syrup is the sap collected from maple trees, most famously in North America during the "sugaring" season at the end of the winter when the weather is somewhere between freezing and thawing and so the sap flows. The harvesters collect it by drilling "tap holes" equipped with spouts into the trees. The sap is then boiled up to remove the water, so it reduces to syrup. The principle of this glaze is to create something sweet and sticky, combined with something spicy, to give the ham a rich, deep flavor and a crisp outside. The classic glaze is a mixture of mustard and brown sugar, or honey. Alternatively, you could brush the ham with marmalade mixed with ras el hanout or a little chile powder or paprika.

INGREDIENTS

For 4

2 ham hocks (unsmoked)
1 medium onion
1 bay leaf
6 black peppercorns
2 tablespoons maple syrup
2 teaspoons ground mixed spice

FOR THE VEGETABLES

4 large Maris Piper or Russet
   Burbank potatoes
2 parsnips
8 large carrots
2 large onions
2 large shallots
1 whole garlic bulb, plus
   3–4 garlic cloves
few sprigs each of thyme
   and rosemary
2–3 tablespoons olive oil

Bertinet Basics

✳ **Why use onions and shallots?**
See page 118

✳ **What does "reducing" a sauce actually mean?** *See page 141*

PREPARATION

✳ Ham hocks can sometimes be quite salty. Also, if the meat has been sealed in a bag, you want to get rid of the taint of plastic and any liquid that may have gathered around it. So rinse them well under running water for 10–15 minutes.

✳ Cut the onion into quarters.

METHOD

1 Put the hocks into a large saucepan, cover with cold water, and add the onion quarters, bay leaf, and peppercorns. Bring to a simmer, skim off the white foamy "scum" that rises to the top, and cook gently for 1½–2 hours, depending on the size of the hocks. They will take roughly 15–20 minutes per pound. You don't want to overcook them because they are going to be roasted in the oven next. They are ready when the meat just starts to fall away from the bone. Preheat the oven to 425°F.

2 Meanwhile, prepare your vegetables. Cut them all into pieces roughly the same size so that they cook evenly. Scrub or peel the potatoes and cut each into four wedges; peel the parsnips and cut each into eight lengthwise; peel the carrots and cut each in half lengthwise; peel the onions and cut into eight; peel the shallots and cut each into four. Leave the skins on the garlic cloves, but lightly crush them with the flat edge of large knife just to release the flavor. Strip the leaves from the thyme and rosemary.

3 Put all the vegetables in a bowl, drizzle in the oil, add the rosemary and thyme, and mix together. Spread out over a big roasting pan (you are going to put the ham on top shortly).

4 Once the hocks are cooked, lift them out of the saucepan and put them in a colander to drain. Keep the cooking water, which will now be really good stock. You are going to use a little at the end, but you can keep the rest for use another time (see page 56).

5 Put the vegetables into the oven for about 10 minutes and then turn down the heat to 375°F. Keep an eye on them and turn them a couple of times. They should start to turn golden brown.

6 While the vegetables are in the oven, lay the ham hocks on a clean work surface. Some hocks have a very thick layer of skin and fat, so take off the outside layer if necessary. With a sharp knife, make crisscrosses in the skin/fat.

7 In a small dish, mix together the maple syrup and spice and then rub the mixture all over the hocks, deep into the crevices you have made in the skin. Take the pan of vegetables out of the oven, put the hocks on top and return the pan to the oven for another 30–40 minutes. Stir the vegetables around if necessary, since they may blacken and crisp around the edges of the pan. If they start to get too dry, sprinkle over a little of the ham stock—just enough to moisten them.

8 Lift the meat onto a big, warmed serving dish and put the vegetables all around. Spoon a few ladlefuls of the ham stock into the roasting pan and put it on the stove over medium heat. Let it bubble up for a few minutes and reduce down and thicken, while you scrape up all the sticky bits from the base of the pan. Pour into a pitcher and serve with the ham and vegetables.

Pork fillet stuffed with Gruyère, sage, and bacon, and braised Little Gem lettuce

28

INGREDIENTS

For 2

2lb whole, good-quality pork
   fillet, preferably locally reared
   (see Q&A)
4oz Gruyère (or Emmental)
2 large sprigs of sage
4 strips of bacon or pancetta
2 tablespoons light olive oil or
   canola oil
sea salt and freshly ground
   black pepper

TO SERVE
1 small Little Gem lettuce
3oz butter
100ml red wine
2–3 tablespoons water

Q&A...

WHY IS IT IMPORTANT TO TAKE MEAT OUT OF THE FRIDGE AN HOUR BEFORE YOU COOK IT?
It will take much longer to cook from the fridge, because it is cold, and you won't achieve that lovely browned, almost sugary sweet outside and tender inside that you should get from a pan-fried or griddled piece of meat. People often describe this as "caramelization," which really only involves sugar—instead, this browning is called the Maillard Reaction, after Louis Camille Maillard, the French physicist who identified this complicated reaction between carbohydrates and amino acids that produces that lovely browning. The same goes for any meat that you are broiling or grilling.

This is similar to the Italian dish of veal scallop, stuffed with mozzarella and prosciutto. I have been making this all my life, so I think nothing of it—but in the classes, I find people are sometimes unsure about stuffing cheese into raw meat. However, when they taste the finished dish they love it.

I find that in Britain especially there is something of an obsession with cooking pork for a long time. Of course, you need to cook it through, but not to the point of it being leathery. It still needs some moisture in the middle, and stuffing it with cheese and bacon really helps to keep it from drying out, as well as adding flavor.

PREPARATION

✳ Take your pork out of the fridge about an hour before you want to cook it.
✳ Preheat the oven to 425°F.
✳ If the pork fillet has been vacuum-packed, drain off any liquid that has collected, and pat it dry. With a small knife, clean off any excess bits of sinew.
✳ Cut the cheese lengthwise into thin slices.
✳ Pick the sage leaves from their stalks.

METHOD

1 Imagine the pork fillet is a baguette and you are going to cut it in half lengthwise to make a sandwich: cut it almost all the way through, but not quite, leaving it hinged at one side, so you can open it enough to put the filling inside.

2 Slide in two of the strips of bacon, followed by the cheese slices and sage leaves, and then the rest of the bacon. Close up the pork around the filling and tie with butcher's twine. If you find it easier, you can just tie it at certain points along the length, knot it, and cut it, or you can use one long piece of twine and cut only at the end, which, once you get the hang of it, is much quicker to do. Follow the step-by-step instructions on page 130.

3 Get a big frying pan (that will transfer to the oven) really hot on the stove. Rub the pork with the oil and seasoning. Put into the pan, with the knotted string-side down and let it get really brown. With a pair of tongs, turn the meat over and brown on all sides. Transfer the pan to the oven for around 18–20 minutes. To check that the pork is done, pierce it with a skewer at the thickest part. If the juices run clear, it is ready. The bacon in the center will make it look quite pink, but don't worry about this—don't be tempted to put the pork back into the oven, or you will overcook it and it will become gray and chewy.

Step-by-step: Stringing a joint of meat

I often find it is easier to demonstrate this using a rolling pin, rather than a joint of meat—since you can see the knotting more clearly.

1 Put the joint on your board so that it is facing you vertically, then loop one end of a ball of butcher's twine under the end of the joint farthest from you and secure with a double knot.

2 (If you are right handed) hold the length of string in your right hand and loop it over and then under the fingers of your left hand (keeping your palm upward).

3 Now, turn your left hand over so that the palm is facing downward and you close the loop.

4 Pull this loop backward toward the edge of the joint nearest to you.

5 Slip the loop underneath the joint at the edge nearest you.

6 Slide the loop away from you along the length of the joint, back toward the knot you made in step 1.

7 Pull on the string with your right hand to tighten the loop around the meat, about 1 inch away from the knot.

8 Pull the string back toward the center of the joint and make the next loop as before, starting at step 2.

9 Repeat until you have a series of loops all the way along the length of the joint, about 1 inch apart, then tie the end of the string tightly to the last loop and cut the string.

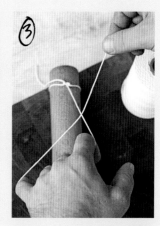

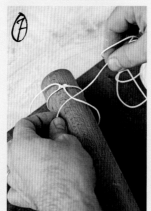

4 Take the pork out of the pan and put it on a plate by the side of the hot oven, covered with foil, to rest for about 10 minutes while you prepare the lettuce.

5 Cut the lettuce in half and wash and dry it.

6 Take another frying pan, heat 1oz of the butter and, when it starts to bubble up, put in the lettuce, cut-side down. Let the halves brown for 2–3 minutes, and then turn them over. Add the red wine, 2–3 tablespoons water, and the remaining butter and cook for about 2 minutes so that the wine becomes a little syrupy and glossy.

7 Take the string off the pork and slice it as thickly or thinly as you like. Serve the lettuce alongside and spoon the red wine sauce over the top.

Bertinet Basics

✳ **How is pancetta different from bacon?** *See page 63*

✳ **Why do you rest meat?** *See page 136*

✳ **What kind of wine should I use?** *See page 118*

Q&A...

WHY BUY LOCAL PORK?

There's so much good that can be said about buying local produce and meat, in this case pork. The most obvious being that buying local supports the local economy, is better for the environment—in that the fuel costs of transportation are eliminated—and you know the what, when, and where of your pig's life and in what kind of conditions the animal was reared. The same of which can't be said of store-bought pork. What you may not realize, however, is just how much of a difference there will be in the flavor of the meat. There is no comparison between the quite pale, sometimes flabby, mild-tasting meat that comes from animals reared intensively indoors, and the much more richly flavored, sweeter ,and darker-colored meat from traditional animals that have been allowed to grow slowly out of doors, often feeding on fallen apples and excess garden produce, and just coming inside straw barns for shelter. In terms of flavor, you get out what you put in. When you buy a pig, or part of it, from a local farmer you pay the farmer a set price per pound for the "hanging weight." This is the weight after the pig has been gutted, skinned, and the head removed, so hanging weight includes the meat, fat, and the bones. The cost is a bit higher, but well worth it. If you can't buy locally, ask questions of your butcher about quality and rearing conditions.

Rack of lamb with herb crust

When I first learned to prepare racks of lamb, I was taught to clean and scrape every little bit of meat from the bones so that they would look pristine. If you have time to do that, fine, but otherwise don't worry about it.

The idea here is that you have a lovely crunchy, herby crust on top, to give a great contrast of texture with the soft lamb, which is kept moist during cooking, thanks to this protective topping.

A rack of lamb is at its best cooked pink—do try it, even if you think you like your meat well done. But if you really prefer it cooked longer, you could halve the racks before putting them in the oven. Just cut between the bones to make four smaller racks that will cook through more quickly.

I love this rack of lamb with the garlic potatoes on page 161 and green beans on page 200.

INGREDIENTS
For 4–6

2 racks of lamb, each French-trimmed with 8 bones (ask your butcher to do this for you)

FOR THE CRUST
4oz hazelnuts (or walnuts or almonds)
1 cup fresh bread crumbs, from good bread
small bunch of sage
bunch of curly parsley
3–4 sprigs of thyme
4 tablespoons heavy cream
2 large egg yolks (preferably free-range)
2 heaping tablespoons Dijon mustard
sea salt and freshly ground black pepper
2 tablespoons canola or light vegetable oil

Bertinet Basics

✳ **Why is it important to take meat out of the fridge an hour before you cook it?** *See page 128*

✳ **Why do you rest meat?** *See page 136*

PREPARATION
✳ Take the meat out of the fridge about an hour before you cook it.
✳ Preheat the oven to 400°F.
✳ Cut off the flap of thick skin and the fat that clings to it from each rack with a sharp knife—it should all come off in one piece. If there is still a layer of fat left behind you can trim the excess off, if you like.

METHOD

1 Put the nuts and bread crumbs into a food processor and pulse, then add the herbs and pulse again until well blended.

2 In a bowl, mix together the cream, egg yolks, mustard, and seasoning, and then add to the nuts. Again, just briefly press the pulse button, because you just want a coarse, moist herb mixture that will stay together easily if you press a bit into your hand. If it is too dry, it will crumble away from the lamb, so add a little more cream; if it is too wet, add a few more bread crumbs.

3 Get a large, heavy-bottomed pan hot on the stove. Rub the lamb with oil and season it. Put the racks one at a time into the pan, bone-side down first, and let them color for about a minute, then turn onto the other side. Stand them on each end, too, so they are browned all over. Take out and put into a roasting pan, bone-side up.

4 Leave to cool for 5 minutes, and then press the bread crumb mixture over the top of each rack, into the meat right to the base of the bones. Put into the oven for 14–15 minutes, which will give you a crispy crust and pink, tender meat.

5 To check that the meat is done to your liking, press the side of the meat and use my guide on page 145. If you prefer it cooked longer, put it back into the oven for a minute or so until you are happy (cover the crust with foil to prevent it from getting too brown).

6 Take the lamb out of the oven and cover with foil (if you haven't already done so). Allow to rest next to the hot oven for 5–10 minutes before serving.

Q &A...

WHAT DO YOU MEAN BY "FRESH" BREAD CRUMBS?

When I say fresh bread crumbs, what I mean is crumbs made from bread that is a day or so old that has dried out a bit—as opposed to crumbs that have been toasted in the oven until they are golden and crispy. (You might use these, tossed in olive oil and a little sea salt, for sprinkling over pasta, or on top of a vegetable in cheese sauce—a gratin—before putting it under the broiler, if you want a crispy topping.) I was brought up making bread crumbs from every bit of leftover bread. In France, you go to the boulangerie at least once a day, because bread is made to be eaten right away, rather than kept—you know how hard a baguette is even a day after you have bought it. So there would be plenty of end pieces left to make bread crumbs. The easiest way is to cut the bread into chunks, put them in a blender, then pulse briefly until you have crumbs. If you have only very fresh bread which is too soft to make crumbs—i.e., the bread is quite moist, so it will clump together in the blender—cut it into slices and put it in a very low oven (110–125°F) for about 45 minutes to dry out first. I usually sift the bread crumbs, to separate out the fine ones from the coarser ones, both of which I store in jars—or you can keep them in bags in the freezer. I might use the finer ones for coating goat cheese or meat for baking or frying, whereas the bigger ones are good for the crust in this recipe. If you don't have a blender (or food processor) put the dry pieces of bread in a plastic food bag, tie it, then crush with a rolling pin.

Roast leg of lamb

This is roasting in the true old-fashioned sense of the word. Unlike in the recipe on page 132, where the meat started off on the stove and finished inside the oven, this goes into the oven raw. Roasting on the bone keeps the meat nice and moist, and it will always be slightly pinker in the center.

In our meat classes, one thing that people always comment on is how long we rest the meat. They can't believe how much more tender the meat is after, say, 10–15 minutes of letting it relax. No matter how many times they may have seen it in a recipe book, most people don't rest their meat because they are worried about it not being served piping hot. Sunday lunch is a prime example: people panic about having roast meat and lots of vegetables ready to go, and keeping everything hot in the oven, whereas I would much rather let the meat rest, while I put out the potatoes and vegetables. Then, by the time the family comes to eat, everything will have settled down and all the flavors will be coming through. You can only really taste food properly once it has cooled down a little, so don't worry.

To keep things even more relaxed, instead of having potatoes roasting, and vegetables boiling or steaming, I would serve a mix of roasted vegetables (see page 126) alongside a roast leg of lamb.

Most lamb packaging, in my view, suggests cooking it for too long, as a safety net, and, as a result, I feel the meat is often too dry on the outside. So instead of the guidelines of 30 minutes per pound plus 30 minutes, I would cook it for 20 minutes per pound—this should give you lovely pink meat, which will be really tender and succulent once it has rested. Of course, if you really prefer it well done, you can cook it for longer.

INGREDIENTS

For 6–8

6lb leg of lamb
6 garlic cloves
about 6 tablespoons olive oil
sea salt and freshly ground
    black pepper
few sprigs of rosemary and thyme
½ bottle red wine

PREPARATION

✳ Take the meat out of the fridge about an hour before cooking, so that it is not stone cold in the middle.

✳ Preheat the oven to 375°F. Do this a good 30–45 minutes before cooking, so that it is thoroughly hot. If it has only just reached temperature when you open the door to put your meat in, it will take longer to come back up to temperature and the meat won't cook as quickly.

✳ Cut each garlic clove lengthwise into four—so you have little spears.

✳ Rub the meat with olive oil along with a good tablespoon each of salt and pepper. Don't be scared to really massage the meat. It sounds silly, but think of having a massage yourself when you feel tense. Well, this relaxes the meat after the fibers have tensed up in the cold fridge.

✳ Put the lamb in a big roasting pan. Using a small knife, make regular incisions into the leg of lamb, at a 45-degree angle through the skin and into the meat, about 1 inch deep. Slide a spear of garlic into each one, along with a little sprig of rosemary or thyme (or both).

Q&A...

WHY DO YOU REST THE MEAT?

Whenever you cook meat relatively quickly at high temperatures—for example, broiling, pan-frying, or roasting—the sinews tense up and toughen, so it is important to let everything relax again before eating, so that the meat becomes tender. For steaks and small joints, such as a pork fillet, 5–10 minutes is enough, but you can happily leave larger joints for up to 30 minutes. The other thing people often ask is where is this "warm place" that you are always told to rest your meat. Well, it is just by the side of the warm stove. If you cover the meat with foil—just on top; don't wrap it or tuck it in—it will retain heat while it rests, but don't be afraid of it cooling down a bit. In France, we don't worry so much about serving food piping hot. I believe that if it is too hot, all you experience is heat and you can't properly taste the food—in the same way that excessive chiling dulls down taste... think about it: you can't fully get the flavors of a white wine until the chill comes off it, or of an ice cream until it starts to melt a little.

METHOD

1 Roast the lamb for about 1¾ hours (or 20 minutes per pound if you have a different-sized joint), covering it with foil for the last 30 minutes so the meat becomes really tender without browning too much.

2 Take the meat out and leave to rest on a warmed plate by the side of the stove for at least 15–20 minutes, still covered in foil.

3 To make your gravy, put the roasting pan onto the stove, add the red wine, and allow it to bubble up while you scrape all the bits of meat from the bottom of the pan. I like all the little bits of meat and herb in the gravy, but you can strain it if you like.

Bertinet Basics

✳ **Why is it important to take the meat out of the fridge an hour before you cook it?** *See page 128*

✳ **What kind of wine should I use?** *See page 118*

Lamb casserole with baby vegetables

In this dish, I use finely diced vegetables at the beginning of cooking as a "base layer" and then add chunkier or whole ones later. The diced vegetables soften into the stew, giving it flavor, while the chunkier ones added toward the end keep their shape and individual flavors. As you can see from the photograph, in springtime I like to use baby vegetables, which look quite impressive—at other times of the year, just substitute the baby vegetables with four large carrots and two medium-sized turnips, cut into neat pieces. I always get people to try to visualize the finished dish before they start cooking—what do you want it to look like? In this casserole, the baby vegetables or chunks are very prominent, so think about their shape when you are preparing them, since what you put in is what you will see at the end.

INGREDIENTS

For 4–6

2¼lb boned shoulder of lamb
1 large onion
1 large carrot
12 baby carrots
12 baby turnips
12 baby onions
12 small new potatoes
3 garlic cloves
sea salt and freshly ground
    black pepper
2oz butter
2 tablespoons olive oil
1 teaspoon sugar
¼ cup all-purpose flour
¾ cup dry white wine
1 quart chicken stock
1 bouquet garni (a sprig each of
    rosemary, thyme, and a bay leaf,
    tied together with butcher's twine)
10oz small fresh or frozen peas
    (petits pois)
small bunch of flat-leaf parsley

PREPARATION

✷ Cut the lamb into 1 inch chunks.
✷ Cut the large onion and large carrot into small dice.
✷ Prepare the baby vegetables (if using). The funny thing in classes is that unless I preempt them, most people are so used to cutting the ends off vegetables like carrots that they automatically do it with baby ones, and then they lose the point, which is to see the whole vegetable, in miniature form. So, for the carrots, leave the pointed tip and an inch or so of green stalk intact (assuming this hasn't already been taken off). Don't peel them; just wash them and the skins will slide off once they have been plunged into boiling water (step 7 on page 141), leaving them looking a brilliant orange.

✷ Leave the skin on the turnips, too—again, it will slide off easily once they are cooked.
✷ Peel the baby onions (tedious, I know!) and scrub.
✷ Scrub the potatoes. If you are substituting the baby vegetables with larger carrots and turnips, peel them, too, and cut them into neat chunks.
✷ Leave the skins on the garlic cloves, but crush them with the flat edge of a large knife to release the flavor.

Bertinet Basics

✷ **What is the best way to slice or chop an onion?** *See page 60*

✷ **Why do you sometimes crush garlic rather than chop it?** *See page 29*

✷ **What kind of wine should I use?** *See page 118*

✷ **Do I need to make my own stock?** *See page 201*

"The baby vegetables or chunks are very prominent, so think about their shape when you are preparing them."

Q&A...

ARE FROZEN PEAS AS GOOD AS FRESH?

Of course, nothing can beat the unbelievable flavor of the first peas of the season, straight from the pod, picked in the garden, but a young frozen pea is the next best thing. We tend to have a confused idea of frozen food: that it is somehow inferior to "fresh" or chilled, which, in terms of produce or fish, can actually mean about 5 days old. However, what many people don't realize is that some foods that appear to be "fresh" in the supermarket chiller frequently have some sort of preservative in them. Freezing, on the other hand, is a time-honored natural preservative. Personally, I would rather have a pea picked in season and frozen within an hour of harvest than an old "fresh" pea from the supermarket, at the end of the season, which will have become bitter rather than sweet, and will need sugar in the cooking water to sweeten it... just as I would rather eat a fish, frozen immediately after it is caught at sea, using the sophisticated technology fishermen have these days, than a so-called "fresh" fish from a supermarket counter that could actually be up to a week old.

Bertinet Basics

✳ **Why is it important to simmer, rather than boil?** *See page 59*

METHOD

1 Season your lamb just before you are ready to cook it, so that the salt doesn't draw out any moisture, which will toughen up the meat.

2 Heat the butter and oil in a large frying pan (with a lid). Usually, I prefer to oil the meat rather than the pan, but not here, since I'm using butter, too. Listen to your butter: as it melts and heats it will "sing"—when it stops and becomes quiet, that is the point when you put in your meat, a few pieces at a time. Don't pile all the lamb in together, or the coolness of the meat will bring the temperature down and it will boil rather than sizzle and brown.

3 Let the lamb pieces brown underneath, and then turn them over and brown on the other side. Take out the first pieces and keep them on a plate beside the stove while you brown the rest.

4 Put all the pieces back into the pan and sprinkle over the sugar. Turn the pieces of meat in the pan as it melts. Now you are actually "caramelizing" the outside of the lamb as opposed to browning it. Take out the meat and place it on your plate by the stove.

5   Add the diced carrot and onion to the pan and cook in the meat juices until soft. Stir in the flour and cook for a couple of minutes, stirring all the time until it is absorbed into the juices. Add the wine, stock, garlic, and bouquet garni and bring to a boil, stirring to prevent lumps.

6   Return the lamb to the pan, cover with a lid and turn the heat down to low so that it simmers gently for 45 minutes, or until the lamb is tender. To test it, take off the lid and turn it over to use as a plate, then take out a piece of lamb, put it on top, and use a wooden spoon to press down on it (see center left). If the meat is soft and starts to shred easily, it is ready; if it is still quite tight, put the lid back on and cook for another 5–10 minutes before testing again.

7   While the meat is cooking, briefly cook each baby vegetable (or your chunks of vegetables) in boiling salted water—do this one type of vegetable at a time, lifting them out with a slotted spoon when they are just tender. (The potatoes for 12-15 minutes and the carrot and turnips for 1-2 minutes.) Once they are cooked, drain them in a colander under cold running water to stop them from cooking any more (this is what is meant by "refreshing" vegetables). Put the peas in last, for just a minute, then drain.

8   Once the baby carrots and turnips are cool enough to handle, carefully peel away the skins.

9   When the meat is ready, lift it out with a slotted spoon and put it back on your plate by the stove, covered with foil, to keep warm.

10   Spoon off any fat from the surface of the sauce, and then put the pan back onto medium heat. Allow the sauce to bubble up and "reduce" until it is thick enough to coat the back of a spoon.

11   If you want an extra-smooth sauce, at this point you can strain it through a fine strainer into a bowl and then pour it back into the pan—it is up to you. Put the lamb back into the sauce, taste, and season a little at a time, until the flavor comes alive.

12   Put the baby vegetables or chunks into the pot and simmer for another 5 minutes. Chop the parsley, sprinkle on top, and serve.

Q&A...

WHY USE A BOUQUET GARNI?
The idea is that you put together a little bundle of fresh, woody herbs in their entirety and then lift them out at the end of cooking, rather than having hard leaves in the finished dish. They infuse the casserole with a much nicer flavor than dried herbs, which may have lost their edge by sitting in the pantry. Usually, you use rosemary, thyme, and bay (add some sage leaves, if you like). You can buy ready-made sachets filled with herbs—but it is the simplest thing to tie your own. Either tie the herbs together with butcher's twine, or use a strip cut from the outer layer of a leek.

WHAT DOES "REDUCING" A SAUCE ACTUALLY MEAN?
When you cook liquid, usually containing wine or other alcohol, over high heat, some of it evaporates and, as it thickens, it concentrates in flavor as well as texture. Often recipes say, "Reduce by a third or a half." If you have a dark-colored sauce containing red wine, you can clearly see a "tidemark" around the inside of your pan that shows you how far your sauce has reduced, but it isn't always that easy to gauge, other than by keeping a mental note of the level of sauce you began with. I think it is more helpful to describe the thickness of the finished sauce—which is what I have done throughout this book—so you know what you are looking for, rather than worrying about fractions.

32

Hanger steak and fries with garlic and herb butter

In my classes, I joke that this is for the people who look in a cookbook and shy away from long lists of ingredients. This is essentially steak, potatoes, and the simplest accompaniment in the world: perfect!

That said, a great steak and fries relies on everything being cooked just right. People say they never know whether to cook the fries first, or the steak, or both together. My way is to part-cook the fries first, then cook the steak and, while it is resting, finish off the fries.

Of course, you can use any cut of steak; the one I like is a very underused one, which used to be known as "butcher's steak," but is now often referred to as "hanger steak." In France, we call it *onglet*. Along with *bavette* (a flank steak), this is the cut that is used for the classic *steak-frites* you find in every local brasserie. It is a cut from just under the kidneys, which, if it is cut too thin, can be a bit stringy but, when you cook a big chunk of it rare, it is beautiful, tender, and good value.

For a long time, I couldn't find this cut in Britain. Then the chef Mark Hix came to the cooking school to give a class and described the cut he wanted to a local butcher, and we have been buying it from him ever since. But now I'm beginning to see it everywhere. Buy steak that has been hung properly, since it will have a much better texture and flavor and, if you are not used to cooking it, check out the Q&A section on page 145 before you start cooking so you know how to tell when it's done to your liking.

The classic garlic and herb butter is used in every restaurant in France for all kinds of dishes, especially snails. This recipe will probably make more than you need, but you can keep the rest in the freezer, then you can just take it out, defrost it, and use it to top any grilled meat or fish. Or, to make the best garlic bread, slice into a baguette, smear the butter inside, and bake at 350°F for 6–8 minutes. The other great sauce to have with steak is Béarnaise—see page 201.

Fries are one of the first things I ever learned to cook at home with my parents—we used to have them on Sunday for lunch with roast chicken. The way I cook them has been passed down through my family, and I think it makes for perfect fries: crunchy on the outside and fluffy inside. I like them cut medium, not in matchsticks or *pommes alumettes*.

Q&A...

WHY MARIS PIPER OR RUSSET BURBANK POTATOES?

These are all-purpose potatoes, not too waxy or too floury. You need a little waxiness, so that the potato holds together and crisps up nicely. (On the other hand, the extreme waxiness of a new potato gives the wrong texture.) A little flouriness is good, too, for that perfect crisp outside and fluffy inside. I buy loose, earth-covered potatoes that look as if they have just been dug up, rather than pristine ones packed in plastic bags, which seem to go green more quickly.

"The way I cook fries has been passed down through my family, and I think it makes for perfect ones."

INGREDIENTS

For 4 (or 2 if you are very hungry!)

1 piece of hanger steak (it will weigh
   about 1–1¼lb)
2 large Maris Piper or Russet Burbank
   potatoes—or as many as you like,
   since you can never have enough
   fries
light vegetable, sunflower, or peanut oil,
   for deep-frying
sea salt and freshly ground
   black pepper

FOR THE GARLIC AND PARSLEY BUTTER

6–8 garlic cloves
1 large shallot
9oz unsalted butter
large handful of curly parsley
large sprig of thyme
pinch of salt
4 tablespoons extra-virgin olive oil
½ lemon

Q&A...

**WHY DO RESTAURANTS PREFER TO
SERVE STEAK RARE TO MEDIUM RARE?**
*If a chef has sourced a good piece
of steak, he or she will want to
show it off at its best: rare, tender,
and moist. Serve steak well done
and it can be chewy and tough.
However, you may have friends
who like it well done. If you ask
them, it is usually the sight of the
bloody juices running out on the
plate that puts them off. So I have
a trick that will solve the problem.
Wrap a good thickness of paper
towels around the steak and press
down onto it really hard using
one hand on top of the other, so
that the red juices soak into
the paper. Unwrap the meat
and it will look as if it has
been cooked well done, but
will still be beautifully tender.*

PREPARATION

✳ Take your steak out of the fridge about 1 hour before cooking it.

✳ Make the butter several hours or even the day before you want to use it.

✳ Remove the green germ from each garlic clove. Finely dice the shallot. Take the butter out of the fridge to let it soften, or, alternatively, bash it with a rolling pin, then cut it into pieces.

✳ If you have a food processor or blender, you will get the best greeny color and distribute the flavors evenly by just blending all the garlic butter ingredients together—if you don't have a gadget, just mix them all in a bowl.

✳ Cut a square of plastic wrap or parchment paper large enough to wrap up the butter. Spoon the butter into the middle and form it roughly into a sausage shape, then roll it up tightly in the plastic wrap or paper and twist the ends. Put into the fridge to set and chill.

✳ Cut along either side of the central sinew of the steak. This will leave you with two long pieces of meat, one a little thicker than the other. Trim off all the fat and cut each piece in two crosswise.

✳ Peel the potatoes, then cut lengthwise into slices ½ inch thick. Cut each slice lengthwise into fries ¼ inch wide. Keep in a bowl of cold water until you're ready to use them. The fries will stay firm and some starch will leach out, helping them crisp up nicely.

METHOD

1 For the first stage of the fries, heat some light vegetable, sunflower, or peanut oil, ideally in a deep-fat fryer, to 250–275°F. Alternatively, put the oil into a large pan (don't fill it more than a third full), using a cooking thermometer to test the heat. Have ready a fry basket so that you can lower the fries in and out easily.

2   Drain the potatoes through a colander, then, with a clean kitchen towel or paper towels, dry them really well; dampness makes the oil spit when you put them in. Lower the fries into the oil in batches—a handful at a time, so as not to reduce the temperature of the oil by overcrowding. Cook very gently for about 3–4 minutes, until the potato is soft, but not colored.

3   Lift out and drain well on paper towels, then transfer to a bowl and leave to cool until you have cooked your steak.

4   My favorite way to cook steak is on a ridged griddle pan. You don't need any oil. Just get the pan very hot before putting in the steak. If you are using a frying pan, get the pan hot on the stove first, then just before cooking brush the steaks with oil.

5   Season the steaks just before they go into the pan—not in advance, since the salt draws out the juices and makes the meat tougher. Put all 4 pieces of steak onto your griddle or into your pan. Don't move them for around 2–3 minutes, until you can see the edges starting to color; they will have sealed and will move easily without sticking. Then you can turn them over and finish to your liking.

6   Take the steaks from the pan and keep them warm by the stove, covered in foil, for at least 5-6 minutes. This lets the meat rest and gives time to cook your fries. Again, do them in batches. It seems quicker to cook all the fries at once, but, in fact, it takes longer, since they will lower the temperature of the oil. The first batch will stay crisp in a warm bowl for a few minutes while you cook the rest.

7   Reheat your oil, this time to 325-350°F, and plunge the fries in for 2–3 minutes, shake them around well, then lift them out. Let the oil come back up to temperature, then plunge them back in again and fry for another 2–3 minutes until crisp and golden. When you shake them, you can tell when they are beautifully crispy because they rattle.

8   Lift the fries out, drain on paper towels, then put them in a bowl, and cover with foil to keep them warm while you make your next batch. Sprinkle with a little sea salt before serving with the steak. Cut 4 slices of cold butter and put 1 on top of each piece of meat.

Bertinet Basics

✳ **Why is it important to take meat out of the fridge an hour before you cook it?** *See page 128*

✳ **Why do you remove the germ of the garlic?** *See page 23*

✳ **What is the best way to chop or slice a shallot?** *See page 60*

✳ **Why do you rest meat?** *See page 136*

Q&A...

HOW CAN I GET THOSE PERFECTLY CRISSCROSSED "BARBECUE" MARKS?

By using a griddle pan. However, if you are cooking steaks in a frying pan or broiling them and you want to have the same effect, hold some metal barbecue skewers over a gas flame, then press them onto the meat. You can do this with tuna or scallops, too.

HOW CAN YOU TELL WHEN A STEAK IS DONE TO YOUR LIKING?

Don't pierce the meat, or you will release more juices. Instead, you can gauge when the steaks are very rare (or "blue"), rare, medium-rare, medium, or well done just by touch. I have a little trick I show people to demonstrate what the steak will feel like at each stage. Try it before you begin cooking.

Start by just touching the fleshy pad at the base of your left thumb with the forefinger of your right hand. If you want your steak to be very rare (blue), you should feel a similar softness when you press down on the meat in the pan. Keeping your right forefinger on the pad, press your left forefinger and thumb together. The stretch causes the muscles to tighten a little, so the fleshy pad will feel a little less soft. This is what rare steak should feel like. Next do the same exercise using your middle finger and thumb. This is what medium-rare steak should feel like. Repeat with your ring finger, to correspond to medium meat, and, finally, your little finger. Feel how much tighter and harder the pad has become. This is what well-done steak feels like. (You can use this guide for rack of lamb on page 132 and loin of venison on page 153.)

Hanger steak and chips with garlic and herb butter

"When you eat a good pie you know that a lot of heart, soul, and pride has gone into it."

33

Beef and ale pie

The word pie just says Britain to me—from pork pie to shepherd's pie, meat pie and apple pie, there is something so comforting, homey, and British about a great pie. I like the fact that people take pride in passing their recipes down through the generations, so everyone looks forward to Auntie Nelly's wonderful meat and potato pie, or my wife Jo's great great-grandmother's (Nana Harrod's) famous apple pie. It is a very humble dish in a way—you don't necessarily need expensive ingredients, but when you eat a good pie you know that a lot of heart, soul, and pride has gone into making it.

I like to buy local produce, so for the ale in the recipe I use a beer brewed by Bath Ales, sold in Bath and Bristol pubs, whose brewery is only 20 minutes away from my home. I also use Somerset Cider Brandy, but you can use whatever brandy and ale are available in your area or that suit your tastes.

My tip is to cook the meat and leave it in the fridge for a day before you make the pie, since it will taste even better once all the flavors have had time to mingle and develop.

You will see for the pastry I use 1¼fl oz of cold water—the amount is very specific, but when it comes to baking, whether it is bread, cakes, or pastry, it is important to be as accurate as possible. When you are cooking the beef for the pie, it really doesn't matter too much if you add a little more or less ale, but if you were to tip a few extra tablespoons of water into your mixing bowl when you were making the pastry it would make a difference. The touch of turmeric is optional, but it just gives a nice warm golden color to the pastry.

Note: This makes enough pastry to cover an oval pan 9–10 inches long. If you are using a larger, shallower pan, make a bigger quantity of pastry rather than trying to roll it more thinly. You can make the pastry in advance and keep it in the fridge for up to a week before using it—or in the freezer for up to six weeks. You can also make up the pie completely and put it in the fridge the day before you want to bake it, but you will need to add an extra half hour or so onto the baking time.

INGREDIENTS

For 6–8

3½lb beef shank

7oz pancetta or strips of bacon

4 large onions

6 medium carrots

large sprig of thyme

large sprig of rosemary

2 bay leaves

3 garlic cloves

sea salt and freshly ground
    black pepper

3 tablespoons tomato paste

½ cup Somerset Cider Brandy,
    Calvados, or brandy

8 black peppercorns

4 cloves

3 pints real ale

good handful of curly parsley

1 egg (preferably free range)

FOR THE SAVORY PASTRY

4½oz lard (or 2½oz lard and 2oz butter,
    if you prefer)

2 cups all-purpose flour

½ teaspoon ground turmeric (optional)

¼ tablespoon salt

1 medium egg (preferably free-range)

1¼oz cold water

PREPARATION

✷ The lard (and butter, if using) needs to be cold for making the pastry.

✷ First, make the pastry: cut the lard (or lard and butter) into squares.

✷ Put the flour, turmeric (if using), and salt into a mixing bowl. Add the lard (or lard and butter) and rub it lightly into the flour between your fingers and thumbs until you have big flakes. Stir in the egg and water. Use your hands gently to bring everything together into a dough, but as soon as it comes together, stop—don't overwork the pastry.

✷ Form the pastry into a rough square. What I always do is pick up the square of dough and drop it down onto the work surface from a height of about 12 inches on each of the four sides of the square—I don't know why I do it exactly, but it feels as if it somehow knocks all the ingredients together.

✷ Wrap the pastry in parchment paper. I prefer this to plastic wrap, which can make the pastry a bit sweaty. You can wrap it in its parchment paper in an outer layer of plastic wrap, or in a freezer bag. Leave to rest in the fridge for at least 1 hour.

✷ Cut the beef into large chunks, about ¾–1 inch. Cut the pancetta or bacon into large dice, or pieces, leaving the fat on.

✷ Peel each onion and cut into 8 wedges.

✷ Peel the carrots and cut into large chunks.

✷ Tie the thyme, rosemary, and bay leaves together with butcher's twine to make a bouquet garni.

✷ Crush the garlic cloves lightly with the flat edge of a large kitchen knife just to release the flavor, and then peel off the skins.

METHOD

1 Put the pancetta or bacon into a big, heavy-bottomed pan (with a lid) and heat it up from cold over medium-high heat until it browns and releases its fat. Quickly season the pieces of beef with salt and pepper. Make sure the bacon is sizzling nicely, and then add the beef to the pan and brown the meat on all sides. When there is no raw meat showing, stir in the tomato paste and then add the brandy. You can flame it if you like (see page 76, step 3)—otherwise, just let the brandy bubble up to burn off the alcohol. Add the onions, carrots, garlic, bouquet garni, black peppercorns, and cloves; stir well.

2 Now pour in the ale. Bring everything up to simmering point and then leave it to cook very slowly over low heat for 3 hours, with the lid propped halfway over the pan so that the liquid reduces a little but the meat still stays moist. To test whether the meat is done, take out a piece and put it on the underside of the lid, press it down and if it comes apart a little and doesn't bounce back, it is ready.

3 Finely chop the parsley and add to the pan, along with a little extra seasoning, if you think it needs it.

4 Now take the pan off the heat and leave it to stand for an hour so that the flavors develop.

5 Preheat the oven to 350°F.

6 Take the pastry out of the fridge and lightly dust your work surface with flour. When I say a dusting of flour, I mean that if you were to run a bread scraper or a table knife over your floured work surface you would hardly gather up any flour at all. It is very easy to throw an avalanche of flour all over the place, but remember that it will be absorbed into your pastry, which will then lose some of its lightness and become more dense.

7 Lightly flour your rolling pin, too, and when you roll the pastry, keep your fingers lightly on the outer edges of the pin. Move the rolling pin backward and forward in short, sharp rolls so that you don't press down on the pastry too hard or stretch it, and, most important, keep lifting the pastry up (turning it through 15 degrees or so) to create an air cushion underneath and stop it from sticking to your work surface. Roll it until it is about ¼ inch thick and large enough to drape over the top of your pie pan, leaving an overhang all the way around. Don't roll the pastry any thinner, or it will droop and get soggy in the middle, and then it won't be very appetizing. You can make it thicker if you like, and it will be more like a dumpling, but you will need to cook it for a bit longer.

8 Pile the meat into the pan. If you have a porcelain pie funnel you can put it in the center to help hold up the pastry—or what I often do is lodge a large piping nozzle in among the meat with the hole facing upward. However, you have a very dense meat mixture and quite substantial pastry, so don't worry if you don't have either.

9 Beat the egg and use a little of it to brush around the rim of the pie pan. Drape the pastry over the top and press it onto the rim so that it sticks. Brush the top of the pastry with the rest of the egg.

10 Make a hole in the middle of the pastry for steam to escape—if you are using a pie funnel or piping nozzle poke the tip of it through and it will keep the hole open nicely.

11 Put the pie pan onto a baking sheet before you put it in the oven. That way you can easily move it onto a different shelf if the pastry is coloring too quickly or too slowly, and you can also turn it around if the pastry seems to be baking more on one side than the other—every oven is different, so it's just a case of getting used to the way your own works.

12 Put the pie in the oven for about half an hour, or until the pastry is golden brown. Remember, the meat is already cooked, so you don't have to worry about that.

Q&A...

IS IT TRUE THAT PEOPLE WITH COLD HANDS MAKE THE BEST PASTRY?
I know a lot of people swear by this, but I think it is just an old wives' tale. What is more important is that you don't overhandle the pastry. It doesn't matter how ice-cold or warm your hands are, if you keep pushing and pummeling it rather than treating it lightly, it will react—the butter will melt and the pastry will start to toughen and become greasy.

WHY DO YOU PUT THE PASTRY INTO THE FRIDGE BEFORE ROLLING IT?
Letting it rest for a while before rolling allows the gluten in the pastry to relax and makes the pastry more elastic and easier to roll. Once it is rolled, if you are using it to line a pie pan or plate, it is also a good idea to put it back into the fridge before baking it—again, this relaxes the gluten and makes the pastry less likely to shrink in the oven.

Bertinet Basics

✳ **How is pancetta different from bacon?** See page 63

✳ **Why is it important to simmer, rather than boil?** See page 59

✳ **Why use a bouque garni?** See page 141

The perfect ground beef

Such a versatile thing, ground beef, isn't it? You can use it in shepherd's pie, chili, lasagne, with pasta… You are probably wondering why I am even including a recipe for it—after all, even people who hardly ever cook can usually rustle up a Bolognese sauce. There's nothing to it, really: just brown the meat in a pan with some chopped onions, maybe some carrots and celery, add a can of tomatoes and some herbs, and simmer for half an hour or so (although the temptation is often to cook it for less!). Well, yes and no. Try this longer, more slowly cooked version, which is a variation on a recipe I discovered in an old Italian cookbook, using milk to help tenderize the meat. You'll find it really rewarding; the milk pulls all the flavors together into something much richer and more flavorsome and softens the ground beef, which can sometimes stay chewy if it is cooked for a shorter time. Because you are going to cook it for 3 hours, it is worth making three times the quantity and freezing some for another day.

Buy good-quality meat, and don't go for the super-lean stuff. You need a bit of fat to add flavor and keep everything moist.

INGREDIENTS

For about 6

3 celery ribs
3 medium carrots
1 medium onion
1 shallot
large sprig of thyme
3 tablespoons canola oil
small spoon of butter
1 bay leaf
1lb good-quality ground beef—
    not too lean
sea salt and freshly ground
    black pepper
6 tablespoons whole milk
1½ cups white wine
1 whole nutmeg, grated (or a large
    pinch of grated nutmeg)
3–4 x 14.5oz cans whole plum
    tomatoes

PREPARATION

✳ Cut the celery into three lengthwise, then cut each length into small dice.
✳ Peel the carrots and dice them (see page 118) so they are about the same size as the celery.
✳ Finely chop the onion and shallot.
✳ Pick the leaves from the thyme.

METHOD

1 Put the canola oil and butter into a big, heavy-bottomed pan. Add the onion, shallot, and thyme, and gradually heat everything up over low heat—starting from cold means you have less chance of burning the onion and shallot. Keep stirring and cook slowly for about 10 minutes. Add the celery and bay leaf, stir well, then add the carrots and stir very well again.

2 Add the meat and turn up the heat to medium. Season with salt and pepper and cook for 10 minutes, stirring regularly, so that the meat colors. Pour in the milk, stir again, and cook for a couple more minutes. Now add the white wine, followed by the nutmeg and canned tomatoes. Stir everything again well, then bring it all up to simmering point. Turn the heat down very low, so that little bubbles just break the surface, and cook, uncovered, for about 2½–3 hours, stirring from time to time. It shouldn't get too dry, but if it does, add a little water. Over the long cooking time, you will see globules of fat clinging to the sides of the pan that you can remove with paper towels. Once the ground beef is cooked, allow it to cool, then store in the fridge for 4–5 days or freeze for up to 3 months.

Bertinet Basics

✳ **What is the best way to slice or chop an onion?** *see page 60*
✳ **Why use onions and shallots?** *See page 118*
✳ **Why is it important to simmer, rather than boil?** *See page 59*

Q&A...

HOW CAN I USE THIS GROUND BEEF?
Serve it with tubular pasta, such as penne, or use for lasagne—layered with sheets of pasta and Béchamel sauce (see page 98), finishing with Béchamel and a thick layer of grated Parmesan, baked at 375°F until crispy on top. Alternatively, you can use it as a base for shepherd's pie—pile it in a dish with mashed potatoes over the top, as for the fish pie on page 96, grate over some cheese, and cook in the same way. To transform it into chili, add some chopped chiles, ground cumin, and coriander, some drained and rinsed canned kidney beans, simmer very gently for another 15 minutes or so, and serve with rice.

"I like to serve duck breasts with spinach—one of the easiest of all vegetables to prepare."

Duck with cranberry and clementine compote

The cranberry and clementine compote is a handy recipe just on its own, since you can serve it with any kind of meat, hot or cold; it is also beautiful with Stilton cheese at Christmas. If you make a larger quantity it will keep for a few days in the fridge.

Don't worry about the thick layer of fat beneath the skin of the duck breasts; it doesn't mean they will be fatty to eat. I agree, chewy duck fat is not very appetizing, but the key is to sear the breasts, skin-side down, in a dry pan over high heat, so that the excess fat comes out and the skin really crisps up. Then you can put the breasts into a hot oven to finish cooking. I like to serve duck breasts with spinach—one of the easiest of all vegetables to prepare because you just have to let it wilt in the pan.

PREPARATION

✳ Preheat the oven to 375–400°F.
✳ Peel the satsumas or clementines and separate them into segments.
✳ Wash the spinach and leave to drain in a colander.
✳ Score the duck skin in crisscrosses, about 1 inch deep, with a sharp knife—this will help the heat penetrate the meat more quickly and it will encourage the fat to melt so that it runs off and the skin gets really crisp.

METHOD

1 For the compote, put all the ingredients into a pan over low heat and cook gently for about 20 minutes, until the cranberries start to pop and the compote becomes thick and jammy.

2 Get a large, dry frying pan (that will transfer to the oven) really hot—no oil. Season the breasts on both sides and put them into the pan, skin-side down. The skin will shrink back very quickly and the fat will run out into the pan. Be careful because it might spit. Cook for at least 3 minutes over medium heat until the skin is brown and crisp, and then turn the breasts over. If there is a lot of fat in the pan, drain off the excess carefully (keep it for roasting potatoes). Put the pan into the hot oven for 10–12 minutes, depending on the size of the duck breasts, or until the meat is cooked but still slightly pink and moist. Take the duck breasts out of the oven and put them on a rack to drain, skin-side up (over the pan in which you have cooked them). Leave to rest by the side of the stove for 5–10 minutes, placing a little piece of foil loosely over the top to retain the heat.

3 While the meat is resting, put the butter into a large pan with the washed spinach and grate the nutmeg over the top. Put the lid on and cook over medium heat for 5 minutes. Take off the lid, stir the wilted spinach well, then drain it through a colander, and squeeze gently to get rid of any bitter juices.

4 Slice the duck breasts thinly and lay them on top of the spinach on your plates, with some warm compote on the side.

INGREDIENTS

For 4

1¾lb spinach leaves
4 duck breasts, about 5–7oz each
sea salt and freshly ground
   black pepper
large spoon of butter
½ nutmeg, to taste

FOR THE COMPOTE
4 satsumas or clementines
2 tablespoons Grand Marnier or
   Cointreau
7oz cranberries, fresh or frozen
1 tablespoon sugar

Q&A...

DOES POURING BOILING WATER OVER DUCK SKIN HELP IT TO CRISP UP?

This idea is part of the traditional Chinese way of preparing a whole Peking duck—the boiling water opens the pores, starts to break down the fat, and shrinks the skin, before the duck is hung up to wind-dry and painted with a mixture of sugar and soy sauce.

If you are roasting a whole duck at home, you can still get a good, crispy skin, provided you put it into a hot oven—pricking the skin will help, too, but make sure you don't go right through to the flesh. If you are just cooking duck breasts, none of the above is necessary. Simply put them straight into a dry, very hot pan, skin-side down first, and finish them off in the oven.

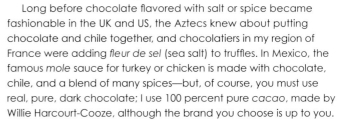

Venison loin with chocolate, cinnamon, and chile

This recipe is all about being bold with flavors. I love venison, I love good chocolate, and I love those warm Christmassy spices like cinnamon and caraway. So why not put them all together?

Long before chocolate flavored with salt or spice became fashionable in the UK and US, the Aztecs knew about putting chocolate and chile together, and chocolatiers in my region of France were adding *fleur de sel* (sea salt) to truffles. In Mexico, the famous *mole* sauce for turkey or chicken is made with chocolate, chile, and a blend of many spices—but, of course, you must use real, pure, dark chocolate; I use 100 percent pure *cacao*, made by Willie Harcourt-Cooze, although the brand you choose is up to you.

Venison is a great meat to combine with chocolate and spice, because it is rich and lean and can cope with the bold flavors. I like to serve it with carrots and salsify (also called oyster plant)— which is quite an underused vegetable. If you aren't familiar with it, it is a root that is a bit similar to horseradish, with a thick, darkish skin, which you need to peel off first. I grew up with it and I love it. Usually we had it in cans; we would drain the chunks of salsify and then toss them in a pan of *beurre noisette*—a spoon of salted butter heated until it turns golden brown. Sometimes, though, we would be able to buy it fresh from the market, which was a real treat. It has a flavor that is hard to put your finger on: it's a little bit nutty, a little like asparagus, but really it has a flavor all of its own. You need to marinate the venison for 12–48 hours before cooking.

PREPARATION
For 4

1¼lb loin of venison
1 fresh red chile (or 1 large teaspoon
  dried chile flakes)
2 teaspoons caraway seeds
2 teaspoons ground cinnamon
2 tablespoons grated good-quality
  chocolate (70 percent cocoa
  solids, or 100 percent pure cacao)
2 tablespoons canola oil, plus
  1 teaspoon
4 long stems of salsify
about 8–12 baby carrots in season
  (or 4–5 big carrots)
spoon of butter
1 tablespoon sugar
dash of Madeira or sweet sherry
sea salt and freshly ground
  black pepper

PREPARATION
✳ Lay a sheet of plastic wrap on your work surface, with the venison on top.
✳ If using fresh chile, finely chop it, removing the seeds if you don't like it too hot.
✳ Combine the spices, chile, 1 tablespoon of the grated chocolate, and the 2 tablespoons of canola oil in a little bowl to make a paste. With your hands, massage the marinade all over the venison. Wrap it tightly in the plastic wrap and twist the ends like a candy wrapper. Put the roll into the fridge for a minimum of 12 hours and up to 2 days, so that the spice mixture has time to flavor the meat well.
✳ Take the venison out of the fridge about 1 hour before you are ready to cook it.
✳ Peel the salsify under running water, because the skin is very sticky. If the roots are small, just halve them lengthwise; if they are bigger, cut them into chunks.
✳ Peel the baby carrots and leave them whole. (If you are using big carrots, cut them into long wedges.)

METHOD
1 Put the carrots in a steaming basket or colander over a pan of boiling water, cover with a lid, and steam until just tender—about 2–3 minutes. Drain under cold running water to stop them from cooking further. Steam the salsify until it is also just tender—it will probably need a minute or so longer than the carrots.

2 Unwrap the venison. Rub the extra teaspoon of oil over the base of a large frying pan and put it over low-medium heat (you need very little oil because there is already oil on the venison). When it is hot, but not smoking, put in the meat and fry for 4 minutes on each side until it is well browned. You need to do this quite gently because you don't want the spices and chocolate to burn and become bitter-tasting. This timing will give you meat that is medium-rare—see my "test" on page 145. You can cook it for a little longer if you want, but really keep an eye on the heat to prevent the venison from burning.

3 Lift the meat out of the pan and put it on a plate, loosely covered with foil, to rest for 5–10 minutes by the side of the stove. Keep the pan to one side ready to make the sauce.

4 While the meat is resting, melt the butter in a separate pan with the sugar until it is syrupy. Put in the vegetables and toss them in the pan so that they are heated through, glazed and shiny.

5 Place the venison pan back on medium heat. Add the Madeira or sherry and use a spoon to scrape up all the bits and pieces of meat that have stuck to the bottom of the pan. Let the sauce bubble up and start to thicken, and then stir in the remaining tablespoon of grated chocolate. Check the seasoning and add a little salt and pepper if you think it needs it.

6 Slice the venison loin and arrange on your plates, pour the sauce around, and serve with the glazed vegetables on the side. Sprinkle with good-quality sea salt, if you like.

Bertinet Basics

✳ **Why is it important to take the meat out of the fridge an hour before you cook it?** *See page 128*

✳ **Why do you rest meat?** *See page 136*

Q&A...

WHAT DOES "70 PERCENT COCOA SOLIDS" MEAN?
We've all become a lot more aware of chocolate; we know it should have at least 70 percent cocoa solid and that the higher the percentage, the more rich, but bitter the chocolate will taste. But what do these percentages actually refer to?

During the chocolate-making process, after the cocoa beans have been roasted, the outer layer is taken off, leaving broken pieces of the seed known as "nibs." These are the cocoa solids from which chocolate is made, and they are milled to form "cocoa liquor." In a separate process, some of this liquor is pressed to separate out the fatty cocoa butter, leaving the rest for grinding into cocoa powder. Some of the cocoa butter is then added to the original liquor (which in good chocolate accounts for around 70 percent), along with sugar, and sometimes soy lethicin, which makes it more smooth. Milk chocolate also has milk added to it. However, during the process of making cheaper, mass-produced milk chocolate (that has long been a favorite in Britain and the US) much of the cocoa solid and cocoa butter is replaced with vegetable fats, oils, sugar, and artificial flavorings, so it can end up containing as little as 5 percent cocoa solid, and up to 5 percent vegetable fat instead of pure cocoa butter—something that prompted a big battle with the EU over the whole definition of chocolate.

Roast pheasant with Savoy cabbage, pancetta, and chestnuts

You could use this recipe for guinea fowl, partridge, or squab... although the cooking times will vary according to the size of the bird. I always think the sauce that goes with the roasted bird is a good illustration of the way a dish is the sum of its parts. It is easy sometimes to look at the list of ingredients in a recipe, or on the menu in a restaurant, and be put off if you see something you don't like: mustard and port, for example. But that is where the alchemy of cooking comes in. You might not like mustard on its own, but put it with other ingredients and it works differently, as do other strong-flavored ingredients, such as horseradish, which you could substitute if you like. It's always good to keep an open mind; more often than not, you will be pleasantly surprised. That said, not everyone likes sauces, period, and the worst thing is to impose your taste on someone else, so I would serve the sauce separately.

While chicken always has to be cooked through and not served pink, game birds are very different. There is nothing worse than a dry, overcooked pheasant, pigeon, or guinea fowl, so it is fine for the meat to still be quite pink and moist.

PREPARATION
✳ Take your pheasant out of the fridge an hour before you are ready to cook it.
✳ Preheat the oven to 400°F.
✳ Slice the cabbage finely into shreds, discarding the core.
✳ Cut the pancetta into small strips.
✳ Break up the chestnuts (each one into 3–4 pieces).

METHOD

1. Rub some oil and salt and pepper all over the pheasant. Put it into a roasting pan over medium heat on the stove and fry for 5 minutes on each side until the skin is brown and crispy.

2. Cut the orange in half, squeeze the juice into the cavity of the pheasant, and put the squeezed halves inside, with the rosemary, thyme, and bay leaves.

3. Put the pheasant into the oven, resting on one side (i.e., on one of its legs). Roast for 15 minutes on the first side, and then turn it onto the other leg for another 15 minutes, or until the juice runs clear from the thickest part of the legs if you pierce them with a skewer. (The legs take the longest to cook, and by doing it this way, each leg is in direct contact with the heat of the pan for half the cooking time, which will speed things up. If you roast the pheasant conventionally on its back, the breasts often dry out too much and become chewy while you wait for the legs to be done.)

4. When it is cooked, take the pheasant out, remove from the pan, and put on a plate beside the stove to rest, with foil over the top to keep it warm.

INGREDIENTS
For 2

1 oven-ready pheasant
1 small Savoy cabbage
7oz pancetta
7oz cooked chestnuts (vacuum-packed or canned— or cook your own, see next page)
a little vegetable or canola oil
sea salt and freshly ground black pepper
1 orange
sprig of rosemary
sprig of thyme
2 bay leaves

FOR THE SAUCE
6 tablespoons port
1 generous teaspoon Dijon or English mustard
1 cup heavy cream

Q &A...

HOW DO YOU COOK RAW CHESTNUTS?

You can roast them in a dry frying pan. Cut a slit or cross in each nut, to let the steam escape and stop them from exploding, and then cook them over medium heat, turning regularly, for about 10–15 minutes. Or put them into a hot oven (around 400–425°F) for about half an hour. When they are cool enough to handle, peel them and also take away the thin inner skin. Check that none of the nuts have worm holes in them, and if they do, discard them. If you want a softer texture, you could simmer them in boiling water for 10 minutes first, drain them, and then finish cooking them in the oven.

5 Pour away the excess fat from the roasting pan, but don't wipe it clean— you just want to be left with the meaty bits and juices. Put the pan back on the stove over medium heat. When it starts to sizzle, add the port, stirring and scraping the bottom of the pan to amalgamate all the meaty bits, then add the mustard, again, stirring well.

6 When the sauce is bubbling nicely, add the cream and stir well. Reduce the heat and cook very gently for 2–3 minutes until the sauce thickens and becomes deep pink. Take the pan off the heat, take a little spoonful of the sauce, let it cool down briefly so you can taste it well, and check your seasoning. You may not need any extra salt, because you have already seasoned your pheasant. What you are looking for is a flavorsome sauce that doesn't shout one particular flavor at you. What salt does is bind the taste of all the ingredients together into one, so it shouldn't be overly sweet (from the port), too rich (from the cream), or too spicy (from the mustard)—all of those sensations should be well married together with a resulting mellowness. If necessary, add a little salt and pepper. If it should happen to be too salty, a little extra cream will neutralize the sauce. If you feel it is too creamy, let it reduce a little longer so the flavor intensifies at the expense of the creaminess. When you are happy with the flavor, cover the pan with foil to keep the sauce warm while you sauté the cabbage. (Alternatively, pour it into a warmed pitcher and cover with foil.)

7 Heat a large sauté or frying pan (or a wok) over medium heat without adding any oil. You want a wide pan with a big surface area so that all of the cabbage pieces come into contact with the pan—that way, they will cook really quickly. Put in the pancetta first and let it sizzle so that the fat comes out. When the pancetta starts to become brown, add the chestnuts. Stir really well, then add the cabbage. Cook for a few minutes, stirring, until the cabbage softens. It will stay nice and green, but will just start to brown around the edges. Taste it—you probably won't need to season it because the pancetta will give enough salt.

8 Pile the cabbage mixture around a warm serving plate, put the pheasant in the middle, and serve the sauce on the side.

Bertinet Basics

✳ **Why is it important to take meat out of the fridge an hour before you cook it?**
See page 128

✳ **How is pancetta different from bacon?** *See page 63*

✳ **Why do you rest meat?** *See page 136*

✳ **What does "reducing" a sauce actually mean?** *See page 141*

Creamy garlic potatoes

Warning: this dish is addictive. You can never make enough. For me, this is a supper dish in itself with a simple salad on the side, but it is equally great with the ham hock on page 125, or instead of roast potatoes with a joint of meat or a roast chicken; it's so addictive we leave any leftovers by the side of the stove and by the time we've done the dishes everyone has had another forkful. If by any chance there is any left over, it is fantastic the next day fried up in a pan.

This dish is similar to the classic potato dauphinoise, excluding the nutmeg, and is simple as anything—you don't need to layer the potatoes carefully. I start off the potatoes and cream on top of the stove, all mixed up together, and then simply pile them into an oven-proof dish and finish them in the oven.

Everyone has different-sized and shaped dishes and it's not easy to work out how many potatoes you need: the trick I have, which always works, is to get the oven-proof dish you want to use and then put in as many whole, raw potatoes as you can fit in a single layer—and that is how many you will need. It is important to slice the potatoes all to the same thickness so that they cook evenly, so it is worth investing in a good Mandoline to make all the slicing quicker and easier.

Bake the gratin a good hour before you want to eat it, to let it cool down, since it will taste much better warm than hot. You can make it a day in advance, put it in the fridge, covered with foil, then reheat in the oven gently at 275–300°F.

PREPARATION

✳ Preheat the oven to 400°F.

✳ Peel and wash the potatoes, then cut into very thin slices—the easiest way is with a Mandoline. If you are using a knife, the safest way is to cut the potatoes in half lengthwise, then put each half, cut-side down, on your work surface and slice crosswise.

✳ Remove the garlic germ, if necessary. Crush the garlic clove(s) with the flat edge of a big knife and then chop finely—the more you crush, the more garlicky the flavor.

✳ Chop the parsley.

METHOD

1 Heat the oil in a heavy-bottomed pan over medium heat. Put in the potato slices and stir with a big wooden spoon so that every slice is covered in oil. Season and stir again. The potatoes might catch a bit on the bottom of the pan, but that is normal; just keep moving them around. When all the potato slices are well coated in oil and you see them becoming sticky as they release their starch into the pan, add the garlic and pour in enough cream to cover the potatoes; no more. Turn the heat down and cook until you see the cream thickening a little—about 5 minutes—then take the pan off the heat, and check on your seasoning.

2 Stir in the chopped parsley and pour everything into your oven-proof dish. Put the dish on a baking sheet—that way, it is easier to slide it in and out of the oven; also, it will protect your oven if the cream bubbles over. Bake for 20–30 minutes, depending on the thickness of the potatoes, until the top is golden brown and you can pierce the potatoes easily with a small-pointed knife. Leave to cool down before serving.

INGREDIENTS
For 8

enough whole potatoes to fill an
    oven-proof dish, roughly 10 x 7 inches
    (about 8 medium potatoes)
4 garlic cloves (or 1 if you don't like a
    lot of garlic)
small bunch of curly parsley
about 4–5 tablespoons vegetable or
    olive oil
sea salt and freshly ground
    black pepper
about 2 cups heavy cream

HOW CAN I VARY THE RECIPE?
To make it into a quick version of dauphinoise, just substitute the garlic and parsley for a handful of grated Gruyère and add it to the cream along with a grated whole nutmeg. Then just before it goes into the oven, sprinkle some more cheese on top and bake in the same way.

Bertinet Basics

✳ **Why do you remove the germ of the garlic?** *See page 23*

✳ **Why curly parsley?** *See page 99*

Vegetable stir-fry

This is just a simple dish of stir-fried vegetables, which owes very little to Chinese cooking, beyond the concept of slicing vegetables very thinly so that they cook quickly and retain as much of their flavor and goodness as possible. It is a great way of serving lots of vegetables at the same time without having to boil or steam them. I like to serve this with fish or roast meat (you could replace the braised lettuce in the pork fillet recipe on page 128 with stir-fried vegetables). Of course, if you want to make a main course, you could add some thin strips of pork, chicken, or some raw shrimp—stir-fry them before you add the vegetables. And you can bring a more authentic Asian feel to your stir-fry by adding some finely sliced ginger, chile, and soy sauce.

INGREDIENTS
For 4–6

1 leek
1 small or ½ large white cabbage
2 carrots
1 zucchini
about 7oz button mushrooms
1 red bell pepper
1 tablespoon canola or light
   vegetable oil
either sea salt and freshly ground black
   pepper or a few dashes of soy sauce

PREPARATION
✳ Trim the green "flags" from the top of the leek and discard them. Cut the white part into sections of about 2 inches, then cut these "tubes" in half lengthwise. Slice again lengthwise into long, thin strips.
✳ Cut the cabbage into quarters, cut out the hard "core" and slice the rest into fine shreds.
✳ Peel the carrots and cut them in half widthwise. Now use a vegetable peeler to take off fine strips from each chunk.
✳ Slice the zucchini into very thin rounds.
✳ Slice the mushrooms finely if large or quarter them if small.
✳ Cut the pepper in half, remove the seeds and stem, and then cut into long thin strips.
✳ Mix all the vegetables together in a bowl—at this point you can cover them in plastic wrap and keep them in the fridge if you are not ready to cook them just yet.

METHOD
Heat the oil in a wok or large frying pan. Fry the vegetables over high heat, a handful at a time, for about a minute, moving them around the pan constantly. Take each handful out and transfer to a serving dish, then put in the next handful. You can either season them with salt and pepper while they are in the pan, or just add a sprinkling of soy sauce at the end.

Q&A...

WHAT IS THE BEST OIL TO USE FOR STIR-FRYING?
When you stir-fry the oil needs to be heated to a very high temperature. All oils have a different "smoke point" and if you heat them beyond this, they begin to burn, losing their beneficial antioxidants, character, and color, as well as taking on a bitter flavor. Olive oil doesn't have a high enough smoke point, so choose vegetable or canola oil, which I like since it is one of the few "single" oils (not a generic cooking oil) that can be heated to stir-frying or deep-frying temperatures without breaking down.

Bertinet Basics

✳ **Are red peppers sweeter than green?** *See page 51*

Lemon curd

My absolute favorite way to eat lemon curd is on top of toasted sourdough: that's the ultimate. Next is dipping madeleines into it! I also like to make a dessert using lemon curd that is similar to trifle, but layered with cream and ladyfingers like a tiramisu. I smear some ladyfingers with lemon curd, put them in the bottom of a glass bowl, sprinkle with alcohol—Limoncello, Grand Marnier, Cointreau, and vodka are all good. add a layer of cold custard, then follow with a layer of whipped cream. I then repeat the layers until I have filled up the bowl and chill it in the fridge for an hour or so before serving. You can add layers of fruit, too, if you like: some passion fruit is lovely, or even some drained, canned apricots.

You don't need to pot the lemon curd into jars, but I like to make a big batch, keep some, and give some away to friends. If you are going to put it in jars, make sure you sterilize them first. The easiest way is to put them through a dishwasher cycle, and then put them in a preheated oven (225°F) for 15 minutes to dry completely. Pot the lemon curd while it is still hot, seal, and then leave to cool.

INGREDIENTS
Makes enough to fill 5 medium (8oz) preserving jars

6 medium unwaxed lemons
5 large eggs (preferably free-range)
2 cups superfine sugar
9oz unsalted butter
¾ cup cornstarch

PREPARATION
✳ You will need a heat-proof mixing bowl that will fit over a saucepan with the base of the bowl clear of the bottom of the pan.
✳ Zest the lemons and squeeze the juice.

METHOD

1 Whisk all the ingredients together in your mixing bowl.

2 Bring some water to a simmer in your saucepan over a small burner—you want enough water to come close to the bottom of your bowl when you sit it on top, but not actually to touch it.

3 Put the bowl over the simmering water and heat gently over low heat, whisking all the time. Be patient, or you will end up with scrambled eggs (if this should happen, put the mixture through a fine strainer very quickly, then back onto the heat). Keep watching and whisking all the time, making sure you move all of the mixture around in the bowl, so that none sticks to the sides. Once it starts to thicken—it will look a bit thicker than heavy cream—cook it for 1 minute more, continuing to whisk. It should be ready now: to test, put a little dollop of the mixture onto the inside of the bowl toward the top. It should stay still without dripping.

4 Take off the heat and leave to cool.

Bertinet Basics

✳ **What is the best way to juice a lemon?** *See page 102*

✳ **Why buy unwaxed lemons?** *See page 103*

Q&A...

HOW DO I STORE THE CURD?
If you plan to eat it fairly quickly, you can keep the lemon curd in a bowl in the fridge for about a week, covered with a lid or plastic wrap. Alternatively, place it into sterilized jars (see introduction) and store in the fridge for up to 2 months.

"My absolute favorite way to eat lemon curd is on top of toasted sourdough: that's the ultimate."

Crème caramel

Crème caramel might sound like a retro dessert—all the rage in the sixties and seventies—but I think it is having a bit of renaissance, and it is one of the most popular desserts in our classes at the cooking school.

It is also a useful way of getting familiar with the technique of cooking in a bain-marie—which is a "water bath."

You can use either a whole vanilla pod or vanilla sugar. You can buy vanilla sugar now in supermarkets—or make your own by simply storing a clean, dry vanilla pod (you can use ones that you have split and from which you have scraped out the seeds) in a jar of superfine sugar. If you like a really gutsy flavor of vanilla, you could grind your pod and sugar together into a fine powder; or you could add a few drops of good vanilla extract (not essence) to plain superfine sugar.

"You can use whatever shape of mold you like, such as a dariole, above, or the typical restaurant one, right."

Q&A...

WHY DO CUSTARD RECIPES ALWAYS SAY TO BEAT THE EGGS AND SUGAR UNTIL PALE AND CREAMY?

One of the earliest things I had drummed into me when I was an apprentice in the patisserie section of my first bakery was that you must always mix your eggs and sugar together correctly before you add any other ingredients. The change to a pale straw color and more creamy, mousselike texture shows you that you are there. My old boss used to say, "Don't burn your eggs!" What he meant was that if you just give your sugar and eggs a quick stir, they won't amalgamate correctly—if you were to set them aside for a few minutes the sugar would darken the color of the eggs and they would look as if they had been burned (the same thing happens if you add salt to beaten egg for an egg wash; the salt acts on the egg to darken it). Try a little experiment at home and you will see what I mean. Take 2 eggs, break them into separate bowls, and add 1 teaspoon of sugar to each. Mix the contents of one bowl briefly, then whisk the other one really well. Leave the bowls alone for a while, and you will see how the badly mixed one darkens to a burned-looking color. If you are making a sponge cake and you haven't mixed your eggs correctly, it won't rise as well; if you are making custard, the finished result will often be uneven and heavy.

INGREDIENTS

For 6

spoon of butter, to grease the molds
1 large vanilla pod or 2 small ones
 (alternatively, omit the vanilla pod
 and substitute the 2½ tablespoons
 superfine sugar with vanilla sugar,
 see introduction)
2 whole eggs and 2 egg yolks
 (preferably free-range)
2½ tablespoons superfine sugar
10fl oz whole milk
10fl oz heavy cream

FOR THE CARAMEL
6 tablespoons superfine sugar
squeeze of lemon juice

PREPARATION
✳ Preheat the oven to 325°F.
✳ Butter six metal molds and have a deep roasting pan ready.
✳ If using a vanilla pod, split it in half lengthwise.

METHOD

1 For the caramel, put the 6 tablespoons of superfine sugar and a squeeze of lemon juice into a heavy-bottomed pan with 3 tablespoons water over medium heat. Use a small burner and take your time, rather than putting your pan over a big flame because you are in a hurry—if you do that, the flame will heat the sides of the pan and burn the edge of the caramel. A word of warning here: always be very careful with caramel and be aware that any splashes on your skin burn very badly, so keep the children clear. Never leave the pan unattended and have a bowl of cold water next to the stove, so if the caramel starts to burn you can lift off the pan and put the base into it to bring the temperature down—only the base, though, never let any water get into the pan, or it will spit, and you run the risk of being splashed with red-hot caramel.

2 Let the sugar dissolve and cook gently, watching all the time, until you have a golden-brown caramel. However impatient you are feeling, don't stir it; leave it alone—otherwise, the caramel you push to the edge of the pan will burn. Pour an equal quantity of caramel into the bottom of each mold and set aside.

3 In a mixing bowl, beat together the whole eggs, egg yolks, and the 2½ tablespoons superfine sugar (or vanilla sugar, if using) until they turn a very pale straw color and have a creamy, mousse-like appearance.

Q & A...

WHY ARE LIQUIDS MEASURED EXACTLY IN FLUID OUNCES IN THE BAKING RECIPES, WHEN ELSEWHERE IN THE BOOK MEASUREMENTS ARE OFTEN IN CUPS OR APPROXIMATED?

For baking and desserts, I am careful to measure exactly for each recipe. For general cooking, a little more or less liquid usually makes little difference, but desserts often rely much more on science to help things to set, rise, amalgamate, etc., so it is important to be precise.

4 Heat the milk and cream gently over low heat with the split vanilla pod (if using) until it comes to just below boiling point. As soon as it looks like it is shivering, and tiny bubbles are about to start forming, take it off the heat. Scrape the vanilla seeds into the milk and discard the pod. Pour the milk slowly onto the beaten egg and sugar mixture, whisking well as you do so, and then pour into the molds.

5 Boil a kettle of water. Put the filled molds into a deep roasting pan, preferably with handles, and pour boiling water around them to come halfway up the outside of the molds. Carefully put the pan into the oven on the middle shelf until just set—about 15–30 minutes, depending on your oven. The way to check is to take the pan out and wobble it just a little. The cream should be just set, but quiver like jelly. It might color slightly or form a little skin, but that is fine. Just be careful not to let it overcook, because a firm crème caramel doesn't hold a candle to a soft, wobbly one.

6 Leave to cool for at least half an hour, and then chill in the fridge for a few more hours—ideally, overnight. Once the cream has cooled, it will be easier to turn out.

7 To serve, either run a round-ended knife around the inside of each mold to loosen or, if you don't feel confident about doing this cleanly, use a cocktail stick. Hold a plate over the top and then turn the mold and plate upside down together and lift off the mold. Hopefully, your crème caramels will slide out beautifully intact.

Q&A...

WHAT IS THE DIFFERENCE BETWEEN VANILLA EXTRACT AND ESSENCE?

It's funny how little people know about vanilla. Vanilla pods are the cured beans of a climbing orchid that originated in South America. These days, they are grown around the world, but the most famous production area is Madagascar. Highly prized by the perfume industry, vanilla is very complex, and the best way of extracting the flavors and aromas from the pods is to use traditional cold processing in which the beans are steeped slowly in pure alcohol and then filtered and bottled (sometimes there is added sugar or glycerine, so check the label). Cheap vanilla essence or "flavoring" is produced synthetically in the laboratory and is nowhere near as rich and subtle.

WHAT IS THE POINT OF A DOUBLE BOILER OR BAIN MARIE?

In France, a double boiler is known as a bain-marie: Mary's bath, or a water bath. Who was Mary? One story says that it refers to the sister of Moses, who was supposed to be an alchemist; another that it was named after the Virgin Mary, considered the ultimate symbol of gentleness, since the whole point of using a double boiler is gentle cooking. The water bath protects the cream from harsh, dry heat around the molds. These days, many chefs cook sous-vide, a method in which the food cooks inside a pouch in a water bath—the same principle. In this recipe, even though you pour boiling water around the molds, when the molds go into the oven at 325°F, the water settles down below boiling point (212°F), which lets the custard cook and set more gently so that it stays soft and quivering.

Bonus recipe:

How to make crème anglaise (real "English" custard)

This is made in the same way as the custard for the crème caramel recipe, but with a different ratio of ingredients (and using just milk instead of milk and cream). You can spoon it over poached fruit, fruit pies, etc., or use it in bread and butter pudding, or to make ice cream. To make a good pitcherful, use 5 egg yolks, ¾ cup sugar, and 16fl oz milk.

Step-by-step

1-4 Whisk the eggs and superfine sugar together until they have a pale straw color and mousse-like appearance. Make sure you use your wrist to whisk in large circles to get as much air through as possible.

5 Add the milk, which has been heated in a pan to just below boiling point, pouring slowly and whisking well as you do so.

6 The final custard should fall in heavy drops from your whisk.

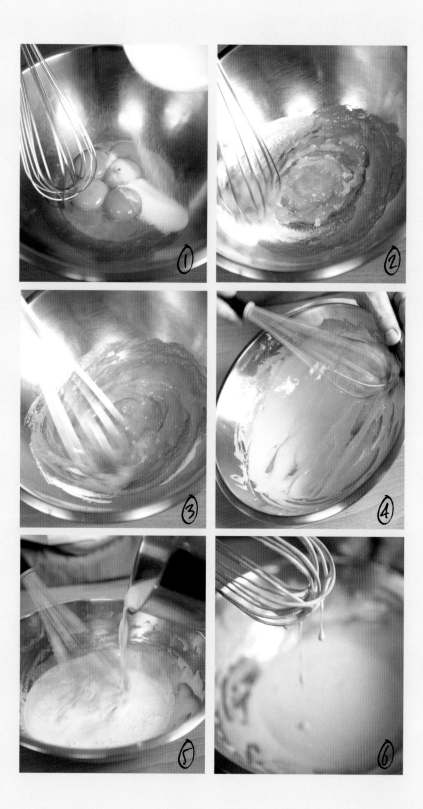

Crème brûlée

The skill is first in making a good crème. There is a whole family of custards and creams that are very similar, but have a slightly different ratio of ingredients (especially concerning the quantity of eggs and yolks), depending on the way they are to be used and how thick or set the crème needs to be. This one is thicker than the crème for the crème caramel in the recipe on page 168, which is why we use all cream rather than cream and milk to make it, and egg yolks rather than whole eggs—both of which will help to set it more; however, it shouldn't be set solid like a mousse, so you will need to keep an eye on it while it is in the oven. If you are wondering why I use a mix of light and heavy cream, an old pastry chef at Chewton Glen showed me this ratio many years ago, and the balance is just right, so I have followed it ever since, never daring to change it. If you have a great recipe that works, why tempt fate and mess with it?

The second skill is getting the burned-sugar topping (which gives the dessert its name) just right. The perfect crème brulée has a very thin, brittle caramel on top that will just snap when you crack it with your spoon—so you get that great contrast with the rich, melt-in-your-mouth cream underneath. Once your crème is made, the trick is to get it really cold before you sprinkle it with sugar and then caramelize it, preferably with a kitchen blowtorch, so that you can melt the sugar as quickly as possible without heating the custard underneath and turning it to liquid. If you don't have a blowtorch, you need to get your broiler as hot as you can, so that you can flash the pots of cream underneath very quickly. In the old days, people used to have flat brûlée disks, like irons, which you would get red hot in the coals before pressing them onto the sprinkled sugar on top of the custard, so that it would instantly melt and caramelize.

Having said all of that, I know some people love the rich cream but don't like the crunchiness of the caramel topping—it can wreak havoc with your teeth! So on occasion, instead of sprinkling the top with sugar and caramelizing it, I have played it safe by making some caramel as for the crème caramel on page 170, and then pouring it into a very thin layer over some waxed paper laid on a baking sheet. Once it starts to set, I take a round cutter the same size as the tops of my crème brûlées and just rub the rim and inside edge of the cutter with a little vegetable oil to stop it from sticking to the caramel, before cutting out a disk for every pot of crème. I let the disks set hard, and then when I serve the ramekins of crème I prop a disk of caramel on the side, so those who want to can pop it on top, and those who don't, can opt out.

Bertinet Basics

❋ **Why do you measure liquids exactly for dessert recipes and not elsewhere in the book?** *See page 170*

❋ **Why do custard recipes always say to beat the eggs and sugar until pale and creamy?** *See page 168*

❋ **Is there a technique to whisking?** *See page 178*

❋ **What is the point of a double boiler?** *See page 170*

"This is one of my favorite desserts."

INGREDIENTS

For 6

1 large vanilla pod or 2 small ones
4 egg yolks (preferably free-range)
²/₃ cup superfine sugar
10oz heavy cream
10oz light cream
confectioners' sugar, to caramelize

PREPARATION

✳ Preheat the oven to 325°F.
✳ Have ready 6 ramekins or dishes and a deep roasting pan.
✳ Split the vanilla pod in half lengthwise.

METHOD

1 Beat the egg yolks and superfine sugar together in a bowl until they turn a pale straw color and have a creamy, mousse-like appearance.

2 Pour the two creams into a heavy-bottomed pan, scraping in the seeds from the vanilla pod (to give it more of a vanilla flavor, and I like the speckled look) and then putting in the split pod, too. Stir together and heat gently over low heat until the cream reaches the point where it is just shivering, and tiny bubbles are about to start forming—don't let it boil. Take off the heat, remove the vanilla pod, and pour a little of the cream onto the egg mixture, whisking well to amalgamate before adding the rest in a continuous stream, whisking all the time. By starting off slowly like this, you will get a much more homogenous mixture.

3 Return the cream and egg mixture to the pan over low heat. Stir continuously in a figure-eight shape using a wooden spoon. Continue stirring until the cream has thickened enough—about 3–5 minutes; again, make sure it doesn't boil or the mixture will curdle. You can tell when it is ready by lifting the spoon out of the mixture and drawing a line down the length of the back of it with your finger. If this little "road" stays clean, it is ready (see left); if the cream just runs over it, it isn't set enough. If it is ready, pour it into a pitcher right away, so it stops cooking (or you will end up with scrambled eggs), and then leave it to cool for a few minutes.

HOW CAN I VARY THIS RECIPE?

To make a chocolate brûlée, grate 4oz good dark chocolate (at least 70 percent cocoa solids) into the cream as you heat it (step 2). For a coffee brûlée, add 2 tablespoons freshly ground coffee at the same stage, then pass the cream through a fine strainer as you add it to the egg mixture. For a lavender brûlée, add 1 teaspoon lavender instead of the coffee and again strain before adding to the egg mixture. Alternatively, put some fresh raspberries in the base of your ramekins or dishes before adding the cream mixture; or some of the stewed rhubarb from page 186.

4 Put a kettle of water on to boil. Place the ramekins or dishes in a deep roasting pan and divide the cream mixture between them. Fill the roasting pan with boiling water so that it comes halfway up the outside of the ramekins.

5 Put the pan into the oven and cook for 20–25 minutes until the crème feels just set when you touch it gently with your finger. Remove the pan from the oven and carefully take out the ramekins. Cool for 30 minutes, and then put into the fridge to chill for at least 2 hours, but up to 6 hours.

6 When you are ready to serve, sprinkle the top of each ramekin with confectioners' sugar (preferably using a shaker or small tea strainer)—about a teaspoon on each is enough—and then quickly caramelize the top with a blowtorch or under a very hot broiler.

Berinet Basics

✳ **Why is it important not to let milk boil?** *See page 178*

Simple vanilla soufflé

If you have never made a soufflé before, you probably won't believe me when I say it is easier than you expect. There is a kind of mythology around soufflés that makes people scared even to try them, but if you avoid overwhisking your mixture and prepare your ramekins with care, it should all be fine. You don't have to copy the perfect soufflés that rise up in straight lines like chef's hats in Michelin-starred restaurants; the ones you make will look all the more interesting for not being quite so regimented. What should a soufflé be like inside? I don't want a soufflé to be cooked to the point where you feel as though you are eating only air: I quite like a little creaminess inside, so there is some substance to it... remember that the mixture is already cooked before it goes in the oven.

PREPARATION

✳ Preheat the oven to 400°F.

✳ Prepare four ramekins or other small soufflé dishes. Take your time to do this carefully, since it will make all the difference to the easy rising of your soufflés. Melt the butter and brush over the inside of each ramekin, then tip about 2 teaspoons of superfine sugar into each one and roll it around so that the sugar coats all of the buttered surface. Tip out any excess.

✳ Split the vanilla pod along its length.

✳ Separate the eggs. You will need 5 whites and 3 yolks in separate mixing bowls. Make sure the bowl you put the whites into is really clean, because any touch of grease, from handling the butter, for example, will stop them from peaking properly.

INGREDIENTS

For 4

1 vanilla pod
5 eggs (preferably free-range)
6 tablespoons superfine sugar
¼ cup all-purpose flour
8fl oz whole milk
a little confectioners' sugar, to serve

FOR THE RAMEKINS

about ½oz butter
about 3 tablespoons superfine sugar

METHOD

1 Put the 6 tablespoons sugar in the bowl with the egg yolks and whisk for a couple of minutes until they turn a very pale straw color and have a creamy, mousse-like appearance.

2 Sprinkle in the flour, whisking again.

3 Pour the milk into a heavy-bottomed pan over medium heat. Scrape in the vanilla seeds and put the pod in as well. Just before the milk reaches boiling point—that is, when it is just shivering and tiny bubbles start to appear—take off the heat. Pour it over the egg mixture a little at a time, whisking continuously. Discard the vanilla pod.

4 Pour the mixture back into the pan and bring to a boil, whisking all the time. Turn down to simmer and cook for 2–3 minutes, still whisking constantly. Remove from the heat and transfer to a clean bowl.

5 Beat the egg whites until they form soft peaks—either with a wire balloon whisk or with an electric mixer. Again, make sure whatever you use has no grease on it, so that the eggs firm up really well. "Soft peaks" means that the whites will look frothy and hold their shape if you draw them into peaks with your whisk (they won't form "stiff peaks"—that only happens if you add sugar).

6 Using a balloon whisk, quickly mix about a third of the whites into the cream mixture. Don't whisk wildly, since you don't want to knock the air out of the whites; you want to keep the mixture as light as possible. Then, with a metal spoon, gently fold in the rest. This gentle folding-in of the egg whites is key.

7 Put the ramekins on a baking sheet so they will be easy to move. Fill each one to the top and smooth the surface a little. Then, with a piece of paper towel, wipe the rims so that they are nice and clean. This is important, because if there are any bits of mixture on the rim, the soufflés might catch on them and then they won't rise correctly.

8 Put the baking sheet in the oven on the middle shelf and cook for about 15 minutes. For the first 5 minutes, when the soufflés are starting to lift, don't open the oven door because the loss of heat would stop the soufflés from rising evenly. When they are done, they will have risen quite high and be a caramel-brown color on top but still white on the outside.

9 Take the baking sheet from the oven, dust the top of each soufflé with a little confectioners' sugar, and serve immediately.

Q&A...

WHAT IS THE BEST KIND OF WHISK?
There is any number of whisks out there, but look for a medium-large one with seven wires, so that you can get the maximum amount of air through your mixture when you whisk—and use a large bowl. A small whisk, or one with fewer wires, won't work as well.

IS THERE A TECHNIQUE TO WHISKING?
When you whisk, don't just go around and around in the center of the bowl; you need to get as much air as possible through every bit of the mixture. Use your wrist to lift the whisk upward, away from you, and back around through the mixture in a big circle.

WHY IS IT IMPORTANT NOT TO LET MILK BOIL?
If you boil it, you will end up with a skin on the top. Always keep an eye on milk, because there is very little time between it just trembling, before it reaches a simmer and then a boil, when it will rise up and over the side of your pan very quickly as the fat rises to the surface. That is why you should take it off the heat when you see it trembling, to avoid any mishaps.

Bertinet Basics

✳ **Why are liquids measured exactly in fluid ounces for dessert and baking recipes and not elsewhere in the book?** *See page 170*

✳ **Why do custard recipes always say to beat the eggs and sugar until pale and creamy?** *See page 168*

"'Soft peaks' means that the whites will look frothy and hold their shape if you draw them into peaks with your whisk."

Strawberry croustillant

A croustillant is something crispy—in this case, wafer-thin pieces of puff pastry are drenched in sugar and then baked so that they become toffee-ish, before being sandwiched with strawberries and chantilly cream. This is such an easy dessert to make, and yet it looks very impressive. You can vary the fruit according to season: any berries—raspberries, blackberries, blueberries—are lovely, but you could also use mango, passion fruit, whatever you like. A little rosewater in the chantilly cream gives it a nice perfume, which some people like, others don't—so it is up to you whether you add it or not.

INGREDIENTS

For 6

14oz small strawberries (or a mix of
    small and wild strawberries, if you
can get hold of them)
7oz ready-made butter puff pastry
1¾ cups confectioners' sugar

FOR THE CHANTILLY CREAM
1 cup whipping cream
¼ cup superfine sugar
few drops of rosewater (optional)

PREPARATION

✳ Preheat the oven to 400°F.
✳ Line a baking sheet with parchment paper.
✳ Have a wire rack ready for cooling the croustillants when they come out of the oven.
✳ Hull the strawberries and cut them in half.

METHOD

1 Form and roll the puff pastry into a sausage shape, and then cut it into 12 slices, ½ inch thick each.

2 Have your confectioners' sugar in a mound on your work surface and put the first piece of puff pastry, cut-side down, on top of it.

3 Sprinkle some of the sugar over the top of the pastry and then, using a rolling pin, roll it out until it is very thin and see-through, barely thicker than tracing paper. You will need to keep turning the pastry over during the rolling so that it is always coated in sugar and doesn't stick to the rolling pin. Repeat with the rest of the pieces of pastry.

4 Lay the croustillants out on the lined baking sheet and bake on the middle shelf of the oven for 6–8 minutes, until caramelized. Be sure to keep a close eye on them because they burn quickly.

5 Take the tray from the oven and use a offset spatula to lift each croustillant off and onto the wire rack.

6 To make the chantilly cream, whisk all the ingredients together until thick and fluffy.

7 To serve, place one croustillant on each plate with the side that was facing upward in the oven, the rougher side, downward. Spoon or pipe a little chantilly cream along the length of the pastry and cover with halved strawberries. Top with another croustillant—this time, the more textured, bumpy side that was facing upward in the oven should be uppermost.

Sweet flamiche with summer berries

This is a very quick and easy tart that doesn't involve making, or even rolling, pastry—you simply buy sheets of phyllo. It looks pretty and tastes really light.

PREPARATION

✱ Preheat the oven to 375°F.
✱ You will need a heat-proof mixing bowl that will fit over a saucepan with the base of the bowl clear of the bottom of the pan.
✱ You will also need a small frying pan with an oven-proof handle.

METHOD

1 Melt the butter in a small saucepan. Use a pastry brush to lightly butter the inside of your small frying pan.

2 Lay a sheet of phyllo pastry in the frying pan and brush the top with melted butter.

3 Lay another sheet of pastry on top, but this time at an angle to the first sheet. Brush with butter, as before. Repeat with your remaining sheets, brushing the top with melted butter each time. By laying each sheet at an angle to the previous one, you will make a rough star shape with lots of pointed edges.

4 Bring some water to a simmer in the other saucepan—enough to come close to the bottom of your heat-proof mixing bowl when you put it on top, but not actually to touch it.

5 Put the sugar, eggs, and kirsch into your bowl and place it over the pan of simmering water. Whisk the sugar and egg mixture with a whisk over the heat until the mixture is light and fluffy. Add half of the crème fraîche and whisk again, then add the remainder and whisk once more. Take the pan off the heat and carefully lift off the bowl.

6 Place the frying pan lined with pastry over very low heat for 5–6 minutes, until the underneath is lightly browned—you can lift the edges gently with a spatula to check how it is doing.

7 Remove the pan from the heat, scatter the fruit over the pastry, and top with the frothy sugar and egg mixture.

8 Bake in the oven for 15 minutes, until the sugar and egg mixture has set.

9 Leave to cool down slightly, and then dust with confectioners' sugar before serving.

INGREDIENTS

For 4

1oz unsalted butter
4 sheets of phyllo pastry
2½ tablespoons superfine sugar
2 eggs (preferably free-range)
1 teaspoon kirsch
4oz crème fraîche
7oz mixed berries
confectioners' sugar, to serve

Bertinet Basics

✱ **Is crème fraîche a straight substitute for cream?** *See page 59*

✱ **What is the best kind of whisk?** *See page 178*

✱ **Is there a technique to whisking?** *See page 178*

Q&A...

WHY DO YOU NEED TO WHISK THE EGGS AND SUGAR OVER A PAN OF WATER?
Unlike the sugar and egg mixtures in the previous recipes, this isn't a custard or crème; it is more of a batter with crème fraîche whisked in. Half-cooking it like this over a pan of water helps the batter to set quickly when you put it in the oven.

"If you poach rhubarb for just 5 minutes in some syrup, and then drain it, it holds its shape and color."

Rhubarb two ways—
poached and jelly

Rhubarb often gets stewed for way too long, I find, whereas if you just poach it for 5 minutes or so in some syrup, and then drain it, it holds its shape and color much better—especially the early, pink, forced rhubarb. Both of these rhubarb dishes can be made a day in advance and served cold with some crème anglaise (see page 172) or you could use the poached rhubarb at the bottom of a crème brulée (see page 173).

INGREDIENTS
For 6

2 cups superfine or granulated sugar
large piece of fresh ginger
6 sticks of rhubarb
1 x ¼oz package of gelatine
1 lime

PREPARATION
✳ You will need six small jelly molds (or one large one).
✳ Have ready a rack over a baking sheet, to drain the rhubarb.
✳ Peel the ginger, cut it into thin slices, and then again into very thin matchsticks.
✳ Cut the rhubarb on the diagonal into 2-inch lengths.
✳ Squeeze the lime.

METHOD
1 Put the sugar and ginger in a heavy-bottomed pan with 1¾ cups water and bring to a boil, stirring to dissolve the sugar. Turn down the heat and simmer for about 20 minutes to allow the syrup to thicken a little.

2 Add the rhubarb and simmer gently over low heat for 4–5 minutes until it has softened but still offers resistance when you prod it with a sharp knife.

3 Remove the rhubarb with a slotted spoon and lay it on your rack over a baking sheet to drain and cool. Keep in the fridge until you are ready to serve.

4 Add the gelatine to the pan of syrup along with the lime juice. Stir over low heat until the gelatine has dissolved completely.

5 Put your jelly mold(s) on a small tray or flat plate—that way, they will be easier to move around. Pour in the mixture and carefully transfer the tray to the fridge to set for 3–4 hours, preferably overnight. Serve with the rhubarb and some crème anglaise, if you like.

Q&A...

WHAT IS FORCED RHUBARB?
The bright pink rhubarb that appears in February in England is grown in dark forcing sheds in "the Wakefield triangle" in West Yorkshire, between Wakefield, Leeds, and Bradford, in the way that it has been done for centuries. The plants are lifted from the fields at the optimum time and taken into the sheds, where the warmth makes them "think" it is spring. The buds begin to swell, until they pop and the long, pink shoots grow. In the US, commercial rhubarb production is centered in Washington, Oregon, and Michigan.

Bertinet Basics

✳ **How can you tell if a lime contains a lot of juice?** *See page 53*

✳ **Can you juice a lime more easily if you roll it under your hand first?** *See page 53*

French apple tart

A good, full-flavored eating apple with a bit of sharpness is best for this and will keep its shape, unlike a Bramley or Granny Smith apple, which will turn to mush. You might be lucky enough to have your own apple tree or live near an orchard that has some wonderful varieties; if not, the best ones to buy are Braeburn or Golden Delicious. In France, when I was working as a baker, we always used local Golden Delicious because they cooked so well. We would make apple tarts on a daily basis, from September through to April/May, until we moved on to the strawberry season. There are so many different ways of making apple tart, and so many different shapes: round ones, oblong ones, individual ones. This is one of the simplest, made with very thin, crispy pastry. The key to achieving a "professional" look is to cut the apples really thinly, keeping a nice, rounded shape to the slices.

I suggest you buy some good-quality, ready-made puff pastry, because making it can be a challenge; at least make the tart a few times and get used to slicing the apples first, and then you might feel inclined to try producing your own pastry.

You might wonder: why bother using puff pastry when we prick most of the base to stop it from rising, leaving just a puffed-up rim all the way around. Well, even though you don't want it to rise, you still get the crispy flakiness and butteriness that you don't get from any other kind of pastry.

The apple purée for the base (made with Bramley or Granny Smith apples because here you do want it to turn to mush) is simple to make… I do the same thing when I want some apple compote for roast pork (I might add a sprinkling of cinnamon in there, too). But if you don't have any Bramleys or Granny Smiths, a convenient cheat is to use a good-quality, additive-free jar of apple compote, or puréed apple for babies!

I like to leave the tarts to cool, then glaze them with apricot jam to give a golden color and shine, but if you don't want to glaze them, and you prefer to serve the tart hot, try trickling a little Calvados over the top and flaming it, as you would with crepes.

Note: You can make the tarts up to the point of putting them in the oven and then freeze them. When you are ready to bake them, just defrost them for half an hour or so, and bake as described in the recipe.

Q&A...

HOW DO YOU STOP CUT APPLES FROM GOING BROWN?
The old trick of putting the apples in a bowl of cold water with a good squeeze of lemon juice really does work if you are cutting up apples and not using them immediately. However, for this recipe you are using the apples really quickly after slicing them, so it shouldn't be necessary.

HOW DOES PRICKING PUFF PASTRY STOP IT FROM RISING?
Puff pastry is what is known as a "laminated" pastry—like croissant dough, it is made by constantly folding and rolling to create lots of layers, with trapped air in between. When the pastry is in the oven, these air pockets expand, causing the pastry to puff up. However, if you prick the raw pastry all over with a fork, you puncture many of the air pockets and stop it from rising.

INGREDIENTS

For 4

either 2 Bramley or Granny Smith
apples, 1 tablespoon superfine
or granulated sugar and a
splash of brandy or 1 x 4oz jar
apple compote
13oz ready-made butter puff pastry
all-purpose flour, for dusting
1 beaten egg (or a little milk), plus a
pinch of salt, to glaze
4 good eating apples
about 6 tablespoons apricot jam

PREPARATION

* Preheat the oven to 400°F.
* Have ready a nonstick baking sheet, or line one with parchment paper or a
nonstick mat.

METHOD

1 To make the apple compote, peel, core, and chop the apples and put them
in a pan with the sugar, brandy, and a couple of tablespoons of water.
Simmer until the apples are just soft—about 15 minutes—and then blend to a
purée in a blender (or use a handheld one). Keep to one side and leave to cool.

2 Roll out the pastry to ¼ inch thick and have ready a small side plate to cut
around or a large cutter (about 6–8 inches in diameter). Cut out four circles
and lay them on the baking sheet.

3 Using a vegetable peeler or a blunt kitchen knife, mark a border all the way
around each circle of pastry without cutting right through, ¼ inch in from the
edge (or press a smaller size cutter lightly into the pastry).

4 Dip a fork in flour to stop it from sticking to the pastry and prick the central area
of each pastry disk all over (going all the way through the pastry), inside the
border. The area you have pricked won't rise, whereas the outer edge will puff up.

5 Spread 2 large tablespoons of apple compote thinly over the pricked area of
the pastry circles.

6 Remove the stalk and the base from the eating apples. You probably think it
is easier to peel apples from top to bottom, i.e., from the stalk to the base,
but when you come to slice the apples this usually means that instead of slicing

How to peel, core, and slice apples...

into nice, rounded, half-moon shapes, they end up a bit flat and blunt—more like roof tiles! It is probably the baker in me, but I like them to be neater, since it makes the tart look so much nicer, so I always peel my apples going around their circumference, starting at the top by the stalk. The trick is to hold the peeler still and move the apple, not the other way around. You don't have to get the peel off all in one strip—although when I was an apprentice I admit there was always a competition over who could peel their way most quickly through the 2 boxes of apples we used every day, taking the peel off in one piece each time!

7 Once your apples are peeled, use a small, sharp knife to cut each one in half and remove the core. I am always teasing students in my classes, because when it comes to coring apples the work benches end up looking like battlefields, with bits of apple strewn everywhere. If you want nice, neat slices of apple, you just need to take out the actual core, not a crater all around it!

8 Put each half of apple, cut-side downward, on your work surface and, starting at the stalk end, slice downward all the way along, keeping your cuts about ¼ inch apart.

9 Arrange the slices from one whole apple on each of the bases in circles, starting from the outside, and with the largest slices, so that each slice overlaps the previous one by half. Use a pastry brush to glaze the pastry borders with beaten egg (or you can use milk). Bake in the oven for about 20 minutes, or until both the apple and pastry base are really golden brown. They are ready when the tarts lift away from the baking sheet cleanly and crisply with a spatula and the apple slices have dark brown/black tips.

10 Remove from the oven and leave to cool for 15–20 minutes on a rack.

11 Put the apricot jam into a saucepan over low heat, add 2 tablespoons cold water, and stir until the jam melts. Make sure it doesn't boil, or it will thicken and be impossible to brush. Using a pastry brush, glaze the tarts with the jam evenly over the top of the apples; leave to cool.

HOW CAN I VARY THE RECIPE?
To make one big tart, I would use 6 or 7 apples and a little more jam or compote. Roll out a rectangle of pastry, mark out a border, prick it in the same way, and spread the central area with apple compote. With one long side of the pastry facing you, start to arrange your apples in a line from left to right, with each slice overlapping the previous one by half, as before. Then go back to the left and start your second line, overlapping the first line by about a third, and stacking the apples, so they stand up quite proud. Keep repeating until you have covered the whole area, and the tart looks like it has been tiled with apples. Bake, cool, and glaze as before—however, the tart will probably need about 35–40 minutes in the oven, until the pastry is crispy underneath.

French apple tart

Dark and white chocolate brownies

This recipe is from Brett, our trusted baker who runs the night shift for our shop. His brownies are very rich and beautifully gooey inside, like a good brownie should be. The glucose syrup helps keep them moist and you can buy it in any supermarket. Although I suggest using chocolate with 70–85 percent cocoa solids, you can use anything from around 55 percent, if you prefer your chocolate less bitter. You could also use hazelnuts, and add dried fruit or bottled cherries.

INGREDIENTS
Makes 12

4oz good-quality white chocolate
1 cup pecan halves (or walnuts)
9oz salted butter
1½ tablespoons glucose syrup
9oz good-quality dark chocolate
   (70–85 percent cocoa solids)
6 eggs (preferably free-range)
1¼ cups all-purpose flour
1¾ cups superfine sugar

PREPARATION
✳ Preheat the oven to 350°F.
✳ Roughly chop the white chocolate and break the nuts into pieces.
✳ Line the bottom and sides of a deep oven pan, 12 x 8 inch, with a large sheet of parchment paper—snip it at the corners so that it fits neatly inside.
✳ You will need a heat-proof mixing bowl that will fit over a saucepan with the base of the bowl well clear of the bottom of the pan.

METHOD

1 Bring some water to a simmer in your saucepan—you need enough water to come close to the bottom of your bowl when you sit it on top, but not actually to touch it. Turn the heat down low: you don't want to overheat the chocolate or get any steam into the bowl, since this will cause the chocolate to stiffen up and become dull-looking.

2 Put the butter and syrup into the bowl and place it over the simmering water. Let the butter melt, stirring with a wooden spoon.

3 Break the dark chocolate into chunks and add to the bowl, stirring all the time until it is melted and combined. Remove from the heat and stir in the eggs, followed by the flour and sugar.

4 Pour the mixture into your lined sheet and sprinkle the pecans (or walnuts) and white chocolate chunks over the top. Push them gently into the mix.

5 Bake in the oven for 30–40 minutes. The brownies are ready when, if you press them, the tops crack a bit and they feel as if they are starting to set. The worst that can happen is that they will be a bit over-gooey in the middle, but that is better than being dry.

Q&A...

WHAT IS WHITE CHOCOLATE?
Unlike in dark chocolate (see page 153), there is no actual cocoa solid in white chocolate. Good ones are made with milk, sugar, and cocoa butter and look creamy-white; less good ones are made with vegetable fat instead of cocoa butter and usually look whiter.

WHY DOES THIS RECIPE USE SALTED BUTTER?
Usually unsalted butter is used in desserts to give you a blank canvas for your flavors. Where I come from, Brittany, salted butter is much more the norm, even in desserts—and especially in chocolates and caramels, where a little of the local sea salt really brings out the flavor, as in this recipe.

Bertinet Basics

✳ **What does "70 percent cocoa solids" mean?** *See page 153*

Can you melt chocolate in a microwave? *See page 195*

"This is a twist on a classic dessert that is cooked for just long enough for the outside to become spongy, but the inside to be runny."

Chocolate fondant à la Mrs. B

Chocolate fondant is a classic dessert that is cooked for just long enough for the outside to become spongy, but the inside to be runny. Mrs. B, my wife, has always loved it but she thought it needed something else to help it really come alive, so she badgered me into trying one with cherries and kirsch and it was a hit. I like to serve it with crème fraîche because it cuts through the richness of the dessert.

PREPARATION

✳ You need a heat-proof bowl that will fit over a saucepan with the base of the bowl clear of the bottom of the pan. You also need four metal dariole molds.

✳ Strain the cherries into a small bowl, reserving the syrup for the sauce. Pour the kirsch over the cherries: it should cover them. Put into the fridge to macerate, preferably overnight, but a week would be great for a good kick of kirsch.

✳ Preheat the oven to 350°F.

✳ Lightly grease the molds with butter and set them on a baking sheet.

METHOD

1 To make the sauce, put the reserved cherry syrup into a pan over low heat with the 4 tablespoons sugar and stir to dissolve the sugar. Strain off the kirsch from the bowl of soaking cherries into the syrup and let it bubble up and reduce until you have only ½ inch remaining in the bottom of the pan. Set aside.

2 In a mixing bowl, whisk the 6 tablespoons sugar with the whole eggs and yolks until they turn a very pale straw color and have a creamy, mousse-like appearance.

3 Bring some water to a simmer in your saucepan—you need enough water to come close to the bottom of your heat-proof bowl when you put it on top, but not actually to touch it. Turn the heat down low, because you don't want to overheat the chocolate or get any steam into the bowl, which would cause the chocolate to stiffen up and become dull-looking.

4 Break the chocolate into chunks, put into the bowl over the water, and let it melt slowly, stirring. Add the butter and stir well until it has completely melted. Take off the heat and add to the sugar and egg mixture, stirring well until it is all incorporated. Gently fold the flour into the chocolate, sugar, and eggs.

5 Spoon about half of the chocolate mixture into the molds, so that they are half full. Put 3–5 cherries on top of each one, making sure they are in the center of the mixture. If they are touching the side of the mold they will stop the chocolate mixture from enclosing them properly, and the desserts will break apart when you turn them out. You will inevitably add a little of the kirsch with the cherries, but try not to add any more liquid than you have to. Spoon the rest of the chocolate fondant mixture on top.

6 Bake in the oven for 7 minutes until springy to the touch. Don't be tempted to leave them in any longer because the center should be runny. Turn out onto individual serving plates and serve with a few more cherries and a dribble of sauce. (If, by mistake, the desserts do end up cakier than you would like, pour some more cherry sauce over the top of them.)

INGREDIENTS
For 4

1 small jar (about 12oz) dark cherries
   in syrup or kirsch syrup
6 tablespoons superfine sugar
2 large eggs and 2 egg yolks
   (preferably free-range)
6oz good-quality dark chocolate
   (at least 70 percent cocoa solids)
6oz unsalted butter, plus a spoonful to
   butter the molds
¼ cup all-purpose flour

FOR THE SAUCE
½ cup kirsch
strained syrup from the jar of cherries
4 tablespoons superfine sugar

Bertinet Basics

✳ **What does "70 percent cocoa solids" mean?** *See page 155*

✳ **Why do custard recipes say to beat the eggs and sugar until pale and creamy?** *See page 168*

✳ **Can you melt chocolate in the microwave?** *See page 196*

Chocolate truffles

Jess, who works with me in the kitchen, makes these, since I always manage to get covered in sticky chocolate. These little truffles are beautiful. If you like, you can shape the chocolates into neat balls, but I prefer to leave them rough, in different sizes, so people can choose whether they want a little chocolate or lots. I know previously I have said that I like to use salted butter in chocolate recipes, but for this one I don't like a general saltiness spread throughout the truffle. What I do like to do sometimes, though, is wait until the chocolate mixture is nearly cold, and then sprinkle in some flakes of *fleur de sel* so that you get a lovely contrast of sweet creaminess and salty crunch when you bite into the truffle.

INGREDIENTS

Makes 24–30

1¼oz unsalted butter
¼ cup heavy cream
7oz good-quality dark chocolate
   (70 percent cocoa solids)
4 tablespoons rum
strong coffee (see preparation)
about 4oz good cocoa powder,
   for rolling

PREPARATION

✳ You will need a heat-proof mixing bowl that will fit over a saucepan with the base of the bowl well clear of the bottom of the pan.
✳ Cut the butter into small cubes.
✳ Make enough very strong coffee or espresso to give you 2 tablespoons of liquid.

METHOD

1 Pour the cream into a pan and bring to a boil, then take it off the heat right away.

2 Bring some water to a simmer in your saucepan—you will need enough water to come close to the bottom of your bowl when you sit it on top, but not actually to touch it. Turn the heat down low, because you don't want to overheat the chocolate or get any steam into the bowl, which would cause the chocolate to stiffen up and become dull-looking.

3 Break the chocolate into pieces and put it in your heat-proof bowl over the pan. Let the chocolate melt slowly, then remove from the heat and mix in the hot cream, stirring well.

4 Whisk the cubes of butter into the chocolate and cream mixture, and then add the rum and coffee and stir well. Pour the mixture into a shallow dish to cool and set, and put into the fridge to set overnight.

5 The next morning, break the set chocolate mixture into small, irregular nuggets and then roll in the cocoa powder. If you manage not to eat them all right away, you can keep the truffles in an airtight container in the fridge for 2–3 weeks.

Q&A...

CAN YOU MELT CHOCOLATE IN THE MICROWAVE?

Whatever way you melt chocolate, you need to make sure it doesn't overheat and keep it from coming into contact with any steam while it is melting. If either of these things happens, the chocolate will "seize"—i.e., it will stiffen up and look dull instead of glossy and liquid. Some people find the microwave is the best way to melt chocolate, but keep checking on it about every 15 seconds and stir it each time you open the door. Or melt the chocolate in the oven on a very, very low heat (about 225°F), but this can take a long time. I prefer to melt chocolate in a double boiler over a pan of simmering water, so I can keep an eye on it. If you turn the heat down as low as possible, keep the base of the bowl away from the water and take your time, the chocolate won't overheat.

Bonus vegetables,

These are just some quick and useful recipes for when you're stuck for a different vegetable to have with a roast or a piece of fish. There are also some simple stocks and speedy sauces for pasta, and a chocolate and fruit sauce to serve with dessert.

Recipes make enough for 4

Braised leeks

Remove and discard the green part of 2 medium leeks, then cut the white part on the diagonal into batons, about 3 inches in length. Rinse in a colander. Heat 2 tablespoons of light olive oil or vegetable oil in a large pan with a tablespoon of white wine, a spoon of butter, and a teaspoon of sugar, stirring to dissolve the sugar. When the liquid begins to simmer, put in the leeks and cook very slowly over medium heat until tender, turning them from time to time and adding a little more wine if they become really dry. This could take up to an hour, by which time the liquid will have reduced to nothing and the leeks will be golden brown.

Green beans with garlic

Peel a clove of garlic and crush with the back of a large knife. Trim the tops from about ½ lb fine green beans, but leave on the curly tails. Cook the beans in salted boiling water (or steam them) until just tender—the moment the water comes back to a boil they should be ready; they will still have a bit of a "squeak" and a crunch. Drain them through a colander and then tip them back into the saucepan while they still have some moisture on them, with a spoon of butter and the crushed clove of garlic. Stir until the butter melts and coats the beans. The more you prod the garlic, the more it will release its flavor, so it's up to you how garlicky you want the beans to be. Season and serve, removing the garlic, if you like.

Flageolets with shallots and cream

This was the vegetable dish we used to have on Sundays when I was growing up, and it is great with a roast leg of lamb. You can substitute cooked, fresh peas for the flageolets, if you like.

Finely chop a banana shallot (or 2 small ones) and crush a peeled clove of garlic with the back of a large knife. Rinse 2 cans of good flageolet beans in a colander. Heat a little light olive oil or vegetable oil in a pan, add the shallot and garlic, and a sprig each of thyme and rosemary. Cook over medium heat until the onion is soft but not colored, then add a small tub of crème fraîche (about ¾ cup) and stir until heated through. Add the rinsed and drained beans and heat through very gently, taking care not to let the crème fraîche catch and burn; then season.

All-purpose base stock

This is a light and easy base stock that uses up vegetable trimmings left over from cooking, or, of course, you can chop up vegetables freshly if you don't have any trimmings. Once you have made it, you can transform it into a light fish stock, a flavorful chicken stock, or a richer beef stock.

Trimmings or pieces of carrots, onions, leeks, celery, etc. are all perfect—but avoid potatoes, celeriac, rutabaga, or eggplant, since they will make the stock cloudy. Put everything into a pan, add a sprig of thyme and rosemary, plus a bay leaf, and then heat gently— you don't need to add any butter or oil, since there will be enough moisture in the vegetables to sweat them for a few minutes and soften them. Don't add any seasoning, since you want the flavor of the stock to be quite neutral. Then add water: you need four times the volume of the vegetables—bring to a boil, then turn down the heat to simmer, skim off any scum that comes to the surface, and bubble for 1–2 hours. Strain through a fine strainer or muslin. If you are not using the stock right away you can freeze it.

TO TURN INTO FISH STOCK:
Save all your shrimp or crab shells and fish bones or ask your fish seller for some—avoid bones from oily fish, such as mackerel or sardines, since they will add oil and too strong a flavor to the stock. Add the bones and shells to your vegetables and water and continue in the same way, but only simmer for 30 minutes to an hour.

TO TURN INTO CHICKEN STOCK:
Crush the carcass after you have had roast chicken, or chop up the equivalent in chicken bones and add to the vegetables and water. Continue in the same way, but simmer for at least 1½–2 hours, adding more water as necessary. You can simmer it for up to 4 hours if you prefer a more intensely flavored and brown-colored stock.

TO TURN INTO BEEF STOCK:
Chop up several pounds of bones, rub with 2–3 tablespoons of tomato paste, and brown them in a roasting pan in the oven at 400°F for about 30 minutes. Add to your vegetables and water and continue in the same way, simmering for 4–6 hours, adding more water as necessary.

These sauces make enough for about 4–6 people, depending on how you use them.

Béarnaise Sauce

This is the classic sauce to serve with steak (see page 142). The trick is to make it before you cook your steaks—however, if you leave it to cool and then try to reheat it, it will split, so just keep it warm continuously using a double boiler (i.e., put the sauce in a bowl over a pan of just simmering water, making sure that the base of the pan isn't actually touching the water). Or, even easier, do what we used to do in one of the restaurants I worked in and put the sauce into a thermos flask that will keep it nice and warm without splitting until you are ready to serve it. You will need 2 large shallots (finely chopped), the leaves from a bunch of tarragon, and a sprig of thyme, 3 tablespoons white wine vinegar, 3 egg yolks, 5½ oz diced butter at room temperature, and ½ a lemon. Put the chopped shallots in a pan with half the tarragon leaves (you will be adding the rest at the end), the thyme leaves, and the vinegar. Season with sea salt and freshly ground black pepper. Bring to a boil, then let the liquid bubble until it has concentrated and reduced down to a generous tablespoon. Take off the

heat and let it cool a little. In a bowl, mix the egg yolks with a tablespoon of water, put the pan back on the heat, and add this mixture, whisking all the time until the sauce starts to thicken. Add the diced butter little by little, again, whisking continuously. Taste and season again if necessary, then squeeze in the juice of your halved lemon and stir in the rest of the tarragon leaves.

All-purpose tomato sauce

The secret of a good tomato sauce, as any Italian will tell you, is to cook it slowly until it becomes thick and concentrated in flavor—for that reason, it is worth making quite a bit at a time and storing what you don't need immediately in a clean bottle in the fridge (it will keep for 1–2 weeks) or freezing it. All Italians use cans of good plum tomatoes when fresh, ripe, juicy ones are out of season. It isn't always that easy to find fantastically ripe tomatoes, but if you grow them yourself, or can ask your greengrocer for some overripe ones, you can substitute 2 lb for the cans in this recipe. The easiest way is to chop them, skin on, and then strain the sauce at the end to remove the skins.

You need 3 cans of good-quality plum tomatoes. Finely chop a large onion and a clove of garlic (remove the green germ if there is one—see page 23). Heat a little olive oil in a large, heavy-bottomed pan and add the onion and garlic, together with a bay leaf, a sprig each of thyme and rosemary (or oregano), and a pinch of salt. Cook gently until the onion is soft, but not colored. Add about ½ cup white wine and let it bubble up briefly to evaporate off the alcohol. Put in the tomatoes, and break them up in the pan with a spatula. Cook very slowly over low heat until the sauce is thick—about 45 minutes to an hour. Check the seasoning. Either leave the sauce as it is, a little chunky, or if you want a completely smooth sauce, rub it through a strainer using a wooden spoon. You can use this with pasta, to rub over a pizza base, or to serve over meatballs—anything you like, really.

All-purpose cheese sauce

Grate 4 oz Cheddar, Emmental, or other similar hard cheese. Melt 4 oz unsalted butter in a pan, then whisk in ½ cup all-purpose flour to make a paste. Slowly begin to whisk in 1½ cups milk—a spoonful at a time at first, making sure it is all incorporated before you whisk in some more. Gradually, as the mixture loosens, you can start to add more milk at a time. Add the grated cheese and a little grated nutmeg, and season with salt and pepper. Bring to a boil and then turn down to simmer, stirring continuously for about 2 minutes—this length of time is important to "cook out" the taste of the flour. Make sure you keep stirring every part of the sauce, moving it around so that it doesn't catch and burn. Finally, taste and season. You can use this to pour over fish or on top of cooked vegetables such as cauliflower or broccoli (pour over and then put the dish under the broiler briefly if you want to brown the top). Alternatively, make a soufflé by beating 3 egg whites until they form soft peaks, folding them into the sauce and then spooning into one large or four small soufflé dishes. Put these into a preheated oven at 350°F for 25–30 minutes for a large soufflé, or 10–15 minutes for smaller ones, or until risen and golden (see page 177 for soufflé tips).

Chocolate sauce

Warm ½ cup milk in a pan, then add 8 oz good-quality dark chocolate (at least 70 percent cocoa solids), broken into chunks, together with a tablespoon of rum or Amaretto. Stir to melt the chocolate and heat through. Serve with ice cream, poached pears, or doughnuts, or as a very decadent hot chocolate, with whipped cream on top.

Raspberry or strawberry coulis

There are two ways to make a fresh fruit sauce (coulis). The first gives a more intense flavor and is good as a base for a soufflé, or for flavoring ice cream; the second is more of a sauce, good for serving with all kinds of desserts and cakes.

Either: spread 1¼ lb raspberries or strawberries over a baking sheet and sprinkle with ½ cup confectioners' sugar, leave it for an hour so that the sugar draws out the juice from the fruit, then blitz it in a blender. If you are using raspberries and want to get rid of the seeds, push the sauce through a fine strainer.

Or: make a sweet (stock) syrup by putting equal quantities of sugar and water in a pan—½ cup of each if you are using 1¼ lb fruit. Bring the sugar and water to a boil and then turn the heat down to simmer for about 5 minutes until the sugar has dissolved and you have a light syrup. Leave to cool, then blitz your fruit with the syrup in a blender (you could use peaches or apricots rather than red fruit, if you prefer). Again, if you are using raspberries, you might want to push the sauce through a fine strainer to remove the seeds.

Index

As I've mentioned throughout this book, the best way to shop is locally, so try to seek out good butchers, fishmongers, farms, markets, etc. wherever possible. For example, in Bath, where I live and work, I buy my produce from Eades Greengrocers on Julian Road, meat from Bartlett & Sons, the butchers on Green Street, and, a bit farther afield, fish and shellfish from The Scallop Shell in Beckington. Obviously, cooks living in the US won't be doing much shopping in Bath, England. A website that can help you find the best organic food grown closest to you in the United States is www.localharvest.org. The site features farmers' markets, family farms, and other sources of sustainably grown food across the country.

For up to the minute advice on what varieties of fish are sustainable at any time, see www.fishonline.org and when you buy, look out for seafood from sustainable fisheries certified by the Marine Stewardship Council.

Here at The Bertinet Kitchen, we have gathered together some of our favorite things, such as the olive oil we found on a small farm in France, Moulin de Foncabrette, as well as canola oil (Fussels from Somerset) and R-oil from the Cotswolds, Cornish Sea Salt, plus Opinel knives, Eva Trio pans, baking equipment and utensils, and, of course, bread from our bakery: **www.thebertinetkitchen.com**

Here are some useful websites:

CHOCOLATE:
www.divinechocolateusa.com
www.greenandblacks.com/us

CREAM & MILK:
www.organicvalley.coop
www.sustainabletable.org
www.OrganicDirect.com

FLOUR AND SPELT:
www.pleasanthillgrain.com
www.daisyflour.com

GAME:
www.dartagnan.com
www.brokenarrow.com
www.prairieharvest.com

GROCERS:
www.balduccis.com
www.DeanDeluca.com
www.wholefoodsmarket.com

HERBS AND SPICES:
www.penzeys.com
www.thespicehouse.com

PASTRY:
www.dufourpastrykitchens.com

OILS:
www.worldpantry.com
www.organicoliveoilcompany.com

SALT:
www.saltworks.us
www.salttraders.com

SEAWEED:
www.sunfood.com

Conversion charts

WEIGHT

15g	½oz
20g	¾oz
30g	1oz
50g	1¾oz
60g	2oz
75g	2¾oz
100g	3½oz
110g	4oz (¼lb)
150g	5oz
175g	6oz
200g	7oz
225g	8oz (½lb)
250g (¼kg)	9oz
275g	10oz
350g	12oz (¾lb)
400g	14oz
450g	1lb
500g (½kg)	18oz
600g	1¼lb
700g	1½lb
900g	2lb
1kg	2¼lb
1.1kg	2½lb
1.3kg	3lb
1.5kg	3lb 5oz
1.6kg	3½lb
1.8kg	4lb
2kg	4½lb
2.2kg	5lb

VOLUME

5ml	1 teaspoon
10ml	2 teaspoon
15ml	1 tablespoon
30ml	1fl oz
60ml	2fl oz
75ml	2½fl oz
100ml	3½fl oz
125ml	4fl oz (½ cup)
150ml	5fl oz
200ml	7fl oz
250ml (0.25 liter)	8fl oz (1 cup)
300ml	10fl oz
350ml	12fl oz
400ml	14fl oz
425ml	14½fl oz
450ml	15fl oz
500ml (0.5 liter)	2 cups (1 pint)
600ml	2½ cups
700ml	3 cups
850ml	3½ cups
1 liter	1 quart (2 pints/4 cups)
1.2 liters	2½ pints
1.5 liters	1½ quarts (3 pints/6 cups)
1.7 liters	1¾ quarts
2 liters	2 quarts (4 pints)

MEASUREMENTS

3mm	⅛in
5mm	¼in
1cm	½in
2cm	¾in
2.5cm	1in
3cm	1¼in
4cm	1½in
5cm	2in
6cm	2½in
7.5cm	3in
9cm	3½in
10cm	4in
11.5cm	4½in
12.5cm	5in
15cm	6in
17cm	6½in
18cm	7in
20.5cm	8in
23cm	9in
24cm	9½in
25.5cm	10in
30.5cm	12in

OVEN TEMPERATURES

Celsius	Farenheit*	Gas	Description
110°C	225°F	Gas Mark ¼	cool
120°C	250°F	Gas Mark ½	cool
130°C	275°F	Gas Mark 1	very low
150°C	300°F	Gas Mark 2	very low
160°C	325°F	Gas Mark 3	low
180°C	350°F	Gas Mark 4	moderate
190°C	375°F	Gas Mark 5	moderately hot
200°C	400°F	Gas Mark 6	hot
220°C	425°F	Gas Mark 7	hot
230°C	450°F	Gas Mark 8	very hot
240°C	475°F	Gas Mark 9	very hot

* For fan-assisted ovens, reduce temperatures by 25°F